BONES AROUND MY NECK

BONES AROUND MY NECK

The Life and Exile of a Prince Provocateur

Tamara Loos

CORNELL UNIVERSITY PRESS   ITHACA AND LONDON

First published 2016 by Cornell University Press
Printed in the United States of America

Library of Congress Cataloging-in-Publication Data

Names: Loos, Tamara Lynn, author.
Title: Bones around my neck : the life and exile of a prince provocateur / Tamara Loos.
Description: Ithaca : Cornell University Press, 2016. | Includes bibliographical references and index.
Identifiers: LCCN 2016013029 | ISBN 9781501704635 (cloth : alk. paper)
Subjects: LCSH: Pritsadāng, Prince, grandson of Nangklao, King of Siam, 1852–1935. | Princes—Thailand—Biography. | Diplomats—Thailand—Biography. | Thailand—History—1782–1945.
Classification: LCC DS578.32.P75 L66 2016 | DDC 327.5930092—dc23
LC record available at http://lccn.loc.gov/2016013029

Cornell University Press strives to use environmentally responsible suppliers and materials to the fullest extent possible in the publishing of its books. Such materials include vegetable-based, low-VOC inks and acid-free papers that are recycled, totally chlorine-free, or partly composed of nonwood fibers. For further information, visit our website at www.cornellpress.cornell.edu.

Cloth printing   10 9 8 7 6 5 4 3 2 1

For David

Contents

Preface

I was in stubborn pursuit of a different disgraced member of the Siamese elite when Prince Prisdang (pronounced *prit-sa-dang*) Chumsai found me, unsuspecting, in my chair at Bangkok's National Archives. He simply refused to keep quiet. You could almost feel the pressure of his incessant, desperate beseeching. "Disaster and death are waiting for me." "I value truth and honesty." "I'd rather die than break my promises." "My intention [was] to kill myself to prove my honesty to the king." His loud and irrepressible urgency about the injustices he had suffered demanded my attention. Prisdang (figure 1) had been Siam's first ambassador to Europe and the United States in the late nineteenth century, but he vanished from Siam's history thereafter. Yet here he was, protesting that he had "bones hanging around his neck," a reference to a Thai proverb that means being scapegoated. He complained of receiving only reproaches for his tireless and wholehearted diplomatic efforts on behalf of Siam's king and government.

Initially, I leafed through his files with reluctance. The last person I wanted to write about was a member, however distant, of Thailand's reigning Chakri dynasty. Increasingly draconian application of Thailand's lèse majesté laws since the early twenty-first century makes it impossible to write about the king, queen, and heir apparent without risking defamation charges and even imprisonment. The risks are much higher for Thai nationals. I also did not want to produce scholarship that would bring additional attention to a dynasty and an institution that undergird a political and cultural system capable of crushing the public and private expression of dissent. The scholarly political economy in Thai studies is already skewed in the direction of royal hagiography.

However, Prisdang surprised me with his version of the past, which challenges existing accounts of Thailand and its place in global history. His life buzzes like a hub of frenetic political activity, linking together the spokes of Thai nationalism, European imperialism, Buddhist universalism, and transnational anti-imperialism. Yet Thai historical accounts truncate his role in Siam and deny his political activism in transnational Buddhist communities. I wanted to know why.

Prince Prisdang's birth in 1852 and death in 1935 encompass a period in which all territories in Southeast Asia except Siam were formally colonized. As its first minister in Europe in the 1880s when Siam's status as a sovereign state was most intensely challenged, Prisdang negotiated with energetic zeal on behalf of his country and king. To ensure that Siam would not suffer the same fate as

FIGURE 1. Prince Prisdang, London, circa 1882. Courtesy of the National Archives, Thailand.

its neighbors, he took the lead in drafting a blueprint for the massive reform of its governing institutions, including the recommendation for a constitutional monarchy, which he gave to his king in 1885. Through such efforts, Prisdang demonstrated that he was more than a cultural interlocutor and diplomat: he was also midwife to Siam's emergence as a modern state.

To the extent histories of Siam mention Prisdang, it is to highlight these two contributions: as a diplomat and an advocate for a constitutional monarchy. His name rarely surfaces otherwise. Most scholars point to the 1885 proposal as the cause for Prisdang's demise—it allegedly incurred the king's wrath for suggesting a form of rule other than absolutism. However, Prisdang fled into exile in 1890, five years *after* submitting the petition to his beloved monarch. Prisdang himself was at a loss to explain conclusively what caused the rift between him and the king that catapulted him out of his homeland for twenty years. Whatever the cause, which is doggedly pursued in the chapters that follow, Prisdang found himself at the center of ruinous gossip that ran the gamut from adultery and massive personal indebtedness to malfeasance and defamation of the king and ultimately chased him from Siam. He and his alleged lover, a woman whose story remains a mystery, escaped Siamese authorities by absconding through colonial Asia.

Prisdang's experiences in exile were as vibrant and controversial as his life within Siam. After five years living in disguise as a commoner and employee of the British Empire in colonial Southeast Asia, Prisdang resurfaced in the 1890s in British Ceylon, where he was ordained as a Buddhist monk. He quickly gained renown as an outspoken leader and international emissary for Asia's Theravada Buddhist communities in their relations with the British Empire. Foreigners from around the world were drawn to this prince who, like the Buddha, had discarded his wealth and royal status to lead the life of an ascetic. As a monk, he advocated for a pan-Theravada Buddhist movement headed not by him but by the man who had earlier enabled his exile: Siam's monarch. Despite this evidence of his enduring devotion to Siam and its king, national histories ignore Prisdang's international efforts.

The following pages offer the first complete version of Prisdang's entire journey, from childhood through exile abroad and back home. Piecing together these fragmented segments of his life trajectory reveals one pivotal man's subjective experience of global imperialism, the activism roiling Asia's Buddhist ecumene, and the pitfalls of Siam's political culture. Prisdang's drama is a personal and political adventure of a reluctantly rebellious prince and unwitting provocateur who caused a commotion in every country he visited: Siam, countries throughout Europe, French Indochina, and British Malaya, Ceylon, and India. One of his contemporaries quipped about Prisdang that no matter what, "he should not [be] allowed to be *idle!*"

By following a single individual as he rose and fell through the ranks of Siam's officialdom and royal hierarchy, we can begin to understand why some of Thailand's histories ignore or disavow him as a traitor, while others simultaneously celebrate him as a patriot who attempted to moderate royal absolutism. Neither is exactly true, but the following pages reveal how this contradictory appraisal is possible. There are multiple reasons given for his departure, but none offers definitive resolution of why he fled in 1890. After all, he could not explain it. In his personal letters, crippling self-doubt competes with biting invectives hurled against those he blames for his downfall. Even in his autobiography, Prisdang intentionally removed the pages leading up to the moment of his exile. No historian or biographer has discerned or been willing to disclose why Prince Prisdang became the black sheep not just of the royal family but also of the nation.

The fact that we still do not know for certain why he fled is vital to understanding how political power and cultural authority operated in Siam. Secrets are productive generators of the imagination. They also reveal a great deal about the social context in which they gain traction. When Prisdang introduced a mystery— why he had a falling out with the man who sat at the apex of Siam's political and cultural hierarchy—into a political system that lacked transparency, rumors expanded to fill the space of his departure. At one moment, he was essential to Siam's survival as an independent country, and at another he was disavowed as a scandalous betrayer of king, class, and country. Rumors performed destructive political work in the context of absolutism. Prisdang became, literally and historically, persona non grata. All he had were bones hanging around his neck.

BONES AROUND MY NECK

1

STAGING SECRETS
Prince Prisdang Avenges History

Five Buddhist monks gently peeled the clothing off the body of an elderly man who feigned death in an attempt to steal one more year of life. Turning eighty would not be his biggest achievement, but Prince Prisdang Chumsai considered it sufficiently important and uncertain that he had hired the monks to perform a life extension ceremony on his seventy-ninth birthday.[1] Unseasonably dry in February 1930, Bangkok's heat oppressed the royal family members and acquaintances who attended the prince's birthday celebration.[2] The supreme patriarch of Siam's Buddhist order, also a royal prince, gave the sermon. His presence and the monks' talismanic chanting, meant to ward off future bad luck, could do little to change the karmic consequences Prince Prisdang had already reaped during the eight long decades of his life. To that end, he hosted the ceremony, which ultimately succeeded: Prisdang lived five additional years. Open to friends and foes, the event staged the prince's presentation of his vision of the past in the form of a Western style autobiography—the first of its kind in Siam.[3]

Unlike the few other autobiographical types of writing that existed at that point, Prisdang's account was not an episodic, didactic text modeled on the Buddhist life-story (Jataka) tradition.[4] He penned a cradle-to-(near)-grave personal confessional that covered his life from birth until he became ill in the 1920s. Buddhism informed Prisdang's worldview and understanding of his life's larger karmic lessons, as suggested by his decision to excise or downplay all women in his account, his (frustrated) desire to live as a monk from his forties on, and his constant references to his own rebirths. However, Prisdang did not write about his life as a series of mistakes from which he learned clear-cut

Buddhist lessons. Instead, he wrote with a sense of his own historicity—what he did for Siam that changed its history and why he should be, but has not been, acknowledged for it. He did not desire to replace Siam's historical narrative but wanted to be acknowledged for his constructive and central role in it.

As he handed out his autobiography, Prince Prisdang scribbled his signature on each of the one hundred copies that he had printed (see figure 2).

Peculiarly, Prisdang insisted that each recipient sign his name underneath his signature, which was less an autograph than a contract authorizing the recipient to receive the second and third proposed volumes of the autobiography.[5] The signatures must also have served as a validation for Prisdang: face-to-face confirmation that the invitees at his life extension celebration acknowledged receipt of

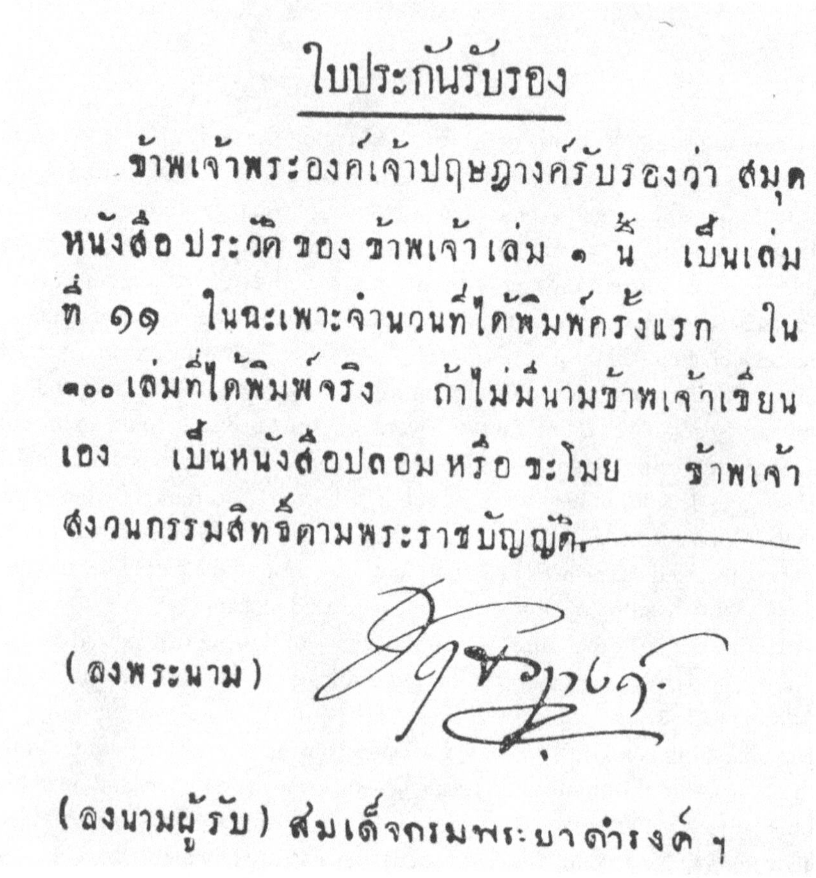

ใบประกันรับรอง

ข้าพเจ้าพระองค์เจ้าปฤษฎางค์รับรองว่า สมุด หนังสือ ประวัติ ของ ข้าพเจ้า เล่ม ๑ นี้ เป็นเล่ม ที่ ๑๑ ในฉะเพาะจำนวนที่ได้พิมพ์ครั้งแรก ใน ๑๐๐ เล่มที่ได้พิมพ์จริง ถ้าไม่มีนามข้าพเจ้าเขียน เอง เป็นหนังสือปลอม หรือ ฉะโมย ข้าพเจ้า สงวนกรรมสิทธิ์ตามพระราชบัญญัติ———————

(ลงพระนาม)

(ลงนามผู้รับ) สมเด็จกรมพระยาดำรงค์ ฯ

FIGURE 2.   Signature page of copy number 11 with signature of Princes Prisdang and Damrong, from Prisdang, *Prawat yo*, 37.

his side of the saga that had many decades earlier ended his diplomatic career and compelled his dramatic and soul-searching twenty-year exile from Siam.

If the presence of powerful men such as the supreme patriarch and Prince Damrong Rajanubhab (Rachanuphap) (1862–1943) serves as any indication, then Siam's political and royal elite probably attended the two-day ceremony, though no guest list survives. One of the most influential men under King Chulalong-korn, Prince Damrong was the former minister of the interior (1892–1915) who masterminded the reforms that centralized the fiscal, territorial, bureaucratic, and legal administration of Siam. By 1930 Damrong had retired and was lead-ing the effort to build the collection at the National Library by accumulating ephemeral texts such as Prisdang's autobiography—this one signed to Damrong is the only surviving publicly available copy.[6]

One wonders what sort of false pleasantries were exchanged between Pris-dang, ill-fitting dentures garbling his speech, and Damrong as together they signed the warranty page on the eleventh copy of the autobiography.[7] They had not been friends. The contrast between the two men could not have been more striking. Damrong, celebrated and powerful even in retirement, stood before the impoverished Prisdang, a former political exile reviled for his alleged betrayal of Siam and its favorite monarch, King Chulalongkorn (r. 1868–1910). This dis-parity was not lost on Prisdang, who hosted the birthday ceremony as a politi-cal event meant to end the speculation about his loyalty to Siam and to King Chulalongkorn.

Curiously, his autobiography hinted at but refused to explicate the "incident" that had caused his falling out of King Chulalongkorn's good graces. Several tan-talizing pages of the narrative leading up to his escape are missing, as if Prisdang had changed his mind and ripped them out just before the autobiography went to press. Yet in the autobiography's foreword, he remarks on the missing pages, purposefully revealing their absence. He worried that those discarded pages "described [things] too tersely. Readers would misunderstand it, so I cut out the entire section . . . and preserved it to place in a future volume."[8] He alerted his pub-lic and intentionally left the gap in pagination intact. No additional volumes were published. Instead, Prince Prisdang staged a political comeback and a mystery simultaneously with this publication. He died without having divulged the secret.

Prisdang's birth in 1852, on the eve of Siam's transformation into a modern, centralizing state, and death in 1935, three years after a coup by nonroyal officials overthrew the absolute monarchy in favor of a constitutional one, offer bookends for this crucial period in Siam's history. But his life cannot be so neatly contained: it engaged in dynamics beyond Siam's borders, where Prisdang spent decades of his long life. His international journey reveals the constraints and possibilities enabled by global imperialism. Prisdang spent most of his life brokering Siam's relationship with the world as his kingdom's mediator and interlocutor, even after he fled into exile.

As Siam's first national representative in a dozen European metropoles, Prisdang stood at the center of the most important imperial maelstroms confronting Siam's leadership. He navigated the diplomatic relationship between Siam and its new imperial neighbors in Southeast Asia. In the mid-1880s, Britain finalized its conquest over all the territory once ruled by Burma's Buddhist monarch, King Thibaw, who lived the remainder of his life in exile in British India. On Siam's eastern borders, France moved north to conquer the rest of Vietnam by 1885. Siamese leaders feared, for good reason, that Britain and France eyed Siam as the next target for conquest.

As Siam's formal regional rivals collapsed around him, an anxious King Chulalongkorn consulted Prisdang, who by then had developed a cultural literacy that made him a skilled interpreter of the subtleties of European diplomacy. Prisdang translated for King Chulalongkorn the colonizing intent behind imperial descriptions of Asian kingdoms as politically backward. He exposed the discourse of civilization as a strategy for territorial and cultural domination. He translated for Siam's ruler the challenges confronting the kingdom as it groped for its new place in the global hierarchy of nations. The advice Prisdang provided included more than suggestions about how to handle international affairs: he offered a comprehensive plan for domestic reform as well.[9]

Prisdang's position as Siam's intermediary continued even after he fled into exile and was ordained as a monk in Ceylon. There he had a second life as a diplomat: he served as an emissary between politicized Theravada Buddhists and officials in the British Empire in an attempt to unify Buddhists under the religious sovereignty of Siam's king. His fluency in English, royal blood, acute intellect, and engaging character earned him an importance in international diplomatic and Buddhist circles that expanded far beyond his reputation in Siam.

Given the significance of the period and of Prisdang's instrumental role as a mediator between Siam and Europe's imperial powerhouses, it is curious that most histories of Siam do little more than mention his name, if that. In part this is because his account challenges royal national histories of Siam that credit King Chulalongkorn exclusively for Siam's narrow escape from colonization. More significantly, his story is omitted because it exposes the dark underbelly of the process by which Siam survived as a sovereign nation. Like other intermediaries and cultural brokers, Prisdang's very ability to communicate between groups rendered him suspect, and his cross-cultural proficiencies came to be seen by the Siamese ruling class as transgressive.[10] Some even thought him a traitor. What Prisdang *did* to deserve this remains unclear, but a rash of rumors within elite society was unleashed to discipline him.

Prisdang's life journey reminds us of the complexities of the colonial encounter and the recalibrations it caused in Siamese political culture. An examination of his ouster from Siam opens a window onto a critical juncture in the development of Siamese political power, when social and political hierarchies dovetailed to create monarchical cultural authority—a construction that continues to shape power and discourse in Thailand today. Prisdang's experiences within Siamese elite society unveil the maneuvering and manipulation of power that can occur beneath the mask of public expressions of loyalty to the monarchy.

King Chulalongkorn cultivated a group of trusted princes and nonroyal officials to help him centralize the administration in the face of domestic rivals and foreign threats. The foreign threats were obvious, but domestically a generational struggle was being waged as well between those allied with King Chulalongkorn, who desired major government reforms, and those affiliated with other factions less favorably inclined toward change.[11] King Chulalongkorn gradually wrested control over the appointment of key posts, filling them with his own trusted men. By centralizing the state apparatus under his control, the king created an absolute monarchy—a system of governance in which one ruler wielded sole power above the law and without reference to other formal political institutions. In practice, absolutism referred not to a single source of power located in the monarchy but to an integrated social and political system built on relationships among trusted individuals—individuals like Prisdang whose connections to each other were complicated by the fact that many in their small elite circles were related through polygynous marital ties. It is this group of individuals—men who held a high enough official position in the government that they had audiences with the king or his closest relatives—who comprised Siam's elite until King Chulalongkorn passed away. It also included some women who were wives or relatives of these men or were high-ranking royalty. Ultimately, however, decision making rested with King Chulalongkorn.

The highest-ranking princes and a handful of men from powerful aristocratic families that had intermarried with the royal family ran most of the important government ministries and departments. For example, in 1883 King Chulalongkorn's brothers and half-brothers, all of whom were princes, headed or were high-ranking officers in the following offices: the Royal Secretariat, the Audit Office, the Palace Ministry and its various departments, four additional ministries, and the courts of law.[12] In this system, the line between public or government business and private or familial matters blurred. Tellingly, the Thai word *luang* referred to both the king and the government. Their distinction had to be consciously constructed. When corresponding to one another, officials, who were also often blood relatives and friends, had to mark their letters "private," using a transliteration of the English word, to designate the content as personal rather than official. Yet their intimacy and emotional involvement were part and parcel of the political administration of the country. To cause an insult would have repercussions in personal and professional realms.

Government officials were ranked differentially according to a number of factors, including their royal birth rank (if they were royal), government position, royally conferred title, marital and familial ties, and sometimes wealth. Individuals rose to prominence on the basis of a combination of these factors and their ability to navigate with tact this complex political and social terrain. However, without institutional checks, the centralization of power in the hands of the king fostered competition among these individuals for the king's favor, which they gained through a variety of means, including serving skillfully in their government posts, respecting social norms regarding deference and obeisance, and bringing to the king's attention the best "intelligence," which also included gossip and hearsay about the personal life of other government officials. This funneling of power tended to insulate the monarch from data and perspectives that would challenge his authority or the hierarchical system itself.

Those who breached protocol or failed to play by these rules risked falling out of favor with entire networks of colleagues, family, and friends, as Prisdang learned. Prisdang was not born into this elite group surrounding King Chulalongkorn; he was a relatively low-ranking and distant royal family member who earned his way into the ruling echelon through a combination of blood ties, education, and innate intelligence. As a consequence, he had to obey rules of etiquette and social status to a degree that a true insider did not. However, he violated the moral and symbolic order by failing to enact his proper place, relative status, and associated behaviors and speech norms. The terms then used to describe an inferior who exceeded the boundaries of his or her social station may have been different, but today the cultural concept is encapsulated in the word *kalathesa*, which means, in practice, to know one's place, relative status, and associated behaviors and speech in a given social situation.[13] *Kala* refers to time, while *thesa* refers to space. It is a deeply conservative and liberating concept that is radically context dependent.[14] When he failed to comply with these behavioral and speech norms, Prisdang unwittingly critiqued the entire social system supporting royal authority. His status superiors, including the king, who had the most to lose from any changes in Siam's social hierarchy, found Prisdang intolerably impudent.

Compounding the significance of his impropriety was the historical context in which Prisdang lived. Siam's social and political hierarchy was under threat from the outside as a consequence of political, economic, and social changes wrought by increased entanglement with foreign powers, global trade, and the imposition of unequal treaties. For ruling elites, it was important to adjust to these transformations while still maintaining their place at the top of the domestic political hierarchy. Prisdang's successes abroad increased his sense of self-importance to Siam's future and also raised a conundrum for leaders in Bangkok who did not have experience abroad. They depended on Prisdang for his talents as an interlocutor with the Western world, but some found him uppity, outspoken, and controversial both for his ideas about how Siamese politics might develop domestically and for personal comportment that exceeded his social station. Prisdang threatened the status quo at a time when it most required stanchioning.

Power and control over elites were more often than not exerted through forms of social disciplining, not through law. The tools of social control used against Prisdang included gossip, rumors, and scandal—extrainstitutional methods that disciplined lapses in emotional and behavioral expression.[15] It encouraged rumors so powerful that he considered suicide. He was accused of all manner of social transgressions, including ingratitude, disloyalty, "courting" a woman in a Buddhist temple, adultery, obsession with European theater actresses, and insanity, alongside legally punishable offenses such as massive personal indebtedness, theft of government funds, misuse of property, and treason. Curiously, the Siamese government never formally tried or publicly condemned him for any of these alleged infractions. Whether or not the accusations were true remains unclear: some of the charges against him are unfounded, but most are a matter of interpretation. Regardless of the truth, the content of the gossip reveals the contours of community for Siam's elites at the time. Rumors performed political work. They were deployed to discipline Prisdang, to put him in his proper (lower) place. They also served to discipline members of a community by defining idealized standards of behavior and jointly held values at the moment they were breached in practice.[16] These forms of emotional control reinforced Siam's existing social and political hierarchy by casting out those who breached its limits. They were at once intensely personal and communal: they delineated in excruciating detail intolerable behaviors allegedly engaged in by a specific member while simultaneously serving as a cautionary tale for all.

The specific content of the rumors is also important for what it suggests about this moment in Siam's history and the anxieties felt by its ruling elite. Prisdang was accused of engaging in sexual and fiscal improprieties. It is no coincidence that these "crimes" were commonly engaged in by Siam's most powerful political leaders and were frequently critiqued by foreigners seeking to deny Siam its sovereignty. By scapegoating Prisdang, the small community of ruling elites expelled a man who hovered at the edge of their boundaries of belonging, enabling them to close ranks and unite against a common threat. It also allowed ruling elites to disavow common practices that fell under increasingly critical scrutiny by imperialists.

Rumors about Prisdang challenged him to prove his willingness to conform and submit to the hierarchical norms governing membership in his social community, even at great cost to his sense of truth, self-worth, and dignity. They required that he admit he had committed the crimes of adultery, malfeasance, lying, defamation, and so on. He refused. This ironic act of self-preservation—ironic because it destroyed his future within Siam—caused his expulsion from the kingdom and excommunication from ruling society. Prisdang's experience demonstrates that emotions—the spite of his accusers and Prisdang's righteous indignation and hurt—are not mere embellishments to history but reflect, maintain, and dismantle power hierarchies.

The costs were high for those who challenged the social and political hierarchy undergirding King Chulalongkorn's construction of an absolute monarchy at the very moment Siam first directly faced the threat of extinction as an independent kingdom.[17] Prisdang suffered disgrace based on rumor and innuendo that followed him to the grave. But let's be clear: Prisdang was not a political radical. He was a maverick, iconoclastic, outspoken, and sometimes brash. But he consistently expressed support for Siam's monarchy. Prisdang valued his regal status and the connections it enabled with some of the era's most powerful individuals, particularly with foreign royalty. He immediately and persistently regretted offending King Chulalongkorn, apologized obsessively, and even wrote his autobiography to serve as a vehicle of self-redemption vis-à-vis this unintended offense.

Narrating this moment in Siamese history through the life experience of Prisdang reveals it as a personal tragedy rather than as a national political triumph, as it is typically known. His story records with excruciating precision the drama and emotional motivations concealed behind history's more measured recording of major political events in Siam, thereby bringing to life the flat interiorities typically associated with colonizing and colonized individuals.[18] Prisdang's human-scale narration grounds the otherwise abstract processes of global imperialism. His life thus offers a vehicle for more than the history of Siam. It also exemplifies how the crisis of colonialism was simultaneously global, national, and personal.

Prisdang moved fluidly in the interstices between Western imperial and Siamese politics, making the most of his role as interlocutor. Liminality has its advantages, and he took every opportunity to stand in between, regulating exchanges between Westerners and Siamese in a perilously significant era. But this very liminality rendered Prisdang's motives and activities suspect to his peers and superiors in Siam. The following pages focus on suspicions about Prisdang's actions, whose meanings remain ambiguous and open to interpretation. Rather than foreclose meaning by settling on one or another interpretation, the narrative below retains the ambiguity present in the source materials. It makes us wonder if Prisdang was a political iconoclast who challenged absolutism or a presumptuous, womanizing spendthrift whose actions so embarrassed ruling elites that they ousted him. Did he and his alleged lover, a widow named Si, commit adultery, flirt in the sacred space of a temple, and then steal money as they fled, or were these rumors spread to irrevocably discredit and banish them from Siam's political and social life? Did he steal relics of the Buddha from a dig in British India or was this yet another attempt by Siamese elites to tarnish his reputation and prevent him from returning to Siam?

Open-ended interpretations fail to serve official history, which quickly imposes meaning upon the events. In Prisdang's case, it was easier to omit mention of him altogether. His contemporaries, many of whom later wrote memoirs and autobiographies, proactively forgot Prisdang and the troubling cloud obscuring the reasons for his departure.[19] Their active forgetting suggests that it behooved them to maintain silence rather than to denigrate him. It suggests that mentioning Prisdang, even to disparage him, would implicate them and, by association, the king and nation. He better served Siam as a scapegoat. He could not tell the whole story in 1890 when he fled or in 1930 when he published his autobiography.

Maintaining silence has consequences for the history of Siam and for Prisdang. Prisdang, who kept quiet about certain aspects of his life for powerful and repressive reasons of his own, became imminently deployable as a symbol for other agendas. He remains an ambivalent figure whose seemingly indeterminate political leanings allow him to be harnessed to various causes that run the political gamut. Prisdang's theatrical last-minute decision to exclude a key segment from his autobiography, which explained why he fled into exile and would resolve the mystery of his political affinities, enabled these contradictory claims on him. No single true story exists. Prisdang may still have the last word. He ends the introduction to his autobiography with a challenge: "Can you see now why I alone must be the one to write [my autobiography] instead of letting friends or foes tell the story, showing off what they think they know as they see fit? In my case, who is dim-witted enough to ask why I would have the arrogance to compose my own history and publish it before I die?"[20]

GULF OF SIAM

Prisdang's Star Ascends

Rarely can a single moment encapsulate all the key elements about to unfold in a person's life. However, the celebration of stars and planets on an unknown beach in southern Siam in 1868, pinpointed exactly at East Greenwich longitude 99° 42' and latitude North 11° 39', encompassed all that for Prince Prisdang Chumsai. The protagonists in his story, including Siam's future king and representatives of European imperial powers, presented themselves on that beach. Then again, almost everyone with any connection to power—French scientists, European diplomats, Siamese astrologers, and Siamese royal and noble elites—convened at this location on 18 August at the request of King Mongkut.[1] The king, an astronomer in his own right, promised them a monumental spectacle: a total solar eclipse. He had independently predicted the eclipse and sought to solidify his reputation as a scientifically minded, enlightened monarch by having his prediction witnessed by skeptics and supporters from home and abroad.

He took this show on the road as well as on a steamboat. Hundreds of people had been invited to join the king, preceded by thousands of laborers who built facilities to accommodate them.[2] Some, dreading seasickness, rode to the seaside on the back of an elephant.[3] A seven-year old Prince Damrong, who decades later helped engineer the vast centralizing territorial and administrative reforms of the kingdom, crowded onto a boat on 8 August as a member of the royal entourage. Once on shore days later, he frolicked in front of the encampment with other royal children, remembering little else about the event except the oddity of shaking his first hand, Western-style.[4] All Europeans residing in Bangkok received an invitation to proceed south to a remote location along Siam's gulf, including the eighty-four foreigners in government employ. Britain's highest-ranking official in the region, Governor Ord of the Straits Settlements in Singapore, arrived just days before the eclipse and was at the other end of young Damrong's first handshake. Mongkut, in his quirky English, personally invited Sir Henry Ord, "My dear familiar friend," who "seemed to be a noble person of best humour and grace" and whom the king was "eagerly and very desirous of meeting . . . in person even once."[5] Nearly a dozen archly competitive French scientists came as well, claiming greater astronomical accuracy and even jostling with King Mongkut to take credit for selecting the best location from which to view the eclipse.[6] Perhaps the monarch should have ceded that claim to them, for the barren beachside south of Hua Hin offered more than a spectacular view. It promised death. The whining buzz of malaria-bearing mosquitoes arose in response to the order to bushwhack the encroaching jungle of ironwood trees. Built in their stead was a "veritable wooden palace with many guest houses and pavilions."[7]

These makeshift dwellings provided some comfort to the Europeans, Siamese court astrologers, royal family members, and nobles on the beach at Wako (aka Hua Wan)[8] in Klong Wan, Prachuapkhirikhan province.[9] All told, about one thousand people and dozens of horses, cattle, and elephants made Wako their temporary home. It cost the king twenty thousand British pounds to house, feed, and transport guests, including the French scientists.[10] Spread out over a few miles, the community sprang to life when the royal entourage arrived. At the northernmost end encamped the king; his leading minister, Jao Phraya Si Suriyawong (Chuang Bunnag) (figure 3); and royal family members, including women and children from the Inner Palace.[11] Consular officials and other European visitors spread down the length of the beach, with the ten French scientists capping off the south end. Sparing no expense, the king brought two brass bands that played most evenings, and he provided food and wine in abundance.

Most of his fellow Siamese, dubious of the king's curious interest in astronomy and collection of Western scientific instruments, whispered out of his earshot that the entire enterprise was a waste of time.[12] Some allegedly still believed that the giant demon Rahu would devour the sun unless they immediately drove him away by raising a deafening din of gongs and explosives.[13] Perhaps as he distractedly slapped at the annoying insects, King Mongkut worried more about the weather than the ubiquitous bloodsuckers. On the morning of the eclipse, clouds appeared and rain pelted onlookers. Anxiety spread throughout the entourage, especially among the French, who wondered if their arduous journey had been for naught.[14]

One might credit science for the king's ability to predict the timing and place to view the eclipse, but only the gods could ensure decent weather. A Siamese astrologer standing near the king could not suppress an astonished "phlup!"

FIGURE 3. Si Suriyawong (Chuang Bunnag) in 1865, photographed by John Thomson. Wellcome Library no. 199561. Courtesy of the Wellcome Library, London.

when, miraculously, the sky suddenly cleared and the crowd on that little patch of cleared land watched the final sliver of light disappear from the sky.[15] They observed nearly seven minutes of a total eclipse of the sun.[16] Young Prince Damrong stared at the stars that gradually sparkled to life as the afternoon sunlight disappeared into an all-encompassing darkness. The king and Si Suriyawong momentarily forgot decorum and ran "like excited boys . . . to and fro between their telescopes watching the spectacle." The king ordered the cannon fired. The band blared trumpets and pipes. Si Suriyawong shouted, in English, "Hurrah! Hurrah!"[17]

Thrilled and relieved, King Mongkut hosted a lavish party that evening in celebration of his scientific acumen. He distributed gifts of money to his entourage to celebrate the precision provided by longitudinal and latitudinal science and bathed ritually in gratitude to the deities for suddenly clearing the skies.[18] Dr. Dan Beach Bradley, an American missionary and longtime resident of Siam, conducted religious services.[19] A French chef prepared meals for the Europeans, and large blocks of ice, brought in for the occasion, chilled their champagne.[20]

Not that the French party appreciated King Mongkut's efforts. It was by no means the first encounter between East and West, but the eclipse provided a unique moment for all parties to reassess these relationships. For the first time, global expeditions to remote locales became de rigueur for Western scientists and their governments, especially those from imperial countries who rivaled one another for scientific firsts. The French forsook their country's new colonies in South Vietnam and Cambodia for the opportunity to scope out Siamese territory from a French gunboat called the *Frelon*.[21] Their lead scientist and director of the Marseilles Observatory, Édouard Stéphan, noted to his compatriots that the Siamese king exercised only nominal control over the southern gulf, and he mentioned promising commercial exploitation, particularly of minerals, if the area were to come under French control.[22]

As a counterweight, King Mongkut had invited Governor Ord and British gunboats to attend. Even though the king paid for the journey and accommodations for his foreign guests, the French remained ungracious in their treatment of Mongkut's scientific acumen, refusing to acknowledge that he had beaten French predictions of the eclipse by two seconds.[23] The eclipse, in any event, provided an opportunity for Mongkut to demonstrate to these two imperial rivals that Siam was governed by an enlightened, scientifically minded leader worthy of ruling a sovereign kingdom.

His domestic situation was potentially more difficult to navigate, in no small part because of the wider imperial context, with Britain already occupying half of Burma and the Malay Peninsula on Siam's west and the French gradually colonizing Cambodia and parts of Vietnam on the east. Mongkut and Si Suriyawong considered the eclipse event symbolic of the need to accommodate the increasing presence of Western imperialists and their technology in the region. The king personally proved that a combination of European science and Siamese astrology could more accurately predict the movement of celestial bodies. It was so important to Mongkut that he be acknowledged domestically for this feat that when he returned to Bangkok on 24 August 1868, he punished the court astrologers who doubted him. They had to scrub palace stones one day, then suffer through eight shameful days of imprisonment, wearing neck-laces made of large snail shells.[24]

They may have had the final word, however, on the ultimate meaning of the eclipse. As the king's party celebrated on the shores of the gulf, malaria spread through the camp and infected dozens, including eight of the French scientists and two teenage boys whose lives were intertwined from this moment forward.[25] Prince Chulalongkorn and Prince Prisdang both accompanied their fathers, King Mongkut and his half-nephew Prince Chumsai, respectively, to witness the eclipse. All of them contracted malaria and fell ill by the time they returned to Bangkok in late August. By mid-September, Prince Chumsai was dead. Two weeks later, on October 1, King Mongkut passed away, confirming the interpretation of the eclipse as a portent of evil to those court astrologers still smarting from their humiliating punishment. The highest-ranking nobles and royalty assembled to mourn the loss of the king and to decide who should replace him on the throne. The opinion of Si Suriyawong weighed heavily. Although a nobleman rather than royalty, Si Suriyawong had no rivals to his power: he commanded most of the army, supervised the government's finances, and occupied (along with his numerous Bunnag relatives) the majority of the key administrative positions. He agreed on the choice of Prince Chulalongkorn as Siam's next king in return for being made regent until Chulalongkorn came of age in 1873. When asked by a relative many years later why he never became king, the regent replied, "'Why should I bother? I have everything a man could desire.'"[26] He remained the "real master of the administration" until his death in 1883.[27]

Orphaned and feverish, the fifteen-year old crown prince became king in October 1868.[28] King Chulalongkorn attempted to fill his father's shoes, but the regent was already wearing them. He recalled this dark moment in his life in a letter from 1893 to his sons:

> When I ascended the throne I was only fifteen years and ten days old. My mother [had long ago] died. . . . My paternal relatives in the Royal Fam-ily had fallen under the power of the Regent. . . . Those who had impor-tant positions did not have the ability to support me in any way. My brothers and sisters were all minors, younger than I. . . . As for myself, I was but a boy. I had no great knowledge or ability in government affairs. . . . I was sick almost to the point of death. I grieved constantly because of my father's death. At that time, I was like a headless person,

my body propped up as a puppet king . . . and there were enemies whose intentions were openly bared around me, both within and without, in the capital and abroad."[29]

During the period of the regency (1868–73), the young king began to build his base of support among the sons of the nobles and princes, whose education in English and modern science he arranged. In this way, he became Prince Prisdang's benefactor: he sent Prisdang to study English in Singapore and later applied engineering in London.

But what of Prince Prisdang? He also lost his father to the disease. Death was no stranger to Bangkok or to other major metropolises at this time.[30] Disease was rampant: smallpox and cholera regularly swept through the city, leaving thousands dead in their wake. According to one doctor who arrived in the late 1890s, somewhere between 70 and 75 percent of children died within the first few years of their lives, and as late as 1880 a cholera outbreak killed thirty thousand in the kingdom.[31] Life expectancy was low even for the wealthy. For example, forty-three of King Chulalongkorn's children lived past the age of fifteen. Of them, only ten lived to be older than fifty and only two over sixty.[32] Perhaps what is surprising is that Prince Prisdang, one of many who contracted malaria, recovered so quickly. Born in 1852, a bit over a year before Chulalongkorn, Prisdang had escaped by a few short years a major cholera epidemic that devastated Siam in 1849, wiping out nearly twenty thousand people in a single month and paralyzing Bangkok briefly.[33]

Before Prince Chumsai passed away, he presented Prisdang to Chulalongkorn as a member of the Royal Page Corps, where all high-ranking nobles and royalty placed their sons in the hopes they would prove themselves worthy of a government post. We know little about Prisdang's inner thoughts at that time, by contrast with those of King Chulalongkorn. Instead, some of what we know comes from the rumors spread about him many years later and preserved in a letter written in 1892 by a British official, who undoubtedly heard the story from a Siamese official.

The 1892 letter incorrectly identified Prince Prisdang's father as "a half brother of the late King [Mongkut]" who "held however no position, being of weak intellect. When he died, he left his family in very poor circumstances & the present King in 1872 sent Mom Jao Prisdang (as he is called, being by birth only of royal descent on the father's side)" to England for an education.[34] The rumors about Prisdang began not with his birth but with his ancestry. This bit of gossip, a single sentence in a longer salacious letter shared among British officials in 1892, found it insufficient to stain the reputation of Prisdang alone: it attacked his royal-blooded father, Prince Chumsai, the progenitor of the Chumsai lineage, for his allegedly imbecilic mind and impoverished position. Neither accusation was accurate. Whatever Prisdang had done later in his life, it had generated sufficient vitriol to make officials in London (and Siam) retrospectively blacken his entire extended family's reputation, regardless of their innocence.

The letter suggested that Prisdang's father was relatively poor, which prompted him to deposit his youngest son, Prisdang, and likely two of his older sons in the Royal Pages Corps just before he died in 1868. Born in 1817, Prince Chumsai was the twenty-first son of Prince Jetsadabodin and a nonroyal consort.[35] A few years after Prince Chumsai's birth, Prince Jetsadabodin became Rama III, ruling Siam from 1824 to 1851. This made Rama III, not Prince Chumsai, the half brother of King Mongkut (Rama IV), contrary to the letter's claim.

The subtleties of royal rank—particularly in the Siamese case, in which polygyny was not just a perk of power but foundational to its operation—are complex. When a single male individual could have dozens of wives and children, who also married and reproduced kin, it is difficult not to use the term *exponential* to characterize the progeny of the royal family and the handful of noble official families that had comprised the "ruling class" since the Chakri dynasty began in 1782.[36] During the reigns of Rama IV and V, a system to limit the ranks of the royal family began to solidify.[37] To control their numbers, membership followed the rule of declining descent "by which status within the royal family diminished by one degree in each generation, until the fifth-generation descendants of kings were simple commoners."[38] Only those born into the first three royal birth-order ranks—Jao Fa, Phra Ong Jao, and Mom Jao—could be called by the honorific titles translated as "prince" or "princess," with the Jao Fa or son of the king by one of his queens ranking highest. Phra Ong Jao princes were born to a king and a lesser wife, while Mom Jao were grandchildren of a king but had commoner mothers. Given that a Siamese monarch often had dozens of wives who gave birth to dozens of sons who then married multiple commoner women, the number of Mom Jao in any given generation was not insignificant: Prisdang was among them. Given the number of Mom Jao and their distance from the court, which favored higher-ranking princes for positions, promotions, and honors, many Mom Jao ran into financial difficulties and engaged in disreputable behaviors. This threatened the honor of the Chakri dynasty. Finally, the latter two ranks of royalty, Mom Rachawong and Mom Luang, were recognized as nominal members of the royal family but were never referred to as prince or princess.

What is important to note here is that Mom Jao were the lowest-ranking princes and princesses in this complex hierarchy. To further distinguish among royal family members, the king presented them (typically princes) with conferred ranks (five different levels, with variation within each) and appointed them to positions in the administration. Symbols (trays made of gold, for example), decorative orders, and other methods signified each person's relative position.[39]

The monarch also conferred a different set of titles on nonroyal nobles who often fathered more children than did kings.[40] The king's power depended on a shifting matrix of loyalties among ranking princes and a few powerful noble families, including—most important for Prisdang's story—the Bunnag family. Managing threats and tensions among royal family members and their allies was simply government by another name for much of Siam's history.

When Rama II passed away, the Bunnag patriarchs considered Prince Mongkut too young and inexperienced by comparison with his half brother, Prince Jetsadabodin, who was a second-class prince (Phra Ong Jao). To avoid a succession struggle, Prince Mongkut was ordained in the Buddhist monkhood, where he studied English and astronomy among other sciences for the next few decades while his half brother ruled Siam as Rama III. Some consider Rama III a usurper who stole the throne from the rightful heir, Prince Mongkut, the son of Rama II by a royal queen. Prince Jetsadabodin, born to a consort rather than a queen, should not have ascended the throne.

In other words, Prisdang's grandfather was a king but not one of the highest royal status, which had consequences for his descendants. While Rama III could not improve his heirs' relative birth rank, he could help ensure their material well-being by arranging marriages into wealthy families. Early on in his reign, Rama III appointed his confidant, Phraya Ratchamontri, to be head of the Department of Royal Pages. As such, he occupied a strategic position that oversaw and registered the sons of the most important noble families in the country to be trained as future government officials.[41] Phraya Ratchamontri, a scion of a noble Ayutthyan-era family, was an extremely wealthy man who lived in a palace (Ban Tha Chang) in close proximity to Wang Tha Phra, the palace in which Rama III resided before he became king.[42]

A marriage was arranged between one of Rama III's fifty-one children and one of Phraya Ratchamontri's dozens.[43] Prince Matayaphitak, the sixth son of Rama III, married a famously beautiful daughter of Phraya Ratchamontri named Mom Noi. The prince's early death left Mom Noi a widowed mother of two.[44] She was still young and beautiful, but likely there were other reasons behind Rama III's "royal wish" that Noi marry another of Rama III's sons, Prince Chumsai. As the daughter of a "millionaire," Noi and her husband would inherit the "vast fortune" of Phraya Ratchamontri.[45] In other words, Rama III arranged for his son, Prisdang's father, to inherit a considerable fortune in addition to the wealth he obtained as a court architect-engineer.

Together Noi and Chumsai had eight children including their youngest, Prince Prisdang (1852–1935), whose title was Mom Jao, or the lowest-ranking prince.[46] Prince Chumsai (1817–68) became an accomplished architect and craftsman under Rama IV, supervising the construction of temples and palaces. In fact, Chumsai oversaw the construction of the Phuwadolthasanai Pavilion clock tower used by the horology-obsessed King Mongkut to display the accurate time and sound the gong on the hour.[47] He was the only individual that King Mongkut appointed to the conferred rank of Kromakhun who was *not* a son of Rama I or Rama II, suggesting that King Mongkut valued him and rewarded him accordingly.[48] Prince Chumsai, as the son of Rama III, was the half nephew of King Mongkut. Moreover, his own niece became Rama IV's queen and mother of Prince Chulalongkorn.[49]

Chumsai had a reputation for being stern and fearless, even in his relationships with higher-ranking royal family members, including King Mongkut and Mongkut's younger brother, Phra Pinklao.[50] For example, Prince Chumsai required passersby to be quiet when outside his palace: if anyone made a racket, he would order his soldiers to apprehend the offender and flog him regardless of who he was. One evening, a drunk man making a ruckus in front of the palace door found himself being dragged into the palace and flogged. He protested that he could not be flogged because he was a soldier of the king's brother, Phra Pinklao. In response, Prince Chumsai ordered his soldiers to double the punishment. Phra Pinklao could do nothing about the beating. King Mongkut would not support retribution, which suggests that Prince Chumsai was a force to be reckoned with. The resentment between the Phra Pinklao and Prince Chumsai was palpable. Once when they both were being carried on palanquins to the royal palace for an audience with the king, they spied each other, jumped off their palanquins, and began a chase, causing a great commotion.[51]

Prince Chumsai's ill temper may have been legendary, but one would not know it from Prince Prisdang's memories of his father. Their home, Tha Phra Palace, bustled with activity and operated as a center for artistic production during King Mongkut's reign. As chief of the reign's craftsmen, artists, architects, and stonemasons, Prince Chumsai sometimes had more than two hundred people working day and night in his palace grounds. All four of his sons, including his youngest, Prisdang, grew up among artists and engineers and eventually joined their ranks. Their family compound was, according to Prisdang, "full of life and chaos: animals trampling all over the place, a whole crowd of people busy working away, children running and playing."[52]

Prince Prisdang was not so fortunate as to inherit his childhood home, a point of contention later in his life. Built in the late eighteenth century for King Taksin's son, Tha Phra Palace was later occupied by Prince Jetsadabodin (later, Rama III), who eventually passed it on to Prince Chumsai, his son. After Prince Chumsai died from malaria in 1868, his wife and remaining children moved next door into their mother's childhood home (Ban Tha Chang).[53] These details demonstrate that Prince Chumsai was far from poor or power-less or imbecilic, despite the rumors spread about him among British officers decades later.

Several of his sons took up the arts, architecture, and engineering in their father's stead. Known jokingly as the "supervisor" when he was seven or eight, Prince Prisdang accompanied his father to the palaces, temples, and homes of officials, where Prince Chumsai supervised the construction and maintenance of these structures. He also went with his father when he had a royal audience with King Mongkut.[54] Prince Chulalongkorn, as his father's favorite son, was also King Mongkut's constant companion after 1866 during royal audiences when official business was transacted, such as those sessions between the architect Chumsai and the monarch Mongkut.[55] Crouching in the traditional manner of showing respect, Prince Prisdang likely first met the young Prince Chulalongkorn during one of these audiences.

As teenagers, they also both watched the eclipse from the royal enclave on the shores of the Gulf of Siam in 1868 and suffered the subsequent loss of their fathers. Prisdang and Chulalongkorn were separated by a slim year and six months in age, but they lived an ocean apart in terms of rank. The status hier-archy in nineteenth-century Siam was a particularly delicate social and political entity that required persistent effort to maintain. That's not to say it was in cri-sis: the changes occurring all around Prisdang and Chulalongkorn were gradual. The very meaning of "power" was shifting as imperialism and global trade made their presence known domestically in Siam and required its leaders to make changes in how they ruled the kingdom. Chulalongkorn, as an underage mon-arch, eventually found himself at the center of a growing dispute among power-ful royal and noble factions about the direction and speed of these changes and the resulting shifts in power and influence that this would cause. In the 1870s, however, the performance of the existing rank and status hierarchy remained in play.

As mentioned above, by the time King Chulalongkorn ascended the throne in 1868, the Bunnag family dominated Siam's political and economic realms. Its patriarch (Si Suriyawong), as Chulalongkorn's regent, was more powerful than the king, who was isolated from the day-to-day workings of government. None of this was lost on the young King Chulalongkorn, who considered abdicating because of the limitations placed on his power.[56] Once he regained his health, Chulalongkorn began to plan and implement his strategy for moving the king-dom in a particular direction that would ideally position him squarely in the seat of power and simultaneously maintain Siam's independence from encroaching imperial powers.

Prince Prisdang played a role in this plan. Born a Mom Jao—that is, a third-ranking prince out of the five possible ranks of royalty—Prisdang was not assured a high position in the government, let alone among elite society. Bewildering to observers outside the system, the decorum, linguistic norms, and protocol of Siam's hierarchy were well known to those who wanted to climb it. Prisdang understood his relative position within the royal and administrative class. In some ways, he was fortunate that one's position in this system did not depend entirely on inherited status—impossible in a polygynous system that enabled some men to have dozens of children—but was also based on ability. As members of the Royal Pages Corps, young men honed and displayed their skills in ways that grabbed the king's attention.

Typically fathers presented their sons to the Royal Pages Corps for them to receive training and education in various aspects of the administration of the government. Working in close proximity to the king, these sons stood a better chance of receiving an official appointment by the king should they reveal themselves to be exceptionally able, as Prisdang did. At age seventeen, he did what most midtier royalty and nobility did: he took up the craft of his father.[57] Shortly after Prince Chumsai's death in 1868, Prisdang took over the restoration of a temple, Wat Nang, and built the top of the entryway for the palace used for King Chulalongkorn's ordination. But King Chulalongkorn had other plans for Prisdang and many other relatives of similar rank. He understood that in order for Siam to move along the path he had in mind, he needed a cohort of men educated in English and various Western sciences. The young king wanted personally to travel to Europe to see modern institutions of rule, but the regent Si Suriyawong forbade it. As a compromise, King Chulalongkorn traveled to European colonies in the region. From these bastions of imperial autocracy, he took his cue.

In 1871 he traveled to British Singapore and Dutch Java. Later that year, he swung back through Singapore on his way to India. On this second trip, his entourage included three Chumsai brothers. Mom Jao Jamroen and Mom Jao Prawit traveled with the king to India; at least one of them was entrusted to sketch images of buildings and places visited on the journey.[58] The king's official travelogue does not mention Prisdang by name, but he must have been among the unnamed Mom Jao whom the king deposited in Singapore to study English at the Raffles Institution.[59] At the time, a suitable English teacher could not be found in Bangkok, so the king sent twenty or so young royal family members to study in Singapore, where they stayed for about six months. Prince Prisdang remembers that he had been married for less than a month before he traveled to Singapore, where he must have studied English with a Briton named Robert Morant, though there is no record other than a photo of him with Morant from 1871 that he included in the appendix of his autobiography.[60] Little else is known about his wife, Mom Sadap, who resurfaces occasionally in Prisdang's letters and autobiography but with no details illuminating much about her background or personality.

The king set up an English school in Bangkok upon his return from India, recalled the students from their short-lived educational adventure in Singapore, and selected three who had excelled to further their studies in London. Prisdang was among them.[61] He sailed to London on a British B&O Company ship called the *Orissa*, which was several hundred feet long and boasted two masts and an old, cranky engine that caused the ship to tremble. They left in November 1871, when storms rocked the Bay of Bengal. He swore the ship would break as it creaked under pressure but noticed that the foreigners on the ship seemed calm enough. The bunks reminded him of a morgue, and he was thankful for once that he was small in stature and could fit on one of the three "sleeping shelves" along the wall in his cabin. Unlike the comparatively luxurious ships made decades later, which Prisdang likened to "multistory floating hotels," his first vessel bounced "like a Chinese dragon dance," causing most passengers (not him, he maintains) to "throw up everywhere."[62]

Once in England, Prisdang studied for a several months at a public elementary school in Streatham Common, London, before the ambassador for Siam, a British man named D. K. Mason, arranged for him to study at St. Paul's College for six months. Then Prisdang took private lessons from a cleric with whom he resided for another year and a half, after which he was ready to attend King's College in London. There in 1876 he became the first Siamese royal family member to graduate with a university degree (in applied engineering) from abroad. Surely the choice of his degree stemmed both from his family background—his father and brothers were architects and engineers—and from the king's ideas about what skill sets might be useful domestically. From all accounts, Prisdang was a genius. He sped through the primary and secondary curriculum before enrolling in King's College, from which he graduated with nearly every honor. William E. Gladstone, who had just completed his first of four terms as the British prime minister, attended the awards ceremony. The attention he received from Gladstone, known already for his oratory eloquence, thrilled the young Prisdang, who worshipped him thereafter. In Prisdang's memory, Gladstone jokingly stated that Prisdang had dangerously hoarded all the awards to himself. "My hands are tired from extending all the awards to him [Prisdang] again and again," Prisdang recalls.[63] The London *Times* did indeed report on Gladstone's presentation of student awards at King's College, where a certain "Chomsai Prisdang, a native of Siam, took the Freake prize for practical work in engineering, the silver medal . . . a Special Certificate of Honour, the first prizes in the arts of construction, manufacturing art, land surveying and leveling, drawing, and a certificate for mathematics and a certificate for geometrical drawing." Gladstone did mention "the formidable and the monopolizing character of the proceedings of that young gentleman to whom he had so often to hand across the table the proof and commemoration of his exertions."[64] Prisdang appears to have been respected by his classmates at King's College, who heartily applauded him at graduation.

Gladstone and Siam's King Chulalongkorn obtained an exalted status in Prisdang's mind and heart, for he understood that he owed his good fortune to more than his native intelligence and his middling royal background. The gossip about him had not yet begun, but one can imagine that he had his detractors, coming as he did from lower ranks of royalty than those of many of his relatives. Rumors are ethereal and ephemeral, like truth, particularly when it comes to pinning them down. They are rather the opposite of King Mongkut's eclipse, which he predicted with precision; he also specified with exactness the geographical location from which it could be best viewed. On Tuesday, 18 August 1868, at exactly 11:36 a.m. and twenty seconds, the sun was in total eclipse as observed by King Mongkut through his telescope on the terrace of his temporary palace on Wako Beach.[65] Had he chosen a site just a few miles north, he would have observed the eclipse in equally clear splendor but avoided the malarial jungle, and perhaps Prince Prisdang's life would have spun off in another direction altogether.[66] But that's not what happened. Historical contingency—the unpredictable trajectories of a limited set of options—brought Prisdang, his father, King Mongkut, and his son to a remote beach, where they all contracted malaria. This set in motion a train of events that were equally unpredictable. All of it began with a mosquito bite.

EUROPE
Prisdang's Controversial Diplomacy

Scholastic awards in hand, Prisdang buoyantly returned to Bangkok in 1876, where he threw a New Year's ball for members of the royal family (figure 4). Prophetically, he dressed up as a combination of the British consul general, Sir Thomas George Knox, and Knox's common-law Siamese wife, Prang. The costume donned by Prisdang appears to split his body into two: on his right half he dresses as a Siamese woman in traditional elite garb, and on his left half Prisdang sports a beard, a sword, and a British military suit. It embodied the tension not just in his ideas about Siam's past traditions and Westernizing future but in his controversial personality as well.

After his return to Bangkok, Prince Prisdang began working in earnest for King Chulalongkorn's government. He joined a handful of other young male elites as part of a select group of men whom the king sponsored and groomed to help advance domestic reform. Prisdang found himself unexpectedly at the center of the most progressive group of young men working within the Siamese administration.[1] This was surprising because of his relatively low position of Mom Jao. So it was unusual that the group of elite princes surrounding King Chulalongkorn accepted Prisdang into their fold. These connections defined his sense of self. When he and the king were younger, Chulalongkorn referred to Prisdang as his "backbone," which was a play on the name *Prisdang*, which means "back" or "behind." It made Prisdang beam with pride to receive this nickname, the designation he used to modify his own name when he signed his autobiography: "Prisdang, the backbone [of the king]."[2]

FIGURE 4.   Prince Prisdang at a New Year's Costume Ball, Bangkok, 1876, from Prisdang, *Prawat yo*, image number 7.

King Chulalongkorn, then a young man in his twenties, cautiously imple-mented reforms that would garner sufficient support from the conservative elite who still controlled many key government posts, while also initiating more pro-found, long-term shifts in the organization of rule—reforms that became known as the Chakri Reformation.[3] This generational conflict dominated the early reign of King Chulalongkorn. In the midst of this delicate domestic shift in power holders, the very real possibility of Siam's direct colonization confronted its leaders.

Prisdang sat at the pivot point of this transition. His experiences reveal the contingent nature of Siam's independence and the monarch's shift to absolutism—it was never a foregone conclusion that Siam would maintain its independence or that it would become a centralized state headed by a native monarch. Prisdang's inclusion in the most exclusive group of ruling elites and his versatile competencies enabled his meteoric rise within diplomatic and political circles in Siam and Europe. Much to his surprise and delight, Prisdang catapulted from the lower ranks of royalty to the limelight of international diplomacy in the mid-1880s during an acute period of danger for Siam, when Britain claimed Burma on Siam's western frontier, France took the rest of Indochina on the east, and both took turns threatening Siamese sovereignty.

Prisdang considered his performance as a royal official exemplary and even sacred: his mission as his king's "spine" was to strengthen both King Chulalongkorn's position domestically and Siam's internationally. He put Siam on Europe's diplomatic map and mingled with European royalty and heads of state. But the context also raised the stakes for Prisdang, whose rapid ascent stirred resentment in some. While his efforts brought him accolades at home and abroad, they also attracted venomous critique in both places. To judge from Western newspaper articles and private accounts about Prisdang, he appears to have boldly staked his and Siam's place among equals despite imperialist perceptions of him and his country as inferior. He also offended some high-placed Siamese for unwittingly arrogating the discourse and manners of his superiors. In the finely tuned social hierarchy that regulated the language and behaviors of differentially ranked royalty and noble officials by government position, royally conferred title, and birthright, Prisdang's conduct rankled the established hierarchy. That he was intelligent and effective as a diplomat made it difficult for anyone to overtly fault him.

Prisdang moved back and forth between Siam and Europe as he rose in the ranks from civil engineer to interpreter to ambassador. What some considered brilliance others regarded as unmerited arrogance. Efficiency became impulsiveness, depending on who interpreted his actions. Indignant, Prisdang responded defensively in private letters to the accusations against him, the basis for which confounded him. The contradictory reactions his presence aroused in European and Siamese circles fueled his eventual expulsion from the center to the margins of Siam's political, social, and diplomatic arenas. His unnamed detractors who had influence with the king began to shred Prisdang's reputation, bit by bit over time, until he raised a gun to his head and considered pulling the trigger.

Prisdang's Meteoric Rise

Prisdang's educational success at King's College, London, brought him to the attention of many in Siamese elite social and government circles. When he returned to Siam in 1876, he received a salary increase from the king and became a favorite of his paternal grandmother, who observed, "You look like your father." It was perhaps the first time she had noticed him, which was sufficiently remarkable that the memory lodged itself in Prisdang's mind, resurfacing decades later in his autobiography. He began working intimately with some of the king's closest relatives. One can imagine the sense of social jockeying in play within Bangkok's high society. Prisdang, a mere Mom Jao and thus barely meriting his princely title, had climbed up the hierarchy through a combination of book smarts and social intelligence.

Riding this euphoric wave, when the whole Siamese social and political world opened before him, Prisdang noted, "All the royal family members were impressed that I still acted and behaved in a traditional Thai way, unlike many others who studied abroad. Many of them became friendly, calling me by my name, *Prisdang*, as if they were talking to a family member."[4] In this way, he first became acquainted with several of the king's brothers and relatives who would come to dominate Siam's administration. They included Prince Naret Worarit[5] (1855–1925) and Prince Devawongse (Thewawong) (1858–1923), the latter of whom served as the king's royal secretary and then as Siam's minister of foreign affairs from the 1880s until his death in 1923. Prisdang mused, "I have this strange fortune that no high level royalty dislike me."[6] His familiarity with European elite cultural norms and fluency in English must have appealed to Siam's king and Prince Devawongse, neither of whom had yet had the opportunity to visit Europe.

In particular, Prisdang cultivated a relationship with Prince Devawongse, the king's half brother, who was also the monarch's most loyal supporter and host to many European royal visitors in the 1870s. When European royalty visited, they sometimes stayed in Prince Devawongse's palace, where Prisdang was also asked to reside. From there, he acted as their tour guide and interpreter. Prince Prisdang reflected on the in he had with Devawongse: "I had to go live in that [Devawongse's] royal palace as well, as the interpreter, and take them around the entire time they were visiting. . . . The prince thereby became acquainted with me, favored me, and used me to run his errands from that point on. Whenever there was an opportunity, he then would take it as his obligation to vouch for me in government service, duties and activities. I was trusted [by the prince]."[7] He also became closely acquainted with Prince Phanurangsi Sawangwong (hereafter Phanurangsi), King Chulalongkorn's younger full brother, who eventually became Prisdang's supportive patron. Prisdang underscores in his autobiography this moment, when the highest-ranking princes like Devawongse and the king were his greatest supporters, portending a later decline in their relationship.

Siam also needed Prisdang's formal training in applied engineering. Soon after his return in 1876, the king began an energetic public works program that he asked Prisdang to oversee, including surveying canals and drafting an irrigation map that would be used to build a system to distribute clean water to Bangkok's residents. The king sent him to help supervise the gold mines in Kabinburi, one of the king's pet projects.[8] There Prisdang no doubt became acquainted with Phra Pricha Konlakan (Sam-Ang Amatayakul), who owned the tax monopoly on gold mining in Kabin and also belonged to a family that strongly supported the king's reforms. His high-placed family brought Phra Pricha into contact with Thomas Knox, whose half-Siamese daughter he eventually married.

Trying to supervise the gold mines and public irrigation projects convinced Prisdang that to do so comfortably, he needed practical training in various public works projects that could be had in Europe. D. K. Mason, the general consul for Siam in London, arranged for a three-year apprenticeship with a British company. With that company, Prisdang received training on railway, port, and hydraulics projects, including one in Holland.[9] He left for his second trip to England in late 1877 and began his apprenticeship early the following year.

Prisdang may have been destined to become Siam's most brilliant engineer, but timing and context intervened to play their typical mercurial roles. A crisis erupted that brought him out of the irrigation trenches and onto the diplomatic stage. Phra Pricha, the owner of the gold mines in Kabin, was arrested for allegedly embezzling funds. Phra Pricha had also married the daughter of Thomas Knox—the very consul that Prisang had masqueraded as in 1876—without first requesting the king's permission as was required by the palace law.[10] Phra Pricha was charged with contravening palace law regarding the marriage of high-ranking officials to non-Siamese and with corruption and murder. Whether these charges were fabricated or real or whether the impudent act of marriage catalyzed the investigation or was the consequence of it is disputed.[11] Most scholars agree that Si Suriyawong, Chulalongkorn's former regent, whose power was threatened by government reforms, engineered Phra Pricha's demise, which is not to argue he was innocent but that the enforcement of law against him was selective and punitive.[12]

Phra Pricha soon found himself irretrievably buried under accusations for which he was imprisoned, along with his father and other relatives who supported the king. Soldiers reclaimed his possessions and those of his wife, Fanny Knox. Allegedly pregnant, she fled to Singapore in late 1878 with two of Phra Pricha's children by a previous marriage.[13] Her father threatened that unless his son-in-law was released, he would send a British warship up the Chao Phraya River to the Grand Palace.[14] This was tantamount to imperial intervention, regardless of the original catalyst.

Knox's egregious diplomatic miscalculations opened up a career in diplomacy for Prince Prisdang. To diffuse the tension, the king sent a small diplomatic mission to negotiate directly with officials in London in 1879–80. He ordered Prisdang to interrupt his engineering apprenticeship to serve as an interpreter for the delegation. In London, Prisdang met, perhaps for the first time, a man who became his dear friend, Jamuen Saraphai (Joem Saeng-Chuto; hereafter Surasak),[15] and Phraya Phatsakorawong (Phon Bunnag), a proreform member of the Bunnag family who had been educated in London.[16]

Their negotiations culminated in a diplomatic coup for Siam and Prisdang: rather than intervening militarily, the British recalled and retired Thomas Knox.[17] Thus began Prisdang's unanticipated ascendance in the field of diplomacy. He worked intermittently over the next two years in Europe as an engineering apprentice and as an interpreter for Jao Phraya Phanuwong Mahakosathipbodi (Thuam Bunnag), Siam's foreign minister, who brought Prisdang with him for audiences with Queen Victoria, the Prince of Wales, the president of the Republic of France, and the crown prince of Prussia (later briefly Emperor Frederick III of Germany).[18] When Siam's foreign minister Phanuwong had to return to Siam, Prisdang remained behind as a broker and general all-purpose man for Siam, ordering souvenirs and other goods for the king and his court. In this way, he began to meet European royalty and learn more intimately their protocol while finishing up his three-year apprenticeship with the civil engineering company. Salary raises, special insignia, and career promotions blessed Prisdang, who had spent nearly ten years abroad by this point.

When he returned to Bangkok briefly in 1880–81, Prisdang was invited to join a secret elite group of the king's most trusted and loyal servants who swore an oath of loyalty and unity before the sacred Emerald Buddha. This league's purpose was to defend the king, ensure that his first son by a high-ranking queen would succeed him, promise eternal friendship and brotherhood, and swear never to serve any other master or seek personal gain from their governmental duties.[19] This tight-knit brotherhood of young men faced serious resistance from established elites who benefited from the existing system of rule and social-political hierarchy, which they sought to reform. *Brotherhood* is an apposite term. Some of the reformers were the king's brothers and half brothers, but more pertinently, they swore allegiance to the king, the heir apparent, and each other, as a band of brothers.

Prisdang had already met fellow oath brethren Surasak and Prince Devawongse.[20] Two additional members of the group would later join Prisdang in Europe: Senae Humphrae, who helped him supervise the Siamese students, and the king's half brother Prince Svasti (Sawat) Sobhon (hereafter Prince Svasti), who was full brother to Prince Devawongse. Because of the group's political nature, its membership remained secret and never numbered more than nine or so.[21]

Prisdang refers to some of these men as his dearest friends, whose relationships were cemented by the sacred vow sworn before the Chakri dynasty's most significant holy Buddha image. He and Prince Svasti were, for a time, very close.

Prisdang was among the most prestigious and progressive members of the elite, something he had never imagined possible given his relatively minor regal status and parentage. His sense of his humble origins and pride in his achievements characterize his autobiographical writings. He ceaselessly refers (in letters) to his gratitude to the king for supporting and advancing him beyond what his parents could have done. In Siam's social hierarchy, no one of his rank, regardless of his brilliant performance in school or as a civil engineer or diplomat, could have come this far without the patronage of the king. For this he owed the king a permanent debt of gratitude.

While Prisdang was in Bangkok in 1881, the king invited him on a trip to Siam's east coast, where he "listened to his [the king's] opinions on politics and other business."[22] It was the most intimate phase of his relationship with the king, who presented Prisdang with another status award and a raise. When the king asked for volunteers to expand the kingdom's reserve troops, Prisdang proudly offered his assistance: "I was the first to take lead (to set an example)" for which the king awarded him the rank of "special colonel."[23] Even though Prisdang never set foot on a battlefield in his life, he brought his uniform and sword with him everywhere, even into exile, and to the monastery where he was eventually ordained decades later. While in Siam, he kept busy with a variety of government projects, including the construction of a new prison in Bangkok.[24] He continued to mingle with his Siamese and European royal superiors, including the king of Hawaii and the duke of Genoa, who visited Siam.

Prisdang had proven his versatility and usefulness. By the fall of 1881, the king sent him back to Europe, appointing him to be a special ambassador to attend the weddings of the princes of Prussia and Germany, where the king also entrusted him to survey military and munitions installations. Nearly a dozen Siamese students and assistants joined him, including two oath brothers: Prince Svasti, who would become a student in London, and Nai Senae Humphrae, who helped Prisdang serve as chaperone. Another nine young Siamese men of the highest birth completed their entourage, which made its way treacherously by boat and train to Europe, where they would attend school and be supervised by Prisdang.[25] They experienced firsthand the discomforts and dangers of modern forms of transportation: seasickness from Singapore to Ceylon, being quarantined in Naples after a passenger died aboard the ship, and a train wreck from Marseilles to London, which Prisdang described in a letter to the king.[26] Prisdang helped rescue some of the injured and, oddly, collected some of the wreckage as a souvenir.[27] Everything to him was worthy of memorializing and collecting as if to substantiate the unimaginable life he was living.

Once he had safely settled the students in London, he met with royalty in Austria and Germany, dancing his way through New Year's at the palace of Vienna's empress. In fact, it may have been the emperor of Austria-Hungary who gave

Siam's leaders the idea of sending ambassadors abroad when he sent a permanent ambassador to Siam.[28] Siam, at the time, did not have resident ambassadors
in Europe but instead typically employed individuals from the country where
they served, such as D. K. Mason in London, who received the Siamese title Phra
Sayam Dhurapaha (later Phya).[29] Monsieur Gréhan, the Siamese consul in Paris,
was known as Phra Sayam-Dhuranurak.[30] The Siamese government would send
special envoys from Siam when a crisis arose that required them to converse
directly with European leaders. This changed in 1882, when Prisdang returned
from the European continent to London to prepare to go home again to Bangkok.

At that moment Prisdang received a life-changing telegraph from Prince
Devawongse, who was then serving as the king's royal secretary: "Do not return.
Plan to stay. I have sent out His Majesty's appointment orders and an assistant
officer. You are to serve as an ambassador to all alliance countries."[31] On 16 March
1882, the king officially appointed Prince Prisdang the first Siamese resident
envoy extraordinaire and minister plenipotentiary to the United States, England,
France, Portugal, Spain, Holland, Belgium, Denmark, Prussia, Austria, Italy, and
Sweden and Norway (which were united at the time). Now Siam had its first resident native Siamese diplomatic representative to the West.[32]

Prisdang served in his new position with zeal. Even the most critical observers would find it difficult to review this brief period of his life without being
impressed by the astonishing number and significance of the activities he accomplished in a demanding imperial context that thwarted the advance of non-
Western countries, many of which were, like Siam, sending their sons abroad to
learn how to catch up with more powerful countries. His diplomatic duties were
broadly conceived, and he did much more than serve as ambassador.

By establishing direct lines of communication between Siam's leaders and those
in Europe, Prisdang bypassed European officials residing in Bangkok who tended
to be prejudiced against Siamese interests. He, by contrast, consistently secured a
better outcome for Siam in diplomatic negotiations. He recommended that the
king appoint Siamese officers to be stationed in each country as a way to sidestep
European representatives residing in Bangkok who consistently took advantage
of Siam. Up to the 1880s, most consular officials for Siam in Europe were Europeans who were honorary appointees and therefore unpaid, with the exception
of Mason in London and M. A. de Gréhan in Paris. They had more power before
Prisdang arrived on the scene because they corresponded directly with King Chulalongkorn or the minister of foreign affairs in Bangkok.[33] More concretely, Prisdang's persistence and perspicacity facilitated the revision of some of the most
egregious unequal treaty provisions regarding alcohol taxation and extraterritoriality privileges. Prisdang proved, moreover, that the new ambassadorial position
paid for itself. For the low expenditure of hiring him to represent Siam in twelve

alliance countries to negotiate the tax on alcohol, which earned profits, Prisdang calculated that the ambassadorial post actually saved money for Siam.

He ensured Siam's entry into global communications networks by standardizing its telegraph and postal system and signing the Universal Postal Convention. His assistance from afar in the establishment in Bangkok of the Post and Telegraph Department (1883), not to mention obtaining Siamese membership in the international post and telegraphic unions, fell outside his duties as ambassador. He helped create Siam's first postal stamps—following the lead of Great Britain, images of Siam's sovereign covered the stamps—which were used in exchanges with foreign countries as official gifts and souvenirs, as well as to pay for mailing costs.

In addition, Prisdang examined European military installations, munitions factories, and public works projects for their utility in Siam. He deployed his practical engineering skills when inspecting European railways, hydraulics, mints and coinage production, mining, military fortifications, torpedoes, public waterways, land and canal surveying, public electricity projects, and postal stamp and medallion design.[34] He was constantly scanning the architecture in Europe's capitals for ideas about how to build and decorate his king's palaces.[35] He also made himself available for consultation about Siamese art and music, which he knew well enough to teach scholar Alexander Ellis the theories of pitches in Siamese musical scales.[36]

In addition, Prisdang supervised Siamese students abroad and sought special tutors for them when necessary, activities that were only tangentially related to his ambassadorial duties.[37] He arranged their study schedules—correspondence reflects his response to the king's concern that they needed to spend more time learning Thai—and he provided their rather limited pocket money.[38] He even dealt with the minutiae of finding a suitable location for the Siamese embassy in London and dealing with the pensions provided to families of British men who had died while in the employ of Siam.[39]

Of all his responsibilities, Prisdang most enjoyed networking and socializing with foreign royalty, linking Siamese royalty with European blue blood. His own royal status enabled a connection that a member of the Siamese nonroyal aristocracy could not have made. As Siam's ambassador, he met with royalty in every country he visited. Prisdang traveled frequently between London and Paris but also to Lisbon, Rome, the Vatican, Vienna, Berlin, Brussels, the Hague, Stockholm, and Copenhagen, where he met the most important leaders of Europe, including emperors and empresses, kings and queens, dukes and duchesses, the pope, one president (France), foreign ministers, and ambassadors.[40] He earned foreign decorations including the British Order of St. Michael and St. George (C.M.G.), the French Legion of Honor, and the German Order of the Red Eagle.[41] Prisdang calculated that he had spent seven years of his life literally in transit, on boats and trains, much of which occurred in this period in Europe.[42] In the era before mass personal communications were possible, his months on board ships and trains gave him time to reflect and to write, which he did prolifically. Prisdang wanted to be known.

He also was intensely aware of being a "first," which meant that sometimes his ambition got the best of him. For example, in his eagerness to present his ambassadorial credentials across Europe as quickly as possible, he ignored important protocols regarding the relationship between the king of Italy and the pope at the Vatican. In the 1880s, the Italian government and the Vatican could not both receive the same ambassador on a single journey, but Prisdang pressed them to do just this: he wanted to visit both the king and the pope on his trip. He was criticized in the British newspapers for his diplomatic faux pas and nearly upset Siam's future relationship with the Vatican.[43]

Prisdang learned to play billiards, tennis, and cards just like a European gentleman. He danced at balls, donated at charity functions, and attended orchestral concerts, the opera, and the theater.[44] Most important, he learned the art of diplomacy. Attending to diplomacy's ephemeral subtleties—wearing the appropriate uniforms, observing protocol, appearing at the key social functions, and joining the right clubs was as significant as formally renegotiating legal treaties. The protocol for the exchange of royal insignia and orders, the seating arrangements at official meals, and the politesse used in diplomatic negotiations operated like a language whose conversation was about rank and hierarchy.[45] Prisdang had to learn it in order to be effective personally and as Siam's face abroad.

Foreign Critiques of Prisdang and Siam

Despite his successes, Prisdang did not execute his duties perfectly, nor did all his royal and diplomatic brethren in Europe accept him with open arms. Some Europeans held him in contempt because of racist and imperial understandings of the world order that had little to do with Prisdang. For example, when the train on which Prisdang and his student entourage were riding crashed into another locomotive, killing eighteen passengers, a malicious *New York Times* article reported that the young Siamese on board "have sat in a corner and gibbered ever since their arrival." "The coffee-colored exotics" attended the opera in Paris, after which "His Highness" (unspecified) made "unparliamentary" advances on the female dancers, who advised these "monkeys" to return to the "Jardin des Plantes."[46]

A private report targeted Prisdang's promotion to special envoy in similarly prejudiced ways that were not unusual for the times. He was, after all, replacing foreigners who had hitherto monopolized the connection between the Siamese government and foreign powers in Europe. William Gifford Palgrave, the British consul-general who replaced Knox in Bangkok from 1880 to 1883, was particularly derisive about Prisdang because of Prisdang's role in negotiations regarding the Thomas Knox affair. In an excoriating letter to a certain H. A.W. Hervey in September 1881, Palgrave describes Prisdang as

> the coxcombical little puppy, who gave himself while here all the airs of the "monkey who has seen the world." . . . Seriously, I trust you will not admit the little mischief-maker to a hearing. While here [London] his influence at Court was very pernicious; and he did all in his power to depreciate England in particular, representing us—I have it on good authority—as a gullable [sic], weak-minded people whose displeasure mattered nothing; and who could be safely trusted never to do Siam any harm: a view readily adopted by "the king and all his ministers," into whom, ever since Prisdang's visit, seven extra demons of refractoriness and trick seem to have entered. The harm done by the (as they imagine) victory of the Siamese over Knox . . . all this harm, I say, exists yet and will exist till a good snubbing lets some of the gas out of these wretched bubbles.[47]

Prisdang had done well by Siam in 1879, which British officials like Palgrave interpreted as harming the interests of Britain. Some wanted to return the diplomatic slight. He did his best to avoid giving them cause, but sometimes this proved impossible. When Prisdang first arrived as the special ambassador accompanying Siamese students to Europe in 1881, he issued detailed letters to King Chulalongkorn that included concerns about the subtleties of diplomatic protocol.

> Once we arrived in London, I consulted with Phraya Sayamthurapha [D. K. Mason, the consul for Siam in London] about how to inquire [with British officials] about various governmental concerns that were suggested by Your Majesty. I expressed concern that we wouldn't be able to ask [these questions] due to some hindrance that Phra Sayamthuranurak [M. A. de Gréhan, the consul for Siam in France] had explained to me. Phraya Sayamthurapha responded that I should not believe in Phra Sayamthuranurak's insights or follow his suggestions. I should just ask [the British government officials] anything Your Majesty has instructed me to ask. If they cannot answer, they will simply say they have to think about it first.[48]

Prisdang brought with him a list of items to address with the British foreign minister, but first he had to pay close attention to codes of behavior such as seating arrangements. He received an invitation to visit the manor of Lord Earl Granville, the British secretary of state for foreign affairs between 1880 and 1885, which indicated that Prisdang had navigated the social scene sufficiently well. There, Lord Granville treated him and Prince Svasti to a meal. "Lord Granville sat at one end of the table, the Countess at the other end. Prince Svasti was seated to the right of the Countess. I sat on the left. Next to me was a lady, then Mr. Sane. Next to him was Lord Chamberlain" and so on.[49] They signed the guest book and played lawn tennis before Lord Granville took Prisdang into a private area to discuss government business. These activities and their sequence were important enough for Prisdang to mention them in detail to the king, as if to explain how diplomatic protocol worked in private settings.

When Prisdang had an audience with Queen Victoria in 1882 to present his diplomatic credentials to her, Lord Granville had evidently not forewarned the queen of his arrival. Horse-drawn carriages arrived at Windsor train station to pick up an entourage from India and their British hosts but not Prisdang. As there appeared to be no other means of transportation available, he asked to share the ride to Windsor Castle and sat with the servants in the back of the carriage. The British aide-de-camp accompanying the India entourage asked Prisdang who he was. The Siamese minister, he replied. Visibly uncomfortable at this diplomatic gaffe, the official had to convince Prisdang to exchange seats, but the prince retorted that he was perfectly comfortable where he sat. Once at Windsor, Prisdang, as a representative of a sovereign kingdom, was ushered in to meet the queen ahead of the Indian party. Either his visit had caught the queen and her attendants innocently off guard or one of the British officials purposefully "forgot" about Prisdang's appointment.[50]

Little slights such as this may have been common, and Prisdang responded with indignant pride though never in front of those who outranked him. As the most powerful imperial nation, England (and more specifically, the Court of St. James) was first to receive Prisdang's ministerial credentials, after which he spent 1883 and 1884 traveling to courts and capitals across Europe to present himself and begin revising the treaties on spirits (see figure 5). Revision of the alcohol treaties and negotiating Siam's entry into the Universal Postal Union (1884) and International Telegraphic Union (1885) occupied Prisdang the entire time he served as minister plenipotentiary, from the moment of his appointment until he left Europe in early 1886.[51] He didn't come home until he had successfully revised them, a task that the French made infuriatingly complex.[52]

While some British officials snubbed him indirectly, the French openly battled Prisdang in negotiations where sharp tongues wagged and tempers flared.[53] Monsieur Gréhan thwarted Prisdang's efforts whenever French interests were

FIGURE 5. Photo of Prisdang in Vienna with foreign officials. Courtesy of the National Archives, Thailand.

involved. The French complicated the seemingly innocuous task of joining the post and telegraph unions by requiring Siam to hire Frenchmen to work on the telegraphic line between Bangkok and French Saigon before they agreed to sign the otherwise unrelated treaty on spirits. Only after intense negotiating was Prisdang able to obtain the signatures of all treaty parties on the alcohol tax revisions even though it meant that Siam had to hire several Frenchmen, known to abuse their positions, to operate that segment of the telegraphic line.[54] Prisdang learned that the French would always demand a quid pro quo in their negotiations with Siam and that international law and diplomacy might appear "universal" but consistently benefited its European progenitors.

Navigating the social scene in Europe, however, rewarded Prisdang as often as it vexed him. He treats high society in detail in his memoirs and his notes taken at the time, embracing his European connections with great pride and even affection. His autobiography skims lightly over the complicated treaty revisions he accomplished, about which scholars have written books. Instead, it was hobnobbing with European elites—ambassadors, ministers, and especially royalty—and collecting the symbols of status that most fascinated him. The seemingly endless exchange of royal insignia earned by attending formal state and royal visits, dinners, balls, clubs, and charity events captivated Prisdang, who described them decades later. "I received the insignia of the Red Eagle Class II," "the king presented me with the insignia of the Crown of Siam Class I," and so on.[55] He was proud of being invited to join the most exclusive clubs in the world. He belonged, and this clearly thrilled him. He attended social functions for diplomatic reasons, but one senses that he personally enjoyed them as well.

Prisdang remarked with pride on his multifarious activities: "I traveled widely, associating with members of the same high social class"; he donated money in support of institutions and societies of higher learning and for the public welfare such as the Pali Text Society, which he subscribed to from its founding in 1882.[56] He "joined clubs in order to associate with and listen to the views and opinions of high class foreigners, and patronized hospitals in every country to the point that the Queen Empress of Germany . . . invited me for a special audience in her quarters . . . to express her gratitude that I had supported her hospital."[57] He was on such friendly terms with the German ambassador that the ambassador personally taught him to drive a horse-drawn carriage. Prisdang fiercely defended his networking as beneficial to Siam and her cause.

For these efforts, King Chulalongkorn presented Prisdang with a reward in August 1883, just two years into his posting as minister plenipotentiary. "The king was extremely pleased that the treaties were successfully completed. . . . The king promoted me to be Phra Ong Jao" and rewarded Prisdang with an additional royal insignia.[58] At the Siamese embassy, then located at 2 Cornwall Mansions, the highest-ranking Siamese princes in London took part in the ceremony that invested Prince Prisdang with the royal (Chakri) family Order of Jula Jom Klao, the Crown of Siam, and a diploma of pure gold that conferred upon him the higher princely rank of Phra Ong Jao (figure 6). He had moved from a third-ranked prince to a second-ranked prince—the highest level anyone not born of a king and a queen could obtain. Prince Naret, Prince Sonabandit, and Prince Svasti—three of the king's half brothers—performed the ceremony before a diplomatic audience that included the U.S., Dutch, and Spanish ministers as well as representatives from the French, British, German, and other embassies.

Prisdang wrote with pride about the promotion in his autobiography. "Because His Majesty graced me by placing immeasurable trust in me, Mom Jao Prisdang was able to change his status, floating up almost to the top . . . as if His Majesty graciously allowed me to be reborn a second time as another person,

FIGURE 6.   From the left: Prince Sonabandit (holding a document), Prince Svasti (holding a ceremonial bowl), unknown foreigner, Prince Naret Worarit (handing over a ceremonial bowl), and Prince Prisdang (kneeling). From the *London Illustrated News*, December 1, 1883, 532.

free from the status of a typical Mom Jao and giving me an opportunity to try to serve him and be rewarded with his favor like this."[59] The ceremony and promotion were crucial to Prince Prisdang, who invited the press to witness the event. A reporter in London sent his glowing piece to the *Straits Times* (British Singapore). "Prince Prisdang, who during his residence here [in London], has won golden opinions for his ability, tact, urbanity, and courtesy, in the highest political, diplomatic, and social circles, is about to remove to Paris as the Minister of Siam to the Continental Powers." The lengthy article noted Prisdang's admirable service, loyalty, patriotism, diligence, merits, and performance and reprinted (in English) the royal command and other related documents regarding Prisdang's promotion.[60] The author also notes the absence of some key officials, such as British prime minister Gladstone, who were unable to attend the ceremony but sent their regrets.

Not all of the reportage reflected positively upon Prince Prisdang. The *Straits Times*' flattery contrasts two farcical pieces published in *Moonshine*, a British weekly. One, entitled "Pris-Dang It All!" mocked Prisdang's promotion in nonsensical poetic form.

> Mom Chow Prisdang Phra Ong Chow
> Phra Wongs Tho'e Bow Wow Wow
> By the grace of King Chom Klao
> (No relation to Cetewayo),[61]
> Had been dubbed a Knight Grand Cross
> Of "The Fifty-Legged Hoss"
> Or some other Order splendid—
> Found which long since eastern men did.
> May be, 'tis the "Siamese-les"
> Or the "Siamese-twin-easels."
> Praise be, then, to Phra Ong Chow
> Phra Wongs Th'oe Bow Wow Wow!
> Also sound the loud tom-tom
> To the Glory of King Chom?[62]

Moonshine published another short piece of mockery the week following the ceremony, in which the author noted that "All of the Cabinet Ministers, and most of the high dignitaries of State were invited to witness the ceremony, but they one and all, for some reason or another, declined." Thereafter, the author contrived a dialogue between Prince Prisdang and the newly appointed ambassador to England and the United States, Prince Naret.

> *H.R.H.* [NARET]. Another refusal. In Siam I would have their heads off in a twinkling.
>
> PRINCE PRISDANG. Ah, your Royal Highness, you've no idea what it is putting up with their airs and graces. I'm heartily glad I'm going to Paris. (Enter Siamese page slowly on his head, a salver in his mouth, on the salver a note.)
>
> *H.R.H.* The German Ambassador is otherwise engaged. I tell you what it is, Prisdang, you've offended these people.... [Four more pages enter with notes explaining other regrets for missing the ceremony.]
>
> *H.R.H.* Ha! Another missive. The Prime Minister, Gladstone the great; even he spits at us....
>
> PRINCE PRISDANG. It is a forgery. He would at least have written himself. He would not have insulted us by getting a clerk to write the refusal.
>
> *H.R.H.* Are you sure the *Daily Telegraph* man will come?

PRINCE PRISDANG. Certainly. Have I not mentioned the luncheon?

H.R.H, Then my wrath is appeased. Place him in a good position and see that the waiters look after him properly. If he describes the feast well we may yet achieve distinction.[63]

It is unclear if Prisdang had a reputation for self-promotion and impudence or if this was simply how the British press and public responded to Asians whose competence threatened to topple a racialized imperial hierarchy. They were not mutually exclusive impulses.

Prisdang's Domestic Detractors

As soon as he was promoted to Phra Ong Jao, Prisdang was transferred from his position in London to Paris. There he was charged with establishing a consular presence and serving as ambassador to France and the continental treaty powers.[64]

The king's decision to promote Prisdang to a higher princely rank may have been an effort to ease the tensions concerning mismatched regal and official rank and to recognize him for his many accomplishments. However, something else was afoot. Soon after the king promoted Prisdang, he removed Prisdang from his post as ambassador to England—the most powerful country in the world. In Prisdang's stead, the king sent his more appropriately ranked (Jao Fa, the highest princely rank) half brother, Prince Naret Worarit, to be ambassador to England and the United States. Prisdang's promotion, in other words, may have been a subtle demotion and an attempt to ease potential disappointment because of the reduction in his portfolio.

The move had been in the works since early 1883. William Henry Newman, the acting consul general in Bangkok, sent a dispatch in August to Granville, noting that he had "for some time been aware of the intention of the king to send this gentlemen [Prince Naret] to Europe in the capacity of Minister to England and the United States of America, Prince Prisdang being transferred to Paris."[65] Then, so as not to disappoint Prisdang by removing him from London, the king issued the promotion in rank.[66] Prisdang moved to Paris, where he found a location for the embassy on Rue de la Pompe, which was renamed Rue de Siam. By this point, his wife, Mom Sadap, had been sent to Europe to join him. Nothing more is mentioned of her or their relationship while they were in Europe together.[67]

Several confidential documents imply that Prisdang's ambassadorial status in London was higher than that warranted for someone with the rank of Mom Jao. Palgrave, who was set against Prisdang as early as 1881, wrote to Siam's head of foreign affairs, Jao Phraya Phanuwong (Thuam Bunnag) that he "did not think it was correct for the Foreign Minister to call him [Prisdang] prince since he was only" a Mom Jao.[68] The British, like most European officials who were still subject to monarchical hierarchy, were highly conscious of the finer distinctions of title and rank. Prisdang's status, however, was based not on rank alone but on achievement.

The issue of rank was not lost on Prince Prisdang, who scribbled an anxious letter to his "dear brother" (*nong than*), who has been identified as Surasak (figure 7),[69] in November 1882. In it he explains that he had received a letter from the "prince in charge of the department" (nai krom),[70] who reprimanded him for "practically everything," including his choice of a first-person pronoun: "It is now deemed obstinate and arrogant when I write to the head of the Department of Foreign Affairs and refer to myself as *khaphajao* instead of as *kha phraphutha-jao*. I really have no idea why. And I've been criticized for many other things."[71]

The pronoun *kha phraphuthajao*—literally, I/slave or servant of the Lord Buddha—is used by a person of inferior status when communicating with a member of royalty of a higher status. When Jao Phraya Phanuwong, a nonroyal aristocrat, was still the head of the Department of Foreign Affairs, Prisdang used *khaphajao*, which was a form of the pronoun "I," to refer to himself: a respectful but less subservient I than *khaphraphuthajao*. But by 1882, Prince Devawongse had assumed the post of Krom Tha, head of the Department of Foreign Affairs (it became a ministry in 1885). Prisdang, by continuing to refer to himself as I/*khaphajao*, was not showing proper deference, for which Devawongse criticized him.

The appointment of Prince Devawongse to this post also signified a major shift in control over Siam's diplomatic affairs from the Bunnag family to the king's group of reformers. Prisdang's appointment in 1882 as ambassador to allied countries and Devawongse's appointment to head up foreign affairs ended the dominance of the Bunnag family in Siam's foreign relations. Even before the Chakri family became Siam's ruling dynasty in the late eighteenth century, the Bunnags had begun intermarrying with them. Over time, the Bunnag family's power was strengthened through marital ties in which Bunnag women were given as wives and consorts to the king and princes. In return, many Bunnag men received lucrative and powerful appointments in the government. Most pertinently, members of the family had controlled the ministry that dealt with foreign affairs and trade since 1822.[72] In this way, Prisdang's appointment as minister plenipotentiary to the treaty countries circumvented and obviated the role of Jao Phraya Phanuwong Mahakosathibodi.

British observers didn't fully comprehend the minor coup occurring under the surface as indicated by one communiqué from 1883 that noted that King Chulalongkorn "deals with Prince Prisdang through his [the king's] brother the Private Secretary [Devawongse] instead of through the proper official channel,

FIGURE 7. Joem Saeng-Chuto, later known as Jao Phraya Surasakmontri, as a young man. Courtesy of National Archives, Thailand.

the Foreign Minister [Phanuwong], and it is worthy of note that the present Siamese Minister in London [Prisdang] is in reality more an agent of the Palace than of the Siamese Government."[73] Although Jao Phraya Phanuwong had led the ambassadorial mission in 1879 that negotiated the Knox affair, it was Prisdang whom Devawongse and the king asked to stay in London and assert an ambassadorial presence in the region. Tellingly, Phanuwong officially retired from his position by 1885, citing ill health, though in fact he was only fifty-five and lived into his eighties.[74] In fact, he had been edged out several years earlier than that, along with other powerful members of the Bunnag family, and replaced by those most loyal to King Chulalongkorn. It is possible that Prisdang, who ruffled the feathers of a few of his superiors, was blamed for a bigger transition in control over foreign affairs. He was expendable: a scapegoat whom the Bunnag patriarchs could target without directly attacking the king or his half brother, Prince Devawongse.

A final concern about Prisdang's questionable behavior in Europe involved his alleged extravagant spending habits. In the same 1882 letter to "nong than," Prisdang fretted about more than his misuse of pronouns. The unnamed prince (Devawongse) who criticized Prisdang dug up all the orders for purchases that Prisdang had placed in the past.

> I was criticized for spending too much on purchasing useless items. All I did was follow instructions to make decisions about buying items I thought were appropriate. I only want to satisfy the king, so I don't know how to respond if he is displeased. I also have the feeling that he [the king] suspects I spent too much money on those things. I believe only that I swore to serve the king and the country with my life. I never try to personally profit. I only try to do my job, but if he doesn't trust me anymore, then everything I do, of course, is wrong.
>
> One thing I am proud of is that I never had any money in my pocket. My wife is living on my salary only. I've never wanted anything more than to benefit the country. All I think about is serving the country, and living on whatever the country feeds me. As long as I live, I wish to serve the king. My life is in his hands. . . . I feel so sorry for my wife who used to have her mother, father, and servants, but she lost all of them after she married me. When I had a good job, I was able to support her. But if I lose my job, I won't be able to do so and she would be in a very tough situation.

He ends the letter: "Now, I have no courage left to say anything else. What I have told you is private. It stays only between the two of us, brothers, true friends. I am at the end of my rope. Fondly, Prisdang."[75]

In his autobiography Prisdang indirectly addresses accusations about extravagant spending in a manner that concurs with letters written in the 1880s. He notes, "While I was serving as an ambassador, I was ordered to implement the king's commands, and purchased many items. I am an active person, never pausing for leisure. If there is something to do, I do it. I was always thinking [about things to do]. However these were all bones around my neck. I never personally benefited or was enriched like others who worked for the king."[76] "Bones hanging around my neck" stems from an adage: Meat you did not eat, skin that did not bear your weight [to sit on]. You get only the bones hanging around your neck.[77] It refers to being scapegoated. In Prisdang's case, he believed he had worked selflessly for others but in return was blamed and punished unjustifiably for mistakes he did not make.[78]

Accusations of Prisdang's extravagance arose among unsympathetic British officials too, in their communiqués, written retrospectively. In 1892, a British official named French who sought to discredit Prisdang noted that "in 1882 he was appointed Minister for Siam in London, the Siamese then establishing a Legation in London & having no better qualified person to represent them. Prisdang however fell unfortunately in the hands of foolish advisors and commenced a life of reckless extravagance & expense which soon got him into difficulties. After being 2 years in London he was sent to Paris as Minister. There however he had the same life as in London & after getting more deeply into debt, there he was finally in 1886, after the scandal of his mode of life had become too notorious, recalled to home."[79]

It was not uncommon for Siamese elite men to become indebted at home or abroad in an era when wearing tailored clothing, smoking tobacco, and drinking fine liquor reflected one's birth, status, and refined taste. A New York Times article from 1891 noted that King Chulalongkorn decided to send six Siamese to study medicine in the United States because "the young men sent to Europe fell into all manner of dissipation. Usually they were the sons of Princes and had plenty of money."[80] Many foreign shop owners allowed these young men to keep a tab at their establishments, assuming their families had deep pockets and would pay up. King Chulalongkorn's half brother and Prisdang's contemporary, Prince Wachirayan, loved fine European-made clothing, an addiction that put him in debt as a young man.[81]

Yet, curiously, Prisdang was known by others to be economical: he gave Siamese students very little pocket money, encouraging them to work hard and spend little. Despite this, one of Prisdang's student charges, a certain Mom Krob studying in Vienna, "was found to be a dandy and in debt, having bought a number of smart suits without the Consul's knowledge."[82] Henry Norman, a journalist with Siamese royal informants, wrote in the early 1890s about "thousands of pounds of Siamese debts in London unpaid at this moment, as several Bond Street tradesmen could testify, and Singapore merchants will only do cash transactions with Siam. It is a literal and unexaggerated fact that most Siamese noblemen could conceive the principles of the differential calculus more easily than the idea that it is dishonourable to evade the payment of justly incurred debt."[83]

Bond Street indeed. A record exists for one debt owed by Prisdang to an establishment located at 25 Old Bond Street. There sat one of the branches of J. W. Benson's jewelry and watch shops, the proprietor of which accused Prisdang of owing him 1,831 pounds for items purchased between 1881 and 1885, which included a whopping 550 pounds in interest accumulated by 1891.[84] The store, founded by the Benson brothers in 1749,[85] made watches and other decorative items for many royal families, including the British, Russian, and Siamese monarchies, a fact that it advertised throughout the British Empire.[86]

Prisdang incurred a large personal debt that began not when he was a student in England but later, when he joined the diplomatic corps in 1881. His pained defense of his integrity in the letter from 1882, his comments about working ceaselessly for the government but earning in return only bones hanging around his neck, and the frequency with which he mentions purchasing items for the Siamese government—from commemorative plates (which Benson's made to order) and stamps to items for the Chakri dynasty's 1882 bicentennial celebration— suggest that he may well have incurred debt for items bought for official use. In fact, his purchases from Benson's for the bicentennial celebration were so large that they were reported in the newspapers as far away as New Zealand. He ordered over six thousand medals to be worn on the occasion by Siamese officials. "Some of these are in pure gold, and others in silver gilt with red or yellow gold, silvered bronze, and pure bronze."[87] The elaborate design on the medals included busts of the first five Chakri kings in full state robes and identified by name and title. One hundred rays of sun embraced their imagery, making for an impressive border around the regal figures. Prisdang "personally superintended the whole of the intricate workmanship." This expense may well have been the target of Devawongse's criticism and Prisdang's umbrage. Prisdang mentions in a confidential memo written much later (1891, for the British) that individual officers of the state incurred enormous personal debt because they displayed wealth as a form of status and competed for the king's favor by purchasing gifts for his children and wives.[88]

Prisdang expressed some confusion over submitting receipts for business expenses versus his ambassadorial account. At one point he asked for 10,000 pounds from the Siamese government for work-related expenses.[89] If his salary was about 2000 pounds per annum, as has been estimated, then the Benson debt (1831 pounds) was proportionally quite high.[90] In any case, he does admit later in confidential letters that he was indebted; however, by the time the Benson debt caught up with Prisdang, he was no longer in government employ. Prisdang never divulged what he purchased at J. W. Benson's store or whether this was for personal or government use. He may have been dressing the part of envoy extraordinaire. Newspaper articles suggest extravagance. One flatteringly reports that "the Prince is about 32 years old, of medium stature, and is well educated. He speaks English and French fluently, and being unmarried, is looked upon as a 'catch' by marriageable young ladies. His dress consists of a derby hat, European coats and vest, the latter buttoned with old buttons up to the neck."[91] This reporter was mistaken about Prisdang's marital status—he was indeed married—and about his ability to speak French, but photos from the period suggest that Prisdang did dress decently. In 1883, he was sighted in Madrid wearing "a uniform partly European and partly Asiatic, consisting of a blue vest edged with gold, wide blue coloured trousers, rose coloured silk stockings, and lacquered shoes. His head was covered by a felt helmet in the Prussian fashion, and he wore, besides, a rose coloured coat of tulee with elegant gold edgings."[92]

The Proposal for Reform of the Siamese Government, 1885

The time kept by a pocket watch, even a brand like Benson's, could not keep up with the pace of events along Siam's borders and in Prisdang's office on Rue de Siam in Paris. In the early 1880s, British and French imperialism brought these countries directly along Siam's ill-defined borders, with the British tightening their stranglehold on the Burmese monarchy in north Burma and the French finishing their conquest of Indochina.

Their competition over territory came to a head when Prisdang served in Europe. While in Paris, he personally witnessed the domestic and international politicking regarding Burma's increasingly limited sovereignty. The French, under the expansionist prime ministership of Jules Ferry (1883–85), were meddling in Burma at the same time that Burmese diplomats had arrived in Paris to enlist French assistance against the British.[93] At the moment that Naret was replacing Prisdang in London, the press reported that the Burmese king was "entertaining some hazy hopes of obtaining aid against [the British in India] from the French in Tonquin [French northern Indochina]."[94]

Prisdang collected European newspaper articles related to Burma and had them translated for King Chulalongkorn.[95] Soon after his arrival in Paris, he invited to his office the leaders of the Burmese embassy. They spent hours debating Siam's and Burma's respective predicaments. Prisdang closely observed the chain of events in Burma among the British, French, and Burmese, but what he noted in particular was the Burmese king's poor decision making based on the undue influence of the king's "inner circle and flatterers." The Burmese ambassador asked Prisdang if he thought Siam would be next to succumb to the same fate.[96]

At some point in early 1884, an understandably anxious King Chulalongkorn asked Prince Prisdang in a private letter for his opinion about the situation in Burma and how Siam might avoid colonization. Prisdang recalls this moment in his autobiography: "I explained to the King how unknowledgeable I was about international politics affairs and how incapable I was to give him any suggestions, and also my fear that I might just cross the line. The King kindly replied that I should not be afraid to speak out, that I should be able to report everything to him to the best of my knowledge. I then took the King's letter, together with my correspondence with him, into a meeting with all three of his [the king's half] brothers and other senior officers in Paris and London. Because they were all senior officers, they would know more than I. We all agreed to write a report for the king together."[97] Without the king's permission, Prisdang had invited others into their private correspondence.

He is less circumspect about the proposal in a confidential memo he wrote to British officials while in exile in 1891. "The King was almost in despair and thought the time had come for him to lose his Kingdom. The writer [Prisdang] took advantage of the situation to advance his earnest wish for remodeling the Government and law, and insinuated to the King that there was only one way of getting out of French influence and saving the country, but that he was afraid to suggest it. The King wrote back almost imploringly requesting him to say what he will and never be afraid as he trusted him. . . . [H]e got all his disciples, whose radical ideas he initiated and whose political views were the same, to assemble night after night to discuss and work out a memorial to the Throne."[98] The four princes (Prisdang, Naret, Sonabandit, and Svasti) met secretly to draft the document, which was later circulated to seven other Siamese officials in London and Paris to sign in January 1885.[99]

The petition offered a comprehensive blueprint for reform that outlined an administrative, legal, and political overhaul of the Siamese administration as the only way Siam could avoid colonization.[100] Its brilliance lay in its realpolitik awareness of how ideas such as progress and civilization operated as a justification for colonization in Asia. European powers might cite governmental mismanagement, the inability to control criminals, the obstruction of trade, or humanitarian reasons such as the failure to provide happiness, justice, and progress to all. The claims would legitimate European colonization. To the petition drafters, the European impulse to "civilize," whether sincere or a ploy, represented the biggest threat to Siam's sovereignty.

Certain reforms, the petitioners noted, would not enable Siam to avoid colonization. For example, going to war would fail because the country was militarily unprepared; offering treaty concessions also had already failed to protect Siam and on the contrary had enabled Siam's exploitation by treaty powers; deploying international law would not help any countries except those that belonged to the exclusive club of the wealthy West; and declaring Siam a buffer state similarly would fail because the British and the French could simply divide up Siam until only a narrow border remained.[101] Also, the claim that Siam had already instituted reforms was insufficient to ward off colonization because these changes had been superficial. "All the reforms we have made thus far have not been to the core foundation, but instead they have been merely supplements to deal with Europeans within the necessary time."[102]

The proposal offered one solution. "We agree that the only solution is to thoroughly Europeanize. . . . There is no path better than this."[103] This entailed a number of reforms, including most audaciously a change in the king's power: "We have to change the current tradition in which the king personally decides every official matter, a tradition the British call an absolute monarchy, to a tradition called a constitutional monarchy, in which the king is the head of the country who decides and issues absolute orders to his high officials, as is the case for all monarchs in Europe who do not have to run everything themselves."[104] Other reforms included a ministerial cabinet (but not a parliament) that would assume responsibility for direct administration of major government departments, a law of succession, equal laws and state obligations for the populace, freedom of speech, a crackdown on corruption, fixed salaries for officials, abolition of outdated customs (an indirect critique of polygyny), and a modern army that would target domestic rather than foreign threats.[105] They reasoned that these changes would protect European commercial interests, which were the foremost concern of foreign powers, and give Europeans no cause for colonization.[106] The blueprint offered Siam a way to escape colonization but only if the king forcefully backed them against the entrenched nobles and royals who benefited from the existing system.

It took King Chulalongkorn several months to respond to the document.[107] In May 1885, he penned a formal response in which he politely explained that he favored many of the suggested reforms but that some could be implemented only gradually. He refused to give up his position as absolute monarch, arguing for Siam's distinctive historical political trajectory:

> Foreign rulers, by which I mean European rulers, have various limitations on their royal power that are due to events that have occurred in their various countries out of the dissatisfactions of the people. So there

are regulations to check the power of kings as a consequence of succes-
sions of events that have unfolded in their countries. These events have
not become, nor can they become, universal. Therefore schemes of this
kind cannot be set down as general schemes for all countries. Siam has
not yet experienced any event to make it necessary to do as other countries have done. . . . In our country it is the king alone who gives thought
to what should be done. It is he who has thought about acting to bring
progress and happiness to the people in general.[108]

The king refused the historicism implicit in the petition: he argued that
Siamese history had a distinct trajectory from that of Europe. This also served his
purposes. King Chulalongkorn was reluctant to enact any reforms that would
weaken his executive power. He had, after all, only recently assumed fuller control of the government after the ex-regent died in 1883—prior to that point,
he reminded the petitioners, all power was in the hands of the ex-regent and
key members of the Bunnag family. He considered change necessary, but some
reforms were simply not appropriate to implement at this time because the country lacked adequate personnel who understood the work of reform.[109]

Notably, the petition did not advocate for parliamentary rule (let alone for a
democratic regime) but instead endorsed the idea of sharing power among elites
like Prisdang, Naret, and others.[110] Still, it may have irritated the king because of
Prisdang's lapse in protocol: Prisdang made their private correspondence a communal conversation, one that required a more formal response from the king.[111]
Or perhaps it shocked the king to receive this blunt advice from the princes—
several of whom were his trusted brothers who had, moreover, sworn a secret
oath to support him—pressuring him to relinquish his place as absolute monarch. Most scholars have surmised that the king was deeply upset, basing this
idea on the fact that soon after he issued a response, he recalled from Europe all
four princes and some of the officials who had signed the proposal. Others have
suggested that on the contrary, the king agreed with the reforms and recalled the
princes so that he would have his strongest reform-minded supporters at home
to begin implementing the changes.

First the king ordered Prince Sonabandit to return. Then he summoned
Princes Naret, Svasti, and Prisdang "for private reasons." Prisdang dragged his
feet. He wanted to finish up his laborious negotiations regarding alcohol treaties,
the telegraph and postal unions, and other diplomatic issues. The king dispatched
a more serious reminder to return, after which Prisdang left with Princes Naret
and Svasti in early 1886. He never returned to Europe.[112]

Frederick Verney, then secretary to the London legation, commented on King
Chulalongkorn's recall of the three "radical" princes in letters to his relative,

Florence Nightingale, in January 1886: "Despotism must degrade a despot unless he is a God, and we know how a God may be degraded by those who attribute despotism to him, and when the selfishness of one man is nursed by all around him, what can you expect but the leveling down to the depths of his own selfishness. Prince Svasti accompanies Prince Naret and Prince Prisdang to Siam. I am glad they are all going together. But the crisis is a great one for all of them."[113] Verney, who as a British official working for the Siamese embassy and hired by Prisdang would have been aware of foul rumors regarding Prisdang, including his alleged spendthrift ways, mentions only King Chulalongkorn's unwillingness to brook any challenge. Prisdang too was unclear at that moment why exactly they were being recalled. He wrote, "At this point, it should be understood that I was only to return temporarily to the country [Siam]. There were notices to every country that I would return to my position [as ambassador]."[114]

Most scholars, to the extent they study Prince Prisdang, point to this proposal for reforms as the cause of his plummet and eventual exile from Siam in 1890. However, his autobiographical recollection and confidential letters suggest that it was not the proposal that forced him to resign but "an incident" or multiple incidents that occurred after his return and that remain a mystery to this day. Prisdang returned to Bangkok to work as the director general of the Post and Telegraph Department, housed, ironically, in the former home of the ill-fated Phra Pricha, son-in-law of Thomas Knox.[115] At age thirty-five, his life had reached what he later referred to as a karmic turning point, a descent from high status and social prominence to which he would never return.

BANGKOK

The Bones around Prisdang's Neck

The ambassadorial entourage reluctantly and belatedly departed from Marseilles on the French steamer *Natal* in late February 1886, arriving in Singapore a little more than a month later.[1] Princes Svasti, Naret, Prisdang, and the latter two men's wives disembarked in the steamy heat of April in Bangkok, a year after the king had recalled them from Europe. Prisdang presumed that the king would send him back to Europe to continue his diplomatic efforts. "However, because of an *incident* that occurred later which indicated my service to His Majesty was no longer needed, someone was chosen to replace me, with a view that 'anyone can be the ambassador because they merely receive and follow orders and simply do what they are told—[in other words, the ambassador is] just a scapegoat for the government."[2] Prisdang took great offense at this dismissive understanding of the ambassadorial role. It inspired him to list in his autobiography a catalog of his achievements above and beyond his duties as a diplomat. Yet despite his efforts, all he received was critique and blame, but for what exactly?

Prisdang refuses to specify the "incident" (*hetkan*, or accident *ubatihet*) in his published work. The issues—for it appears they were multiple—that arose between the monarch and Prisdang motivated Prisdang to escape his stifling situation in Bangkok and live in exile for twenty years, from 1890 until 1911. They have sent many a scholar scurrying to the archives for clues. Most scholars assume that what caused his exile was his role in drafting the 1885 proposal, which advised the king to curtail his power.[3] However, this fails to explain events that transpired after Prisdang's return to Bangkok.

For example, he remained in the king's service in Bangkok for a full five years *after* his recall before deciding, one day in October 1890, to choose the life of a fugitive. In fact, upon their return, the king had appointed Prisdang and his princely proposal cosigners to some of the highest government positions, positions that the king reformed in accordance with some of the suggestions in their proposal. By September 1886, the king had placed Princes Naret and Svasti on the committee for what became the Ministry of the Capital. Prince Naret was then appointed the minister of the capital, and Prince Svasti served briefly as Siam's first minister of justice when that position was established in 1892. For several years Prince Sonabandit served as the king's royal secretary in charge of the highest level of correspondence to and from the monarch, before being sent to govern areas in the north.[4]

Prisdang, who had facilitated Siam's entry into the international organizations associated with the postal and telegraph services, became the director general of the Post and Telegraph Office on 8 April 1887 and served with Svasti and Sonabandit[5] on the Privy Council, a body of the king's closest supporters created in 1874 to serve as His Majesty's eyes and ears.[6] The king also placed Prisdang on the Sirirat Hospital Committee (chaired by Prince Damrong) in 1886 and on a temple renovation committee and appointed him to be a tour guide and interpreter for visiting foreign diplomats and royalty. Socially, Prisdang remained literally at the king's table for diplomatic dinners, along with Prince Svasti and others, suggesting the king's continued high regard for him.

The king's decision to bring these men home may have served a double purpose: to have his most educated and supportive reformers home to help implement domestic change while also keeping closer tabs on their activities to appraise their continued loyalty to the monarch. But it is difficult to discern with certainty. Pointing to the 1885 proposal as the cause for Prisdang's ouster also fails to explain why he alone of those who signed the proposal for reform suffered a fall from grace. If his recall was not a form of punishment, then why did he resign in despair in 1890?

Even loquacious and prolific Prisdang, who confessed to writing over two thousand pages per year, preferred to keep the details of the incident a secret.[7] In 1897, the British Singapore daily, the *Straits Times*, published a letter written by Prisdang that denied the disparaging rumors about the reasons for his departure: "The *Straits Times* or any other paper whatever can in no way know the reasons for my refusing to return to Siam on my return from Japan, unless it be informed by the [Royal] Court of Siam, for no outsiders have yet been informed or ever will be fully informed."[8] In the gap of public silence, private musings ran amok among interested parties: the British, Siamese government officials, and even Prisdang, who groped to understand what was happening to him.

When Prisdang returned to Bangkok in 1886, he found himself homeless. One would assume a prince and government official of his stature could at least take housing for granted—that some palace or mansion awaited his return. In the short stints back to Bangkok during the period he lived in Europe, Prisdang and his wife, Mom Sadap, were allowed to stay in his father-in-law's house.[9] By 1886, however, the king had confiscated his father-in-law's home as a punishment for unspecified crimes against the government or king.

A private letter from Prisdang written in 1882 to his dear friend and confidant Surasak notes that his wife's parents had passed away and that she had no property or possessions.[10] He asked Surasak in 1882 to have Mom Sadap stay with Surasak's family if necessary. By 1883 she had joined Prisdang in Europe, mooting the issue of her residence. When Prisdang and Mom Sadap returned from Europe in 1886, they scrambled indecorously for a place to live. Prisdang initially stayed in a military barracks, which was no place for his wife. He once again asked Surasak to help with her housing. She stayed with Surasak's wife, Khunying Lai, at Ban Saladaeng.[11]

Prisdang did not return to his family home. The palace in which he had grown up, Wang Tha Phra (literally, Phra pier palace), never "belonged" to his father. Royal property didn't quite work like private property: it ultimately belonged to the reigning king, who could redistribute it as he saw fit. Royal relatives and high-ranking noble (nonroyal) officials typically lived in the areas surrounding the Grand Palace, for example, in Wang Tha Phra and on houseboats lining the Chao Phraya River along the royal city walls (figure 8). The king kept officials and their families close. This meant that the buildings, houseboats, palaces, and compounds along the river and royal palace shifted occupants depending on their positions relative to the king and to their government service. As noted later by Prisdang, "As soon as a child is born of a favourite [a royal consort], provision is made for him and a place, such as those now adorning the bank of the river in fine edifices and grand style. . . . All the best sites which can be bought and obtained have been bought and got for Royal children."[12]

The monarch could repossess palaces that doubled as residences and government offices after the death of their princely occupants, regardless of whether the deceased's family still lived in the palace. This was the case with Wang Tha Phra, which a previous monarch had originally given to Prisdang's paternal uncle until he passed away, after which it was bequeathed to Prisdang's father, Prince Chumsai. By fiat, Prince Chumsai's wives and children had stopped living there at some point after he died in 1868.[13]

Prisdang's mother, Mom Noi, still lived in Ban Tha Chang, her wealthy (deceased) father's home, located just outside the royal city gates along the Chao Phraya River.[14] However, when Prisdang returned in 1886, his mother contracted

FIGURE 8.   Photograph of the Chao Phraya River taken in 1866 by John Thomson. Wellcome Library L0055518. Courtesy of the Wellcome Library, London.

cholera. He borrowed a houseboat (a "picnic boat," suggesting it was quite small) and docked it in front of his mother's home, where she likely suffered from the disease's characteristic violent cramping, vomiting, and diarrhea.[15] She succumbed to death two weeks after he returned.

Mom Noi had inherited Ban Tha Chang from her affluent father. Recall that this was one reason why Rama III arranged a marriage between Mom Noi and Prisdang's uncle, Prince Matayaphithak. Once Prince Matayaphithak passed away, Rama III had Mom Noi marry Prisdang's father, intentionally keeping the inheritance in the family.[16] In this case, Mom Noi's inherited home should have gone to her children, all of whom were older than Prisdang and some of whom were still alive in the 1880s. One of his brothers passed away shortly after his mother: he notes in a letter dated March 1887 that "since then I have had much occupation with family affairs that make me forgetful of others [sic] affairs."[17] Prisdang had a complicated relationship with the family property, which eventually ended in a lawsuit, described later. In any case, he did not move into Ban Tha Chang.

So one can imagine Prisdang's relief when King Chulalongkorn bequeathed to him a building referred to as Phumnithet Thahan Na, which was located near Wang Tha Phra. The king issued a royal order stating, "Prince Prisdang has been promoted to Phra Ong Jao but still has no residence that is appropriate for his status. Now, I will bestow that building on Prince Prisdang, but some little things are unfinished. Have Luang Nai Sit contract someone to finish the remaining work first, then once it is done according to the original contract, give the building to Prince Prisdang immediately."[18]

Prisdang mentions the property in a private letter[19] and in his autobiography.[20] Likely because the building had fallen into disrepair, Prisdang did not live there while it was being renovated but stayed on a houseboat parked in front of his mother's home where he could prepare her corpse and arrange for the cremation ceremony.[21] In fact, Prisdang never moved into the Phumnithet property because of the unspecified incident in mid-1887 that aroused sufficient distrust and disfavor that the king decided to repossess it. In his autobiography, Prisdang writes that because of the incident, the "king repossessed the house before I could have it renovated into a three story house. The renovations I had begun on my mother's house for my family also had to stop because of the same 'incident.' Unfortunately, during that time the king's brother, Prince Devawongse, had gone to the Jubilee ceremony for Queen Victoria of England, so I had no one to help ease the situation, as if lacking water to put out a fire. . . . I was severely condemned."[22]

The incident also seems to have destroyed a career promotion that was in the works for Prince Prisdang. Likely because of the support of his patron, the king's younger brother Prince Phanurangsi, Prisdang received an appointment by the king as director general of the Post and Telegraph Department with an initial salary of fifty chang (four thousand baht), plus five chang in royal pension (*biawat*) and a fifteen-chang annual bonus.[23] Prince Phanurangsi had worked with Prisdang since at least 1881, when he requested that Prisdang order Siam's first postal stamps. By the time Prisdang returned to Bangkok in 1886, Prince Phanurangsi was the director-general of Siam's Postal Department and had likely arranged to have Prisdang replace him and work loosely under his supervision as minister of the Postal Department.[24]

One of the administrative reforms under discussion was the unification of various civic works projects, such as those related to the post office, telegraph, and river and canal surveying, under a single Department of Public Works. Prisdang was tasked with drafting the guidelines for the new department, which he did by ordering with personal funds books and reports from British India that might serve as a model. As a civil engineer who had experience in many of these areas, Prisdang was a natural fit to be director of the new combined department. However, the incident ensured that Prisdang would not receive the appointment, which was filled instead by the king's half brother, Prince Naris.[25] Prisdang was appointed secretary. Indignant, he refused this appointment, which he considered a demotion to an essentially secretarial post, and begged to continue to direct the Post and Telegraph Department, where he could at minimum be his own boss.[26]

His autobiographical account continues: "At that time I was very depressed as if I had died from my world of officialdom. I bought a Colt handgun, bid farewell to my wife, and arranged for my corpse to be taken care of by Palat Krom Saeng (he was a trusted relative on my father's side). My wife informed an *older sister* who came crying and pleading with me to cease thinking about ending my life, which is a crime against the dhamma. Because the plan to do this quietly failed, I threw the gun away in the water."[27]

So the incident, which occurred sometime between May and October 1887 while Devawongse was in Europe, was severe enough to compel Prisdang to consider taking his life.[28] There is evidence that suggests the singular incident was actually plural—even the Thai noun *ubatihet* can refer to plural incidents or a singular episode. It depends on context, which remains elusive except through the reconstruction of the scene through long, heartfelt letters by Prisdang written in 1887 and 1890.[29] There were at least two incidents: one involving a man named Mom Jao Pan and another involving Khunying Si hereafter Si or Phi Si, which means elder sibling), the widow of Surasak's brother. The Mom Jao Pan incident came to a head in May 1887, and the rumors regarding Si arose by June 1887. Although Prisdang's published autobiography suggests that his suicide attempt was a consequence of the king's repossession of the Phumnithet property, which relates directly to the Mom Jao Pan incident, his letters suggest it was rumors about an affair with Si that drove him to raise a gun to his head.[30] Very little is known about Si beyond details outlined below.

Mom Jao Pan: Seeds of Distrust Sown

In a letter written by Prisdang in 1890 detailing why he resigned, he offers more evidence about what happened: "Later, when there was this case of inviting Jao Pan to work for the government, he [the king] was so angry that he rebuked me, saying he would rather feed a dog than me because dogs are loyal to their master. Alas, I have become an ingrate. At the time, I didn't understand I was deemed ungrateful. I was extremely devastated. Later, after I figured out the reason, I felt less saddened because I [realized I] had done nothing wrong. Those who spread accusations against me knew I wasn't in a position to defend myself. They are still doing so."[31]

In May 1887, the king repossessed the home he had conferred upon Prisdang and rescinded payment of two chang (160 baht) that Prisdang had received from the king because of his royal status. The letter from King Chulalongkorn to Prisdang about Mom Jao Pan reveals the king's disappointment and distrust in Prisdang based on a complicated scenario. In short, Prisdang appears to have owed money to a woman named Mom Jao Sai, a relative of the king's. Instead of paying her interest or providing collateral for the loan, he was accused of trying to pay off interest by hiring her stepson, Mom Jao Pan, who was already working for Prince Svasti.[32] Moreover, the king speculated that Prisdang had done this in an underhanded manner by trying to arrange the hiring of Mom Jao Pan for the Department of Public Works in a way that implied the king had ordered Pan to work for Prisdang. If the plan had worked, then Prisdang could steal Pan out from under Prince Svasti while justifying it as a royal command that he could not refuse to obey. One reason why Prisdang may have attempted to avoid a direct confrontation with Prince Svasti was that the latter had a reputation for being "the stormy petrel of the family" prone to "tempestuous moods."[33] Regardless, the king put two and two together: Prisdang's loan and the sneaky attempt to hire Mom Jao Pan as a way to return a favor in lieu of interest or payment on the loan. King Chulalongkorn found this an impudent and condescending maneuver.

In addition, the king's suspicions were raised. He began to scrutinize Prisdang's words and deeds. For example, he believed he had caught Prisdang in a lie about whether or not he knew Mom Jao Pan. "The fact that you said in one letter [to the king] that you and Jao Pan knew each other very well and said in the other letter [to Prince Svasti] that you didn't know him: one of these statements has to be a lie. I don't know which one is. . . . If you lied in the letter to me, then that is a greater sin, because lying to the king is also against the law."[34] Ultimately, conversations with others made the king suspicious that the entire Mom Jao Pan affair as manipulated by Prisdang amounted to a form of royal defamation. "I consider this idea of yours to be a genuine defamation of me, even though it is only my conjecture." It would not be the last time that Prisdang was accused of condescension.

King Chulalongkorn had to mention the "plot" directly to Prisdang because "I thought that if I didn't say anything, you would imagine I was so afraid of criticism from those who believe that supreme absolute justice is on their side (which I find too egotistical), that I might not say anything."[35] The king continued, "I am not afraid of crazy preposterous people. Everything I said here is to prove that you always see the worst in me. Therefore, how can I possibly continue to give you your original monthly salary, which I have given out of love and familiarity, when I know that you don't regard me as a sensible person?"[36]

As punishment, the king not only ordered the Treasury to stop paying the extra two chang to Prisdang but also repossessed the Phumnithet property. The king's belief that Prisdang had been dishonest in the line of duty, held a consistently negative view of the monarch, and had attempted to conceal the lender-debtor relationship he had with Mom Jao Sai caused the king to lose trust in him.

Rumors also circulated about Prisdang's misuse of royal-government funds to renovate the property that the king had given him and his maternal grand-father's home, Ban Tha Chang. Prisdang addressed these accusations in an August 1887 letter to the king. He claimed among other things that he planned to com-bine the Phumnithet property with Ban Tha Chang to turn them both into a royal palace area for the crown prince and a trusted senior (royal) adviser to the crown prince, such as Prince Devawongse. He also stated that he planned to divide up the maternal estate among his relatively less well-off siblings.[37] "As for my request to Your Majesty to help fix up the house for my elder siblings, it is only natural that now that I live happily and comfortably, I could not help but think about my neighboring siblings who have been deprived of a proper place to live."[38] Neither the Crown Prince nor Devawongse wanted to live in the Phumnithet property, however, so Prisdang soon found himself accused of aggrandizing his familial and personal properties at the expense of others resid-ing nearby, who had allegedly been rousted from the surrounding area.

His complex housing situation and employment reveal the degree to which Prisdang's fate was tied to the king's opinion of him. Yet his property renova-tions and the Mom Jao Pan hiring scandal were not the only issues that aroused the king's suspicions. The most shaming and obscene incident fails to make it by name into Prisdang's autobiography. It came to a head at about the same time in mid-1887.

Sexual Scandal: Rumors about Si and Prisdang

The immediate catalyst that provoked in Prisdang the desire to end his life was not centrally about his homelessness or languishing government career but about his relationship with a woman named Khunying Si, whom he referred to as "Phi" or "elder sister" in his letter.[39] She was the sister-in-law of his dear friend Surasak through marriage to Surasak's older brother, Phraya Sunthon Songkhram (Jan Saeng-Chuto). Even their own father allegedly described Phraya Sunthon as "dull," and the king had sent Surasak to help his older brother with his gov-ernmental duties in Suphanburi before he passed away sometime between 1883 and 1886.[40] With Phraya Sunthon, Si had had a child.[41] One can locate her on a

branch of that famous Siamese genealogical tree: Si was a member of the ubiquitous Bunnag family. She was the granddaughter of Dit Bunnag, who at one
point under Rama III was Siam's most powerful official, heading the ministries
of war, trade, and foreign affairs. She was also the niece of the former regent, Si
Suriyawong, and daughter of Phra Phromathiban (Jon Bunnag) and his wife,
Nuam. As such, Si was one of hundreds of Bunnag descendants in her generation
alone and therefore was not particularly high-ranking or remarkable on the basis
of heritage. Yet somehow, as a relatively powerless widow, she came between
sworn allies.

Recall that Surasak and Prisdang were not just intimate friends; they also
belonged to the Young Siam Society (samakhon sayam num), formed in the mid-
1870s.[42] This group of men supported King Chulalongkorn, who desired political reforms that challenged the power of Si Suriyawong and his allies at the time.
Prisdang and Surasak may have met as early as 1871 when Prisdang headed to
Singapore's Raffles Institution to study English, and Surasak traveled with King
Chulalongkorn to India.[43] They served together in London in about 1879 (figure 9),
when they met with British officials to resolve the flare-up between the British
consul Thomas Knox and the Siamese regent over the arrest and eventual execu-
tion of Knox's son-in-law, Phra Pricha. In July 1881, the two men swore a secret
oath of loyalty, along with several others, to protect the king, the heir apparent
(Prince Wachirunhit), and each other.[44]

Both men were monarchical loyalists whose fathers, upon their deaths, presented them as pages to the king. They both considered King Chulalongkorn
a parental proxy and patron, even though the king was slightly younger than
they. Both men had reputations for being outspoken—brash even—in word
and personality. One scholar contextualizes Surasak: "In a social milieu of in-
offensiveness and deference to elders, his personality was abrasive."[45] They also
were likely charismatic, given their careers as leaders in the civil and military
service, respectively. Prisdang and Surasak shared more than character traits
and disdain for certain aspects of Siam's social hierarchy; they also held similar
political views about Siam's future. In fact, Surasak refused to sign the 1885 proposal, preferring instead to draft his own, more radical set of recommendations
for reform that he submitted separately to the king. This does not appear to have
harmed his long-term standing in the eyes of the king, who eventually promoted
him to the aristocratic rank of Phraya and then Jao Phraya, the second-highest
noble rank.

Prisdang's intimate connection to Surasak is revealed in the 1882 letter he
wrote from London in which he refers to Surasak as his dear brother and trusted
friend. He begs his "brother," his "true friend," to take in Prisdang's wife, Mom
Sadap, twice—once in 1882 and again in 1886 when Prisdang did not have

FIGURE 9. Surasak (Joem Saeng-Chuto) and Prisdang in London circa 1879, from Prisdang, *Prawat yo*, image number 9.

suitable housing.[46] It also makes sense that Prisdang came to know Surasak's extended family, including his deceased brother's wife, Si.

Sometime after Prisdang returned to Bangkok, Surasak entrusted his own family and property to Prisdang when the king ordered Surasak to quash a rebellion in Luang Prabang.[47] Surasak commanded the First Foot Guard, charged with protecting the capital, royal processions, and the palace and royal commissioners sent to provinces and dependencies on the king's business.[48] His absence enabled the spread of gossip about Prisdang's relationship with Si, which occurred at the same time as rumors about Prisdang's involvement with Mom Jao Pan and his alleged misuse of government funds to renovate his properties. Prisdang notes in a letter explaining his resignation in 1890, "It so happened that I had become very good friends with Phraya Surasak, which at first I thought was a good thing but which turned out very bad. Through his friendship, I had an opportunity to develop such a congenial friendship with Mae [mother] Si, Phraya Surasak's sister-in-law, that I was thought to have committed adultery [with her]. Finally, there was a rift in relations between Phraya Surasak and his sister-in-law and me. Whatever I had done, I did out of honesty and loyalty to Phraya Surasak as a dear friend and to Mae Si as well." Prisdang recounted, painfully, that a rumor had spread that his relationship with Surasak was merely a pretext to gain access to Si. Bangkok's high society considered Prisdang and Si's alleged relationship "vulgar in the extreme. It would be impossible to find anyone as vile."[49]

The gossip spread about the alleged affair with Phi Si was vicious. To find some form of inner peace, Si and Prisdang went "to the temple to make merit and to ease my mind. But it was twisted [into a rumor about] our courting in the temple. Wherever we went, we went together with our relatives and servants, but we were thought to have been courting. I was seen as stubborn, unworthy of serving the king, and devoid of honor, but His Majesty was kind enough to still give me some work, though I could not know his moral judgment of me. If he saw me as dishonest, ambitious, ungrateful, and so on, but continued to let me serve in important matters, it would be really pathetic."[50]

Prisdang believed he could resolve his situation if he were given the chance to prove himself to the king. This opportunity presented itself in mid-1887, just as the Siamese wars against the Chinese Haw forces came to an end. Remnants of the Taiping rebels, the Haw, had invaded parts of northern Vietnam (Tonkin) and areas along the indeterminate border between Siamese and Lao domains. They attacked Luang Prabang, a Lao area under Siamese suzerainty but coveted by the French in Tonkin. Chaos of this sort often enabled imperial powers to intervene and colonize under the justification of providing peace. King Chulalongkorn called on Surasak to lead an army against the Haw, whom he had just vanquished in 1887.[51] After restoring the Lao king to his throne in Luang Prabang, Surasak began the task of reforming the local administration.

Needing assistance, he asked King Chulalongkorn to send Prisdang, who still occupied the position of director general of the Post and Telegraph Department but had diplomatic and surveying experience that could be useful. However, because of the rumors and the king's suspicions about Prisdang, the king refused to send him unless he wrote a letter "explaining and demonstrating my [Prisdang's] trust in Your Majesty's noble wishes, and my faithfulness to Your Majesty."[52] Prisdang saw surveying the disputed territories as his second chance. If only he could prove his innocence, line up the facts, and explain himself to the king, then maybe the king would reinstate him by allowing him to serve the government on this dangerous mission—one that he called a "death trip" (to Luang Prabang)—from which he might not return. "If I cannot make it, if I do not have the opportunity to come back to serve your majesty, there will not be another chance for me to prove my innocence."[53]

In response to the king's request, Prisdang penned a thirty-six-page letter to the king in August 1887. In it, he acknowledges that he has already aroused the king's distrust. He believes one reason for the tension is that the king perceives him as lacking gratitude: "The crucial blemish, that which causes Your Majesty to think of me as wicked, is how ungrateful I am, how I do not recognize the *phradet phrakhun* of Your Majesty."[54] *Phradet phrakun* refers to the expansive generosity of the king for supporting and promoting Prisdang and Prisdang's profound sense of social and moral obligation to the king as a consequence. This hierarchical sense of giving and obligation typifies the relationship between parents and children: it is, for the subordinate, a social and moral debt that eternally defines the relationship. It cannot be repaid, even if the superior stops favoring the subordinate.

As evidence of his gratitude and loyalty to the king and his reforms, Prisdang offers as proof his ardent support of the king. "All government officials who serve together with the same heart concede that I am one person in their gang who is a 'supporter of the crown,' an invaluable designation for me."[55] Paradoxically, Prisdang cites the 1885 proposal as evidence supporting Prisdang's commitment to the king and his plan for Siam. "As for my faith in Your Majesty's noble wishes, I beg to cite the memorandum that we signed and submitted to you from abroad. I was the one who thought it up. This is proof that I have faith in your noble wishes so much that I was able to give Your Majesty that memorandum because I believed that Your Majesty would share the same opinion and would gradually prepare and implement some of these [suggestions] as you wished and considered appropriate."[56]

For Prisdang, the 1885 petition was not what caused his exile, at least as he understood and explained the chain of events in his letters to the king. Instead, it appears that a combination of incidents caused the king to doubt Prisdang's intentions and gratitude, which were placed under microscopic scrutiny. The letter begs the king to punish him or to employ him as the king sees fit. "From now on, I will give up my association with any conspirators whom Your Majesty does not trust.

I will go anywhere you would like me to go, and do anything. I will be able to serve Your Majesty in every way. I beg of you to trust me to serve Your Majesty again."[57]

The letter also reveals the intimacy between Prisdang and Surasak as triangulated through their connection to the king. "If I have an idea to do anything, it will not be out of an intention to defame or betray Your Majesty, who has been most gracious to me. I have always felt that when the time comes, I can just give my life to Your Majesty. And I would not think of myself as royalty, or that I have any 'rights.' It is a firm belief in this. That is why I very much like Phraya Surasakmontri who shares the same thoughts and feelings as me, so much so that we cannot get rid of each other, for there is nothing we lack when it comes to our foundation of trust."[58] The letter ultimately failed to convince the king to send Prisdang to Luang Prabang.

In Surasak's absence and in the midst of these rumors about an affair, the king had ordered Si to move into the king's palace, whether to be his mistress or to return to work there is unclear.[59] Many of her Bunnag female relatives already lived in the Grand Palace as consorts of the king, so Si no doubt was aware of what life within that massive compound was like. She had easy access to information circulating about the king within the small city that encompassed female officials and slaves who managed the town, and the children, unmarried female relatives, consorts, and queens of King Chulalongkorn and past kings. More than 150 women were "gifted" to King Chulalongkorn as minor wives over the course of his long reign; by comparison, 50 women were presented to King Mongkut, who received the second largest number of women of any Chakri king. They often brought with them an entourage of attendants and others, making the population of the inner palace sizable. Si adamantly refused the king's command.

One excerpt from Prisdang's resignation letter (1890), written to Prince Phanurangsi, treats the seemingly platonic but conspiratorial relationship he had with Si. Prisdang considered becoming a monk to end the scandal, rather than continuing on as a government official outside the king's good graces. His debts, however, prevented him from doing so.

> I thought of the way to come up with the money to clear my debts before being ordained. I didn't plan to run away. I wanted to have a good life so I followed the Thai tradition of obtaining a wife with substantial means so we can start a business. Once I pay off my debts, I can become a monk. Phi Si and I came up with the plan to have me flirt with the daughter of Phraya Mae Klong, who is the love of Phra Itsaranuphap. We wrote many letters back and forth and she finally agreed to elope with me. She even gave me her blanket from her bed, and the cloth from her body as a promise that she will be mine. . . . But then there was the

scandal about Phi Si and me. Since she heard about that she has been furious. . . . It was hopeless to pursue this plan. The rumor about Phi Si and me had been widely spread to His Majesty and they all jumped to the conclusion that it was true, depriving me of a chance to find a wife who would enable me to make a living. This is why I have to take leave of you [that is, resign].[60]

Prisdang had hoped that when Surasak returned from Luang Prabang, he would set the record straight with the king regarding Prisdang and Si.

> I was so happy and went to pick him up, hoping that he would help me fend off our enemies, to protect my name, and to [enable me] to continue serving His Majesty for the greater good of the king and kingdom, as we have sworn to do. When we met, he already learned from Phi Si about His Majesty's command that she live in the palace. Surasak was extremely alarmed to learn that Phi Si had refused the king's order. Surasak thought that Phi Si's persistence in ignoring the order would bring calamity to him and myself as well as catastrophe to the whole family and he and I would be dead.

Si refused both Prisdang and Surasak's attempts to convince her to move into the palace. She cited various objections, "saying she would rather die. I [Prisdang] was extremely alarmed and on many occasions had tried to convince her. She wouldn't hear any of it and kept crying profusely. It was beyond me how to fix it."[61]

Prisdang had assumed that Surasak, his most loyal friend, would believe him and Si, with whom Surasak had also sworn an oath of friendship. However, once Surasak heard the rumors about Prisdang and Si, he became cold. He fought with Si "about the money and the inheritance [of his brother, Si's deceased husband]. In fact, the fight was about me. To get to the bottom of it, it must have been about his fear of a wicked person [Prisdang] whose association with him" would bring ruin to Surasak's family. Surasak repossessed "everything that belonged to his brother from Phi Si, and chased her out of the house. . . . He made sure everyone knew that the cause of their fight was because I committed adultery. He wanted to destroy me."[62]

Prisdang continued, "When I had learned about this, I felt that there was no way for me to fight back because he [Sursak] was not attacking me face to face, but instead was stabbing me behind my back. My honesty was no match in this fight because he had secretly conspired against me without ever wanting the real truth to be known or finding out who really was to blame. It was simply to trap me or to blame me for all sorts of things." Siding with Prisdang could, it appears, cause guilt by association. Instead of helping Prisdang, Surasak saved his own skin by turning on him, at least in Prisdang's recounting.

Prisdang suspected that letters he had written in confidence to Surasak and Prince Svasti while in England had been shown to the king and used against him. The letters contained their views, privately shared, about Siam, its administration, and its customs. "Surasak and I used to be very close friends, so we wrote to each other on many important matters just like I wrote to Prince Svasti. Surasak might have secretly given my letters to His Majesty leading to His Majesty's anger and my possible punishment, just like the case of Jao Pan. There was no chance that I could hand in his [Surasak's] letters to His Majesty just as I have never handed in Prince Svasti's letters. The truth remains that when we wrote those letters, we all agreed and thought the same things that were shared in private among close friends who all think alike regarding official matters."[63] Prisdang hinted later, when he was in exile, that the letters dealt with the custom of polygyny as practiced by King Chulalongkorn in particular. Prisdang believed all his former princely allies had turned on him. Prince Sonabandit, who was in London with the regal gang in the 1880s, allegedly reported to the king everything they said in private conversations. Prince Devawongse also showed the king confidential letters about polygyny written to him by Prisdang. "[T]he effect was very electrical [sic] because the letter explained the evil of the [polygynous] system and referred to the palace customs."[64]

Prisdang was out of options and momentarily lost all hope. "I am now at a dead end. I have no friends left at my side. All my good deeds and hope have vanished. I couldn't turn to anyone. There is no one to know the real truth. Hence, I prepared to die. I wrote up my will, went out to purchase a Colt handgun to shoot myself in the head."[65] "I told Phi Si [about the plan to commit suicide], who is the only real friend I have left, and she wouldn't let me do it. She said if I were to die now, then she would die too because she also has no friends left." Prisdang mentioned that Surasak and Phatsakorawong, two of his sworn oath brothers, were plotting to arrest Si.[66] She said she would rather kill herself than die of the humiliation that they had planned for her.

"So I couldn't die because it would be a death with 'dishonor' as it would look like I loved Phi Si and we couldn't live together so we killed ourselves out of desperation. What a great irony, since it would support all the lies that were told about us. . . . My intention to kill myself to prove my honesty to the king would instead be interpreted as an escape from my misdeeds."[67] Letters written in the moment leading up to his decision to flee Siam reveal that Prisdang left because of the vicious gossip about an affair with Si, which led to his abandonment by the king and all his former political oath brothers, men who also served in the highest positions in the kingdom.

Despite these devastating rumors, Prisdang and Si refused to abandon each other. For Prisdang, it was a point of pride:

> I value truth and honesty the most and would remain honest till I die regardless of any suffering and personal loss. . . . If only I did not care for truth and honesty, I could get myself out of the trouble just like everyone else. I am the kind of person who always keeps my word and my promises. If I make a promise to anyone, regardless of who they are, I keep my promise. I'd rather die than break my promise. I had sworn to be friends with Phi Si, and that's why I cannot break my promise with her. I am deemed a wicked person simply because I refuse to break my word.[68]

She and Prisdang suffered through ignominy and shunning at a time when King Chulalongkorn initiated major government reforms, later called the Chakri Reformation, based on many of the recommendations presented in the 1885 proposal. The reforms began to divide ministries along functionally differentiated lines, which not only brought Siam in line with modern bureaucracies in the colonial world but also deprived many of the king's domestic rivals of their administrative sinecures. When the king convened a meeting in March 1888 to announce his scheme for reorganizing the government, nearly all of Prisdang's peers were present and received positions in charge of the new ministries. Prisdang appears to not have been invited, nor did he receive an appointment. The new ministers included two his fellow petition cosigners, Princes Naret and Svasti, and other reform-minded princes among Prisdang's cohort such as Phanurangsi, Damrong, Devawongse, and Naris.[69]

Instead, Prisdang remained in charge of the Post and Telegraph Department, where he bided his time by energetically augmenting Siam's postal services, increasing the number of boats used, and replacing foreign employees with Siamese. He held a banquet featuring a "Victorian menu" for members of the Post and Telegraph Department in the elegant Regency Room at Bangkok's premier hotel, the Oriental, in the fall of 1888.[70] He spent 1889 traveling along Siam's rivers in search of ways to expand the post and telegraph services, collecting handicrafts along the way for a Siamese exhibition in a museum in Paris. He volunteered, along with many of his princely peers, to be one of the directors of the new Borapah (Borapha) Railway Company, Limited, established in September 1889.[71] He also sought to invest in a tin-mining venture but failed to secure funds from the king, even though Prisdang promised to give him up to half of the profit.[72] He was involved in many activities, particularly those dealing with public works and communications, but he no longer had a connection to the royal court.

Prisdang spent some of this time figuring out a way to regain his king's trust, which appeared to be impossible while in Bangkok. So instead he came up with a plan "to escape from persecution so I can speak freely and let His Majesty know the whole truth. . . . Once the king sees that I am loyal, honest, and trustworthy, then I am ready to die for the truth and not because of those damned scandals thought up by those wicked people. I am willing to come back to be his subject and to face any punishment, even if it means my death, or to take up any position whatsoever. I am not afraid to die so long as I can die with honor."[73] That plan involved fleeing Siam. "This is why I had to take my leave [of you]. I am not a traitor who, like Wangna,[74] pledges myself to foreign countries. . . . I wanted to wait for an opportunity to clear my name, to prove my innocence."[75]

He ends his very long letter explaining his decision to resign in 1890 with a veiled threat.

> Should His Majesty be vengeful and seek to punish me, who have done nothing wrong, I will be forced into a corner and have no other choices. In that case, I have already made some preparations to protect myself. My plan will be discreet and will not in any way bring disrepute. If there is no need to use this protection, I would not resort to it. . . . But if danger becomes apparent, I will have to carry out the plan I have prepared to protect myself. I did nothing wrong. I only want to escape from danger. I am what they call a "political refugee." I am not a cheater or a traitor and have not committed any serious criminal offenses. I am not a criminal. There is no cause to arrest or extradite me. And there is no extradition treaty. . . . If there is any imminent threat to my life, the truth no matter what will have to come out to prove that I did nothing wrong. His Majesty the King is well aware that I have done nothing wrong in my job. Relentlessly trying to persecute me will only lead to a scandal.[76]

Prisdang's Critique of Siamese Political Culture

Prisdang believed that people spread the rumor about an affair because it helped them advance their position in the social and political hierarchy by pushing him down. "They only speak in order to please or flatter. They only look up to the sky, never down to earth."[77] He had once sketched a graphic image of this that made Prince Phanurangsi "shout with laugher" and talk about it for days: "The habit and idea of the Siamese of looking up to one above him and never looking down to see those below is the briefest, truest and most comprehensive description of the Siamese from the highest to the lowest. And is here represented graphically by eyes and bottoms."[78] Regardless of Prisdang's clever insights, when the rumors reached the king, the king chose to believe them. "The fact that people took too much interest in this, I feel like they are trying to force me out of the government."[79]

Why would people spread this savage gossip? And why would it matter whether Prisdang claimed Si, a single widow, as his consort in a society in which law and custom endorsed polygyny? It made little sense. Even an official who was ordered to arrest the fugitive Prisdang after he fled into exile commented, "In my humble opinion, I think that for Prisdang, a royal family member who was brought up and very generously supported by the king, to run away only because of the wife, Si, is rather extreme. But . . . I have to do my job."[80] The official thought Prisdang's flight "exceeded the original cause."[81] It didn't add up to observers that Prisdang would flee because of a relationship with a woman, who was, moreover, a widow and therefore a legitimate potential spouse, not an adulteress.

Prisdang had one wife, Mom Sadap, whom he had married in a ceremony that implied the king had given her as a wife to him. In contrast to Si, Mom Sadap is barely mentioned in his otherwise prolific discourse. No other formal marriages appear in the record up to this point, although under the duress of malicious gossip about an affair with Si, Prisdang defends himself by claiming he took two additional women as minor wives: "If I really want to have an affair, I am well known to prefer only young women—my wife would break up with me because of this. I have three wives, and anyone who knows Phi Si knows she would certainly not allow [her husband to have] minor wives [*mia noi*]."[82]

So even though it is possible that Prisdang had an amorous relationship with Si, other facts indicate that he was relatively uninterested in women, unlike many of his peers and status superiors. He was married to Mom Sadap in about 1870, but they never had children, and he spent most of his years abroad without her; he alleged that he preferred younger women, and he had two additional wives; his plan to marry a rich woman stemmed exclusively from a desire to pay off his debts so he could become a monk; and he even suggested that he might be impotent. "Have the king give me a wife and you'll know the truth."[83] As far as the record shows, Prisdang fathered no children.

In any case, the only way his relationship with Si could have been considered an affair was if Si had been partnered with another man, which is not mentioned anywhere. We know only that her husband had passed away and that the king desired her to "work" in the palace. Perhaps there is nothing more deceptive than the obvious: the king had claimed Si as his own against her wishes. That would help make sense of Prisdang's flight, the government's silence, and Prisdang's threat, noted below, to expose a secret. But in a letter he writes from exile, he suggests another interpretation. In it, he explains that the king worried that Si, who knew a great deal about the goings-on within the inner palace, would relay damning information to Prisdang, who the king knew was critical of the custom of polygyny, the influence on the king through polygynous channels, and the excessive spending that supported it.[84] The king may have demanded she return to the inner palace to prevent her from informing Prisdang about questionable activities—financial or sexual behavior, the deployment of influence, or otherwise—happening within the king's inner quarters. Si was the kind of woman who swore oaths of friendship with two of the most outspoken reform-minded elite men, who would bar her husband from having minor wives, and who outright refused the king's orders. The king might have considered dangerous her integrity and ability to feed to Prisdang intelligence collected from the inner palace. Only unraveling the mystery of Si, who has disappeared from the public record, would help resolve this series of inquiries.

For Prisdang, the gossip about the affair unnerved him more than the other rumors. It was linked to his sense of personal integrity and loyalty to the king and his friends, all of whom except Si turned against him. He did not understand as dishonorable his indebtedness and attempt to dupe a wealthy woman into marrying him in order to pay off those debts. He refused to play the game of influence and instead constantly reiterated a principled stance. However, once his relationship with the king soured, he had no refuge because Siam's political and social hierarchies were practically indistinguishable. By skyrocketing to political heights and failing to engage in the competition for influence—through gifting or marital ties or constant ingratiation with the king and his favorites—Prisdang opened himself up to accusations by detractors who curried favor with the king and whispered into his open ears.

Politically, however, Prisdang was promonarchy and devoutly loyal to King Chulalongkorn in particular. In this sense, he was not a political radical. His letters pleaded to be readmitted into the king's good graces. He would follow the king's "noble wishes" if only given the chance again. Yet Prisdang's self-exile was itself a critique of the way power operated under absolutism in its noninstitutionalized form of influence and gossip, particularly through polygynous and familial relationships. Against this shadowy and ephemeral form of influence, good words and deeds were useless.

Prisdang found the name sullying intolerable and compulsively sought to cleanse his reputation. Not even the prospect of suicide offered him relief. Prisdang was so enmeshed in the tangled snarl of scandal that he could not separate the strands. His letters in combination with his autobiography reveal his confusion about what exactly happened and the realization that leaving Siam offered him the only opportunity to clear his name and return, as he fervently desired, to government service.

The opportunity presented itself in 1890 when Prince Prisdang accompanied Prince Phanurangsi, by then the minister of war, on a diplomatic assignment to Japan. Prince Phanurangsi requested the king's permission to allow Prisdang to join the entourage as its private secretary for his knowledge of court traditions and his linguistic skills.[85] Prisdang wrote his lengthy missive of resignation during that mission. From May to August 1890, as he traveled from Bangkok to Kobe (Japan) (figure 10) and on to Hong Kong, he explained the predicament that led to his resignation.

Frantic in pace and repetitious in statement, his letters reveal an anxious and fretful mind. Prisdang had learned while in Japan that Si had also fled Siam, allegedly disguised as a boy and carrying stolen family jewels. Her flight catalyzed Prisdang into action.[86] This news alarmed him enough that he feared danger should he return to Bangkok. "In light of that fact that people were more than ready to accuse us of having an affair though we are not, they will definitely find ways to blame me for the disappearance of Phi Si. I will be completely ruined. . . .

FIGURE 10. Photograph of Prince Prisdang (fourth from left) and Prince Phanurangsi (sixth from left) with their entourage in Japan in 1890. Courtesy of Sumet Jumsai.

I will surely be blamed for it and it does not matter who is behind her disappearance, it will end up solely on my shoulders."[87]

He particularly feared Surasak's reaction, which he believed might be murderous. Surasak, as the commander in charge of the First Foot Guard, was the king's right-hand military man and no stranger to warfare.[88] Prisdang wrote, "I fear for all sorts of danger. Phraya Surasak is like a deadly venomous snake . . . it is like I am walking in a deep forest and I have no way of knowing where the snake is hiding and when it will bite me. . . . One wrong move, they will be all over you till you are dead. . . . I am no match for him. I don't think I could ever harm any of my friends. I have never even thought of destroying my enemies, let alone a friend. This is why I have to run away from death and ruin."[89]

Because he hoped beyond hope that the king might give him a fair hearing and accept him back into the fold, Prisdang begged Phanurangsi to cover for him, to maintain public silence about his disappearance, and to keep the letters private until the king decided what to do. That way Prisdang would have a chance to reverse his decision. The content of the veiled threats to the king are never revealed. "I will have to remain silent unless I am forced and coerced to reveal it."[90]

Prisdang planned to resign after they finished their mission in Japan. On their return journey, however, Phanurangsi became ill en route from Yokohama to Shanghai, which temporarily foiled Prisdang's plans to abscond. He couldn't bear to leave Phanurangsi, who had always been kind to him, while he was ill. To help Phanurangsi recuperate, the entourage made an unscheduled stopover in Hong Kong for about two weeks in mid-September 1890. The *Hong Kong Daily Press* notes that "Prince Prisdang and suite" arrived from Shanghai to Hong Kong on 10 September 1890.[91] On the tenth, he wrote a letter to King Chulalongkorn that his bad karma caught up with him. He sat "between the horns of the buffalo" with danger on either side of him. Prisdang bade the king farewell and promised to remain loyal and grateful to the king until the day he died.[92]

Prince Phanurangsi's illness endured, and over the next days, Prisdang's letters become even more insistent. On 23 September, he wrote, "I have tried many times to leave since we arrived in Shanghai, but couldn't because Your Majesty [Prince Phanurangsi] was still ill. . . . The danger is very near. Now that Your Majesty has recovered, I'd like permission to stay in Hong Kong."[93] Phanurangsi, however, refused to give his permission or to carry the letters of resignation back to Bangkok because he believed that only if Prisdang returned to Bangkok could they clear the air. It also would reflect badly on Phanurangsi if Prisdang disappeared on his watch. Yet Prisdang was not among the entourage when, on 26 September, "Prince Banurangsi [sic] and suites" left their rooms at the Hongkong Hotel and boarded the *Sydney*, bound for Saigon.[94] The night before the boat left the harbor, Prisdang sneaked the letters on board through a Mr. Steven, the head of the Post and Telegraph Office in, presumably, Hong Kong, who deposited them at the last minute with Phanurangsi.[95]

Prisdang attempted to inform the king immediately by telegram to discern how he might be received should he be invited to safely return. On 27 September, the day after Phanurangsi's entourage left, Prisdang sent a telegram to Prince Devawongse explaining in staccato English and more fluid Thai that he was still in Hong Kong and that "I am loyal patriotic still my life honourable in danger but is at the disposal of H. M. the King I shall be ready to submit to his will." To which he received the following reply from Devawongse: "Your telegram 27 September is unintelligible there is no reason to fear. News not reliable. Do not believe it. H. M. the King never mention [sic] a word against yourself."[96]

On 28 September, Prisdang countered from Hong Kong, "Please keep [my present state of affairs] secret and grant me the opportunity to prove my loyalty and usefulness to the country and government service."[97] It appears that the king refused to respond to his requests to either receive a fair hearing or resign because weeks later Prisdang tapped out one last desperate telegram from Hong Kong on 10 October 1890: "Unless I have a reply about middle of next week what his M. the King's pleasure is, I will take it for granted you have abandoned me[.] I must go obtain best possible employment for living in disguise for I am not able to maintain my present position. Will you be [good] enough to inform me by telegraph immediately what has been decided."[98]

No response is recorded.

Phanurangsi returned to Bangkok in early October. The king confiscated Prisdang's property and servants. "When the French consul asked on [Prisdang's] behalf if he had done anything wrong, the reply was that he had done no wrong but had gone mad and run away with a widow. When questions were put if he could return to his country safely, the reply was that he could if he liked but no guarantee could be given as to how he will be treated and at all events he could not be treated as if nothing had happened, and yet nothing wrong was alleged to have been done by him, much less any public offence."[99] The fact that both the Siamese government and Prince Prisdang intentionally maintained public secrecy is itself suggestive. Secrecy must have protected *both* the Siamese monarchy and Prince Prisdang, for there can be little other reason for their mutual silence.

A great deal had transpired in the few short years since the king recalled Prisdang to Bangkok: demotion from being an ambassador, his mother's illness and death, homelessness, indebtedness, the king's perception of his political disloyalty, the alleged misappropriation of royal funds to renovate personal properties, the Jao Pan incident, debilitating rumors of an affair with Si, and his gradual abandonment by former friends and official peers. Each of these issues can be interpreted in multiple ways. Most of the rumors remain impossible to prove or disprove. They are secreted in the letters that remain from the period. Gossip surfaces in Prisdang's correspondence in the form of taunting innuendo, but it does not withstand the same intense scrutiny as facts. The truth, shy and illusive, ran around, behind, and ahead of them all, refusing to this day to be revealed fully. Still, together with other evidence, Prisdang's letters in his defense suggest an alternative narrative about why he left a kingdom to which he was wholly devoted. The 1885 proposal was not what caused him to flee Siam: it takes its place in line as one of many reasons why his "bed became too hot for him."[100]

Written decades later, his autobiography covers his departure from Siam without hinting at the anxiety he expressed in his letters written in 1890. "When it was time to leave from Hong Kong to Saigon, I gave 2 letters to the king's brother, the first one is for the king, and the second one is the resignation from my job. While I was waiting to hear the reply, I traveled around China."[101] Then there is an asterisk noting that "* pages 78 to 82 are missing from the original." His autobiography picks up on his life journey over five long years later, when he is ordained as a monk in British Ceylon in 1896.

In the gap, Prisdang met up with Si in Hong Kong, from where they set out for Indochina to make a living. He eschewed his princely title, adopted his commoner name (Mr. Choomsai), and lived semi-underground for the next five years, surfacing in French Indochina and British Malaya and then finally coming to rest in British Ceylon, or Lanka, as the Siamese called it. Although the Siamese government never issued a public announcement regarding his disappearance, its spies and officials never once stopped shadowing Prisdang.

COLONIAL SOUTHEAST ASIA

Exilic Journey

In this volume of [my] history, I intend to write only the truth and my
sincere views. I do not intend to mislead the readers. Regardless
of my intentions, in the parts where I must mention others, I tried
to speak of them with respect, without causing shame to anyone,
minimizing that which is unpleasant.

—Prisdang, *Prawat yo*, 41.

Despite this caveat in the introduction to volume 1 of his autobiography, Prince
Prisdang found it expedient not just to minimize but to expunge from his life
history the first five years of his exile between 1890 and 1896. He worried that
leaving it in might cause a misunderstanding, so he excised it with the intention of including it in volume 2. Although he never published volume 2 and the
segment he removed has yet to surface publicly, Prisdang alluded to the forces
behind his exile and to his exilic itinerary in the appendixes to his autobiography. These include the table of contents for volume 2, which lists as chapter titles
the places he lived after he absconded: Shanghai, Hong Kong, Saigon, Singapore,
Penang, Perak, and finally "Being Ordained in Sri Lanka." Chapters 15 and 16
are respectively titled "The Truth about the Author Having to Be Ordained," and
"The Truth about Than Si, Wife of Phraya Suphan."[1]

Prisdang's anxious narrative voice, as relayed in his letters and autobiography, subsides to a murmur during his exile. He describes the moment of exile as
being "born again" to his third life—the first being his birth as a Mom Jao, the
second beginning when the king became his benefactor and sent him abroad
for an education and ambassadorship, and the third when the king dismissed
him as persona non grata and he, at age thirty-nine, began working for the British colonial government in Malaya.[2] In reply to his anguished letters to the king,
Prisdang heard only silence. He surfaces in government correspondence, most
of which was confidential, among Siam's officials surveilling his movements.
His disappearance from Bangkok provoked no public remark. Siamese officials
denounced him privately as an embarrassment—an ungrateful royal official and

womanizer who was bankrupt materially and morally. Only later, when considering what to tell colonial authorities, did they base the warrant for his arrest on charges of embezzlement from the Post and Telegraph Department.

Prisdang appears to have harbored an intense internal conflict while in exile. An abiding patriot, he sought desperately to return to his native country but only if the king would consent to hear his side of the story. Yet he not only penned a searing critique of King Chulalongkorn and his method of rule but presented it to British colonial officials in 1891. He defended himself as a "political refugee" because of his expression of views that contradicted those of King Chulalongkorn and the system of patronage that dominated politics in Siam. Was he a traitor, a patriot, a monarchist, or an opportunist? Regardless of one's interpretation, Prisdang caused friction between Siam and colonial governments everywhere he went in exile, even when he tried to eschew his royal and diplomatic identity and go underground in disguise as a commoner. After his stint as Siam's diplomatic face in the imperial West, Prisdang found it impossible to conceal his identity. Foreign governments sometimes considered him an asset and sometimes a threat. In any case, the events that caused him to flee Siam and that occurred during the first years of his exile made it impossible for him to return. They led to his decision to become a monk in British Ceylon for fifteen years. In all, Prisdang spent over two decades in exile.

Bangkok

In the immediate aftermath of Prisdang's refusal to return home with Prince Phanurangsi and the rest of the Siamese diplomatic entourage, a story about him expanded to fill his absence. The Siamese state version never made it into the newspapers but insidiously spread through confidential official correspondence and elite society's churning rumor mill. An urgent Siamese government letter written just after Prisdang resigned and escaped into exile in late 1890 was sent to Siamese officials in Champassak—an area contested by the French and Siamese—who were on the lookout for Prisdang. It alleged,

> Prince Prisdang, the Director General of the Post and Telegraph Department, has been having an affair with Si, the wife of Phraya Sunthon Songkhram, the governor of Suphanburi, for many years, but they feel shameful. Then, in July 1890 when the King's younger brother, Prince Phanurangsi Sawangwong, traveled to Japan, Prince Prisdang went along. However, when Prince Phanurangsi Sawangwong returned [to Bangkok] from Hong Kong, Prince Prisdang did not return with him, but instead absconded [*lopni*] to Hong Kong. As for Si, she had already

taken all the wealth and assets belonging to Phraya Surasakmontri, the younger brother of Phraya Suphan [her deceased husband], which he had given for her safekeeping, and fled to Hong Kong ahead of Prisdang. After Prince Phanurangsi returned [to Bangkok], he then realized that Prince Prisdang and Si had planned all along to elope together. When the work in the Postal Department was investigated, no severe damage had been found except that Prince Prisdang had taken about one hundred chang[3] of government funds from the department for personal use. Also they found out that Prince Prisdang and Si were indebted to many people, both Thais and Westerners [farang], in Bangkok. This might be why they dodged [the debts] and fled beyond the borders of the kingdom. However, Prince Prisdang served as an ambassador in Europe for many years, and earned royal favor for his service, having been promoted by the King to the rank of Phra Ong Jao. Later he became obsessed with European theater actresses. When the King found out, he was anxious that [Prisdang's behavior] would bring shame to Siam's embassy[4] so he recalled him back to Bangkok. Once back, the King continued to support [Prince Prisdang] by providing a government position for him with a royal salary of eighty chang per year. Yet [Prisdang] was not grateful and instead reverted to his former crazed and obsessive conduct.[5]

To the array of questionable activities allegedly engaged in by Prisdang was added his "crazed obsession" with presumably white Western actresses.[6] In this version, he "stole" from the government despite his high salary and fled from his massive debts with his adulteress lover, who also was indebted and a thief. The streamlined narrative of Prisdang made him a criminal worthy of pursuit and incarceration if the Siamese could apprehend him before he caused further damage. He, after all, possessed a state secret, had diplomatic contacts around the globe, and spoke English fluently. No wonder the Siamese authorities tried to track his movements while irreparably destroying his reputation.

French Indochina

Prince Phanurangsi and the Siamese entourage left Prisdang in Hong Kong, where he met up with the renegade Si. Together they decided he would remain in Hong Kong while she would forge ahead to Phnom Penh (in French Cambodia). He planned to join her there later because "no one could follow us" in French Indochina, as they could in territories under Siamese suzerainty. Also Si had a relative in Cambodia, Phraya Montri (Phot Phlong), who worked for Cambodia's King Norodom. Phraya Montri lived in Phnom Penh and would presumably take her in.[7] Si left for Cambodia and Prisdang stayed in Hong Kong until late October, waiting in vain to hear a reply from King Chulalongkorn about his predicament.

His last letter, likely to Prince Phanurangsi, dated 23 October 1890, is from Hong Kong. He writes in unpunctuated English:

> Your Royal Highness, After having fully and truthfully explained my reasons for keeping myself away from malicious intention of doing me harm and the circumstances which had brought on me my present situation ... and doing all in my power under the circumstances to avoid anything which may be unpleasant and regrettable I have now to take for granted that I must be left to my own resource [sic] and [am] not wanted to return for none of my praying has been granted. In taking leave of your Royal Highness I beg to be allowed to acknowledge your past kindnesses to me most sincerely and to assure you that so long as I live, I shall ever remember them and always feel grateful to you.[8]

A dejected Prisdang then took a ship to Saigon, where he resided at the Hôtel de l'Univers until he could arrange a position for himself in Cambodia. Si joined him in Saigon after Phraya Montri died in late November 1890, but she stayed elsewhere, "in a decrepit rented room."[9] Prisdang said, "[I] disguised myself as a commoner, but I got caught. People still knew I was a member of the royal family."[10] The authorities in French Indochina recognized him and did not appreciate his presence in their colony. Prisdang had made enemies outside Siam as well as within.

Siamese and French authorities tracked them both, wary that Prisdang's presence would spark the tinderbox between Siam and the French in Indochina fueled by their violent competition over territory along the Mekong River. The French surveyor and explorer Auguste Pavie habitually stirred up these embers as well. His surveying missions—with dozens of assistants, elephants, and river rafts—mapped areas from Bangkok through Cambodia to the northern borders of Burma, China, and Vietnam. These missions were political as well as geographic in nature and brought Siam and the French into direct confrontation over mutually claimed territories.[11] By the mid-1880s, Pavie served as the French vice-consul of Luang Prabang, where Surasak had fought with the Haw rebels. As a reward for his aggrandizing survey efforts, Pavie was soon thereafter appointed the French resident minister in Bangkok.

In the meantime, Pavie carried out a range of duties across the territories between Burma and Vietnam. These included meeting with Prince Phanurangsi in late September 1890, just after his fraught farewell with Prisdang in Hong Kong. Phanurangsi and the Siamese diplomatic entourage sailed to Saigon on their way back to Bangkok. According to Pavie, both he and Phanurangsi were hopeful that Siam and Indochina could adopt "increasingly cordial relations" and achieve a "broad rapprochement."[12] Their hopes, however, were later dashed because of "incidents provoked by the encroachment of Siamese authorities" in areas Pavie considered belonging to France.

Pavie discusses in his field journals his constant travel between Saigon and Bangkok to negotiate these territorial tensions. On one of these shuttles in late 1890, he journeyed with a Siamese interpreter and messenger, Luang Chamnan-akson, who also served as a spy for the Siamese government.[13] Luang Chamnan-akson reported that two Burmese (likely Shan) men went with Pavie to Saigon to meet with Jao Myngoon, a Burmese prince who had escaped his British captors and was living in exile in French territory.[14] The British had asked the Siamese government to help them recapture Prince Myngoon if he passed through Siamese territory. Pavie, the Siamese believed, would take advantage of the disputed boundaries between Siam, British Burma, and what later became French Laos, to smuggle Myngoon across the Mekong River into Chieng Tung (the Shan state of Kengtung, now in Myanmar) by using a French passport, thereby evading capture.

In the process of tracking Pavie's activities, Luang Chamnan-akson discovered information about Prisdang and Si. He reported that Prisdang had asked Cambodia's King Norodom for a job, that King Norodom planned to hire Prisdang as his royal secretary, and that the king was in the process of building housing for the prince in Phnom Penh.[15] However, once the French authorities caught wind of the plan, they thwarted Prisdang's attempt to find gainful employment by prohibiting King Norodom from hiring him. They escorted him out of Cambodia back to Saigon, where they required that he meet Pavie in November 1890.[16]

Likely these two men knew each other: in the 1880s, the French government in Paris had forced Prisdang to hire Frenchmen to work on the telegraph line between Bangkok and Battambang as part of the alcohol treaty renegotiation.[17] Pavie, who began his colonial career working for French Cochinchina's Post and Telegraph Department, directed the construction of that portion of the line.[18] Given Prisdang's renowned anti-French attitude—"the French know Prince Prisdang's original disposition as one who greatly detests France"—and his status as a former ambassador, the French were wary.[19] They worried he might turn the Cambodian king against them.

Once he learned that King Norodom could not hire him, Prisdang considered another option, one he had been contemplating long before exile. Since he could not escape from being a member of the Siamese royal family, he decided he would become a monk.[20] He initially wanted to be enrobed as a monk in a small town in Cambodia, but the French refused this request, claiming it was an unworthy site for the ordination of a member of Siam's royal family. They feared unnecessarily offending Siam's king at a moment of great tension between the two countries. The French colonial authorities telegraphed Bangkok about Prisdang's desire to be ordained and discovered that the Siamese government would permit his ordination in Battambang, then still loosely under Siamese suzerainty.

But Prisdang became suspicious: why would they allow him to be ordained there? He fired off a couple of letters in quick succession in search of other, safer avenues. On 4 December 1890, from his hotel in Saigon, he sought assistance from a Ceylonese Buddhist monk, the Venerable Subhuti, whom he had encountered many years earlier in Lanka (the Siamese name for British Ceylon). He begged to be allowed to devote his life to the priesthood

> in order to make merit and denounce the world which has been so unprofitable and cruel to me. . . . But I failed to accomplish my object in my own country where political life prevented me. Can you assist me without making it known in the first instant to get into the Order of Priesthood [in Lanka]. . . . If you can manage it please send me a telegram of one word thus
>
> Prisdang
>
> Saigon
>
> Yes
>
> but if not please say No and write to explain what must I do.[21]

A couple of days later he sent another letter to Suhbuti begging him "to be so kind as to treat my letter as private and confidential, whether you can do me the favor I ask of you or not."[22] He then wrote to a former colleague in the Post and Telegraph Department named Phra Satja Phirom, then also living in exile, in a letter dated 13 December 1890 from Saigon:

> I was afraid that they [Siamese] might just harm me in the remote area before I could be ordained. I won't be able to get help since I don't know anyone around here. And whatever happens would be silenced. So, I am hanging [around Saigon] to verify if they will truly allow me to become a monk. If they really allow it and are not tricking me, I will be willing to [be enrobed] because I am so tired of human beings, and tired of my work and everything. Nothing is real. . . . The brownnosers are rewarded like this. I can't stand it and would rather become a monk to get some peace in my life so I will at least have some peace when I die. . . . If I can't be ordained, then I don't know what to do because I do not have enough money to just sit around. No one wants to hire

me for I belong to the royal family. Wherever I run I guess I still cannot escape from being royalty, and might be caught anywhere. So either I am ordained or I die.[23]

A few months later, he wrote more pointedly about his fears in a confidential memo for the British official who eventually hired him. He explained that if the French allowed him to reside in Cambodia, Siam would consider this an unfriendly act. However, if Prisdang wanted "to go into the priesthood he could do so in Batta-bong [sic] (where a murder could be committed without leaving any trace of evidence or be known to the world at large)."[24] He suspected the Siamese might allow or carry out his assassination.

Official Siamese correspondence about Prisdang and his movement in French Indochina suggests less dramatically that he would be arrested as soon as he entered Siamese territory. Siamese authorities followed his movements closely. They knew he feared arrest in Battambang so would not likely head in that direction, but they also knew he stayed in a Saigon hotel, was unemployed, and would soon run out of money. They understood that the French were getting annoyed with him and wanted to expel him from French Indochina.[25] The missives by Siamese authorities repeat the more sordid rumors about Prisdang and Si—their shameful affair and their theft of funds. However, they also introduced a particu-larly lurid bit of gossip: that Si continued to sleep with her husband's corpse after he had passed away. "This Si, she pretends that no woman loves their husband as much as she does. After Phya Suphan passed away, she did not cremate the body, [but] kept the corpse, and has been sleeping with it to this day. It has yet to be cremated."[26] Clearly, this was false. She could not have easily absconded with a rotting corpse, let alone bring it into her bedchamber.

After assassinating their characters, the letters informed Siamese authori-ties along the borders with French Indochina to be on the lookout for Prisdang, who—like a rogue royal charlatan—might cheat people out of money or damage the reputation of Siam. Should Prisdang cross over into Siamese territory, offi-cials were instructed to trick him into remaining there until they received further orders.[27] Ironically, Prisdang's telegraph lines made this speedy exchange of intel-ligence possible.

Prisdang, in any case, was known to be a Francophobe who might turn King Norodom against the French—hence their desire to be rid of him.[28] Si may also have had anti-French tendencies. Prisdang wrote that Si returned to Saigon from Cambodia "because the French might suspect that she is there to instigate the Cambodian royals."[29] He wrote to Phra Satja Phirom, formerly a senior official in the Post and Telegraph Department in southern Siam, who had apparently black-mailed the local populace.[30] From letters Phra Satja wrote to Prince Devawongse,

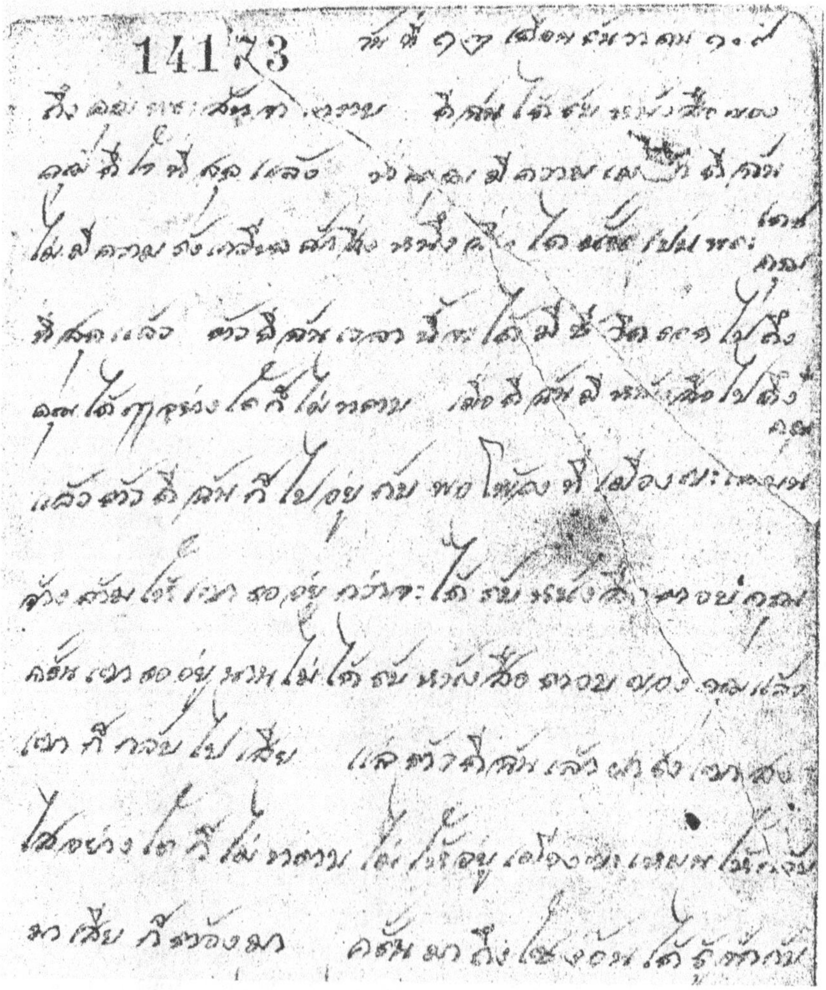

FIGURE 11. NA KT 6.26/2, letter from Si to Phra Satja, 12 December 1890.

it appears that in 1891 he resided in Penang. Prisdang considered Phra Satja an exile like him, except that Phra Satja was wealthy and therefore did not have to rely on others for employment. He attempted to enlist Phra Satja's support by asking him to hire and protect Si.[31] She too wrote Phra Satja a letter asking for a job (figure 11). It is the only source written by her hand that has been found, revealing she was literate. In it, she notes that she was delighted to receive a letter from Phra Satja. Because she could not linguistically navigate French Indochina, she hoped that he could send someone to come pick her up in Saigon and bring her to him. "If I can stay alive until I see you, I will tell you the entire truth about the whole thing and then I won't care if I die. Please be kind and consider hearing the truth from me. You won't regret it. Si."[32]

Phra Satja had been corresponding with Si and Prisdang since October 1890. He too betrayed them by sharing their letters with Siamese officials, presumably in an attempt to be reinstated there. From Penang, Phra Satja forwarded Prisdang's and Si's letters to Prince Devawongse in January 1891.[33] Prisdang's letters express surprise that Phra Satja had taken an interest in him when everyone else had abandoned him. He explains why he cannot return to Siam, including some crucial details that help make sense of his exile. First, Prisdang is confused by the fact that Phra Satja enclosed a letter to Si in the same envelope in which he sent a letter to Prisdang: "I am very puzzled why you did this because Phi Si and I are not together." Prisdang then relays his "side of the story." He had lost all his friends, even sworn friends, who betrayed him—including Prince Devawongse (who was reading the letters), Prince Svasti, and Phraya Surasak—who together swore to serve the government and protect each other. Prisdang continues his story but changes the emphasis in his letter to Phra Satja:

> Then we had the idea to submit a petition signed by all of us to His Majesty the King, proposing that our country should have a *Constitution*[34] and should set up proper government regulations and procedures. Those who disagreed had reported this to HM.[35] His Majesty was not pleased. He thought we were "radical,"[36] trying to reduce the king's power. He was then angry. All my friends were making excuses, and blamed it on me alone. When I returned from abroad, I tried to create a department of *public work*[*s*] and was almost successful, but then Prince Svasti, my sworn friend, stirred up trouble.[37] He showed the king my private letters that I had written [to Svasti]. The king was so enraged that he nearly jailed me. The king confiscated my house and stopped paying my salary.[38] I have been in disrepute since then.... His Majesty remained distrustful, thinking of me as a "radical" who condemns Thai tradition. The truth is, all of us as friends talked, discussed, and commented on many problems in our country.[39]

One wonders whether Prince Devawongse appreciated the layered acts of betrayal: his reading a private letter by Prisdang about the betrayal of friends like Devawongse who gave Prisdang's private letters to the king. What is more curious, however, is Prisdang's return to the petition as the first catalyst that aroused the king's suspicion of his loyalty in particular, rather than focusing exclusively on the sordid rumors regarding his relationship with Si, which he emphasized in his letters of resignation. Highlighting his political views had one unique benefit: it allowed Prisdang to claim status as a political refugee.

His letter to Phra Satja did not ignore the gossip about him and Si but instead shed on it in an illuminating light. "As the rumor never quieted down, the king was worried that Phi Si, who has been in and out of the palace and knows many things [that go on in the palace], may tell me about those things because [the king believed] she was in love with me. Since my friends blamed me alone for critiquing the custom of polygyny and the palace's excessive spending, the king wanted Phi Si to stop seeing me and to disassociate herself from me. He ordered Phi Si to stay inside the palace but Phi Si refused."[40] In the king's view, if she didn't move into the palace, where she had apparently once served, then it would prove the scandal true, that she wanted to be with Prisdang. Even so, Si refused to follow the king's orders.

Prisdang's letter to Phra Satja explaining his circumstances continues. Surasak then weighed in, panicking: "He said if she didn't go to the palace, then we will be in big trouble and even be killed and the whole family will be completely wiped out. . . . But Phi Si resisted and threatened to kill herself because she really hates staying in the palace, and she thinks if she enters the palace, it would imply that we really had an affair. . . . She said she would stay out of the palace to prove that we were right. She really wanted to beat them. She won't budge, no matter how much we begged."[41] Then Surasak abandoned them in order to save his own skin. The lack of viable options suffocated Prisdang: "There's no room to breathe."[42] Separately, they escaped from Siam and Bangkok's stifling elite society.

Not that their reception in the French colonies proved any more welcoming. By early March 1891, French authorities had essentially chased Prisdang out of French Indochina. A missive written by a Siamese official notes that "the French despise him, refuse to let him reside there, and forbid him from going to Phnom Penh to the point that they followed him to arrest him."[43] The king, upon reading the correspondence, concluded that it was unlikely Prisdang would remain in French Indochina.[44]

Indeed, Prisdang was on the move again. On 23 February 1891, he wrote another "Private and Confidential" letter to the Venerable Subhuti in Lanka, who had yet to respond to Prisdang's request for help being ordained. "I am anxious to enter into [the] priesthood in Ceylon if you can still assist me to do so quietly." "In any case should you write to me again, please address me as George Francfort by Poste Restante, Penang, where I am going by the beginning of next month."[45] He ended up residing temporarily near the Thai temple, Wat Chaiyamangalaram, in Penang.

British Malaya

With French Indochina and Siam no longer safe, Prisdang headed to the British Straits Settlements in March 1891. In the first two months, he had avoided Siam's representatives in Penang but made connections with local Siamese speakers. In a revealing letter written in May to the Venerable Subhuti, Prisdang apologizes for not responding sooner and for not immediately entering the monkhood in Lanka:

> The reason is that I have a sister with me whom I must take care and for whose living I must arrange before I can leave for Colombo. . . . I have to find a house for her and a small property on which she can live and to find friends who will be kind to her and assist her in future. She could not go over to Colombo because she does not know any foreign language, but here in Penang there are many Siamese of good standing and Chinese who can speak Siamese so that she can get on and do business here easier than elsewhere. I have now found a house and am about to conclude the purchase of a property and I hope shortly to be able to finally settle all matters in connection with this business, when I will write to inform you of my coming. I regret most sincerely the opportunity of entering the priesthood by the propitious date as proposed by you; and I hope there will be nothing happening to prevent my doing so in the future as my affair is quite quiet now.[46]

Prisdang told a little white lie to conceal any hint of impropriety to the monk by whom he hoped to be ordained. His "sister" was no doubt Si. In the first few months after Prisdang arrived in Penang, he arranged for safe harbor for Si on the island. It is unclear where he received the funding to purchase the house and property on which he settled her, but it may have been the result of a marriage of convenience. In July 1891 Prisdang married "the half sister of Meh Rün [sic] or Koon Naisuan," who is referred to as elsewhere as the sister of the late "Phya Bhuket, the divorced wife of Phya Lakhon."[47] She is identified variously as the elder sister of the last governor of Phuket before it had been incorporated into Siam's new administrative (*monthon*) system, the half sister of Mae Ruen, and the ex-wife of the governor of Nakhon Si Thammarat.[48] Although little else is known about this "wife," it is clear that Prisdang had finally fulfilled his long-stated desire to find a wealthy woman who might help him pay off his debts: "[I]t is believed that Meh Rün helps him with money."[49]

This tantalizing glimpse is all one sees of Prisdang's marital affairs in Penang.

He never mentions this wife in any of his letters or in his autobiography, but *The Bangkok Times* and the *Singapore Free Press and Mercantile Advertiser* did not fail to publicize his new marriage and employment in British Malaya, with great sarcasm:

> Life is full of surprises, pleasant and otherwise, though we believe that taken as a whole *La vie est dure* [life is hard], and in this Prince Prisdang

former Chief of the Postal Department will agree. The noble Prince is now acting as engineer in Perak, under Mr. Davidson formerly of Bangkok. The Prince has taken to his bosom the sister of the late Governor of Junk Ceylon [Phuket]; and we hear that the lady [Si] who followed him from Bangkok is now residing in Pnom-Penh [*sic*]. The only bright spot in the whole miserable business is that Prince Prisdang is able to earn his bread by the sweat of his brow.[50]

The article's inference that Si had stayed in French Cambodia was incorrect—she had followed Prisdang to Penang, where they both likely sought out Phra Satja.

Once in British Malaya, Prisdang and Phra Satja went into business together in Teluk Anson in lower Perak along the west coast of British Malaya. A. D. Neubronner, the consul for Siam in Penang, reported to Prince Devawongse that Prisdang had met with British authorities to discuss cultivating pepper, coffee, and rice in Perak, where he promised to return with Siamese laborers. Rumor had it they would "name the place 'Siam' something or other."[51] In the letter, Neubronner insinuates that Prisdang and Phra Satja planned to lure Siamese criminals, women, and children into British territory, where the women and children would be sold, presumably as prostitutes and slaves, in Deli on Sumatra.

Once King Chulalongkorn learned of this, he issued an order to forbid anyone without proper travel documents issued from the governors (*phraya*) of Songkhla and Saiburi from leaving the kingdom overland. He then asked Prince Devawongse to consider whether or not the order should be rescinded. The ambivalence about sending it appears to have had to do with the degree of control Siam could actually exert over the governors in some of these southern provinces, particularly in Phuket, where Phra Satja had close connections.[52]

Meanwhile, Prisdang had already moved on to other projects. Prince Devawongse penned an urgent letter to the king that he had "some peculiar news" that the British authorities had hired Prisdang in July to work for them in Perak. Robert Morant, by then the tutor to the crown prince and a general adviser to Prince Damrong, was in Singapore having dinner with the governor of the Singapore Straits Settlements, Sir Cecil Smith. Morant knew Prisdang: he had taught him at the Raffles Institution in Singapore briefly in 1871.

Smith reported to Morant that Prisdang's application for a position had been forwarded to him, and he "directed that a post should be formed for him, sufficient to keep him in decency, but that he should not be allowed to be *idle*! He gets $150 in some light engineering work on the roads: he has a lady with him."[53] Devawongse drafted a response to Neubronner in which he stated he "was rather surprise[d]" by this and "could not help thinking that His Excellency [Sir Cecil Smith] may . . . encourage and entice more runaway thieves and the like from

Siam to [the] Straits Settlements."[54] His response amounted to nothing more than a diplomatic slap on the wrist.

In July 1891, Frank Swettenham, the British resident in Perak (and future governor of the Straits Settlements), provided Prisdang a position, salary, and housing, first in Taiping just inland from Kuala Larut on the west coast, and then in "Ponto Tanyong," or what must have been Larut, for three and a half years.[55] Prisdang remained until 1896, when he left for Lanka. Swettenham noted that Prisdang

> has left Siam (for ever he says), and I have given him some work here. He offered to place at my disposal all the information he possesses on any subject, and I thought it might be useful to ask him about the present state of affairs, in view of the reported action of the French [in Luang Prabang]. He has just left me, and what he says is this . . . everyone in Siam, from the King to "rayats,"[56] would prefer British to French occupation, but that they could not get an assurance of protection from the English Government against France. . . . Prisdang also says that the Siamese Government has always told him they wished to claim as much as they could (whether on the French side or in the Malay Peninsula), and hold on to it as long as possible, with the idea that some day they might, like Medea, save Siam or some part of it, by throwing these outlying provinces, one by one, to the pursuers, France on one side, and England on the other.[57]

Swettenham delivered the memorandum in person to the Foreign Office in London in July 1892.[58]

King Chulalongkorn worried about Prisdang's employment by the British for many of the same reasons the Siamese government fretted over his efforts in French Indochina: their geographic borders were as yet indeterminate. Prisdang had been hired to build roads and attract Siamese subjects to Raman, a district under Siamese suzerainty running along the northern border of British Perak. The area was also allegedly rich in ore, specimens of which had been enclosed in some of the Siamese correspondence about Prisdang. The discovery of valuable natural resources only heightened Siam's desire to claim the area. Frank Swettenham was simultaneously reconsidering boundary demarcations because of a long-term conflict between Sultan Idris in Perak and the Raja (ruler) in Raman: "It appeared therefore important to delimit the boundaries between Perak territory and Reman [sic], over which small State the Siamese claimed control."[59] Prisdang entered this fraught geopolitical context just as Siam and Britain were cautiously eyeing their mutual boundary.

The king worried that Prisdang might build a road from the British side across to the Raman side, thereby stirring up trouble along the border.[60] It is not a coincidence that Raman, along with Kedah, Perlis, Kelantan, and Trengganu, were "transferred" to the British in 1909 as a consequence of the development work performed under Swettenham by Prisdang.[61] In the early 1890s, Siamese government correspondence about Prisdang strategized about how Siam might seize him should he step foot within Siam's boundaries when he engaged in his potentially territorially aggrandizing roadwork for the British along the border of Raman. "We can arrest [Prisdang] without having to alert or fear the British because they did not fear the Thai before they hired him. The British will say they hired Prisdang and supported him only because they understood him to be Thai royalty who was without anything to eat, so they were expecting [our] gratitude. However, in terms of international relations, I think we can fight it if it becomes an issue if we arrest him. I ask Your Majesty to issue an order to Muang Raman first so they are aware [of the plan]."[62]

The Siamese government issued an order to the governor of Songkhla in which it accused Prisdang of using funds from the Post and Telegraph Department for personal expenses. It requested that the governor send a spy to Raman to investigate the British government's road construction project, to arrest Prince Prisdang if he entered Siamese territory, and to send him immediately to Bangkok.[63] Letters by the spies sent to gather intelligence about Prisdang explain that during the months of February through June 1892, they met with him. He was living in Larut (Perak) and went by the name of P. Chumsai. They confirm that the British government had hired him to work as an engineer for road construction but also empowered him to persuade people to move to Perak. Prisdang organized the erection of a Buddhist temple to attract Siamese (Buddhist) subjects to live there and even tried to tempt the two men sent as spies to come live in Larut, where he would guarantee them land, a living, and protection from abuse. The governor of Raman had been ill and his administration was chaotic, which exposed it to the risk of outside interference. Prisdang had already attracted about one hundred families from the west side—areas considered dependent upon Siam.[64] The king's frustration and disdain were penciled in the margins of the first letter: "Absolutely cease using *Prince* [to refer to Prisdang], which no one has used for a long time!"[65]

Prisdang's Confidential Memo of 1891

Prisdang, stripped of his princely rank, had made a new life for himself in British Perak. Perhaps he truly believed he would not be allowed back in Siam, and that enabled him to speak his mind about King Chulalongkorn and his methods of rule. He wrote a confidential memo to Swettenham in July 1891, when he was hired. Maybe he felt obliged to write it in return for being offered a job or saw it as an opportunity to vent fully his critique of the Siamese system that had engineered his ouster. In any case, his memo provides a damning evaluation of King Chulalongkorn, the monarch's absorption with family matters, and his increasingly autocratic style of rule. It also presumes that Siam's colonization was "inevitable," a view Prisdang argues was shared by other minister princes.[66] In the 1890s, as Siam aggressively competed for territories along its borders with the French and the British, it might have seemed impossible that Siam would succeed.

Prisdang's memo offers two profound critiques: it details with precision the nature of the problems preventing Siam from reforming its administration *and* offers his ultimate self-defense—one that would reverse the rumors and reveal him as respectable. He was not running away from disgrace. That was the Siamese government's cover story for his real status as a political refugee, based on his stance against Siam's system of rule under King Chulalongkorn.

His first critique was against absolutism. His memo explains that he had advised King Chulalongkorn in 1885 to reduce his absolute authority, which provoked the king's ire. Prisdang does not understand himself to be unique— he shared these views with several other "sworn" friends like Prince Svasti and Surasak. However, both Surasak and Svasti betrayed him, ultimately scapegoating him alone for the ideas expressed in the 1885 petition.

Second, Prisdang's deeper critique of Siam's sociopolitical hierarchy targeted the custom of polygyny, which he dared not place in the 1885 petition "for fear it would upset the king."[67] Remarkably, he and his fellow petitioners felt it easier and safer to request that the king replace an absolute monarchy with a constitutional one than to ask him to consider limiting or ending polygyny. Instead, petitioners like Prisdang denounced polygyny in private letters that Princes Svasti and Devawongse later, after his political demise, shared with the king.[68]

His critique was not protofeminist or about gender equality—after all, Prisdang claimed that he had three wives. He even married another woman while in exile. Instead, it targeted the nefarious operation of influence outside formal institutions of political power through appeal to the queens, consorts, and children of the king and through treacherous rumors fed into and spun within this network. His evaluation stemmed from personal experience of the power of this social and political complex working against him. "The immense power and influence of the favourite Queens works wonders and plays an important part, though indirectly, in political and social affairs of the country. It can make and unmake a man, and can frustrate . . . those who devote their life to public affairs."[69] It is "an open secret that the influence of some of His Majesty's favourite wives is a factor in the well-being and success of a man in the service of the Government."[70] "No man can hope to succeed very well unless backed up by this influence, and those who have succeeded never know when they might fall out of favour, because it all depends upon their wives' or relatives' skill and cleverness to maintain the favour or influence of one favourite of the King without offending others."[71]

Influence worked in two ways: through offering gossip and gifts. Instead of focusing on running the government, the king "listens to and enjoys scandalous and exaggerated stories of his officers' domestic concerns and takes great trouble to acquaint himself with them," while his palace favorites "do not forget to vent their spite on their enemies."[72] A foreign doctor who worked in the courts even noted, years later, that under King Chulalongkorn the court was alive with "its constant change and movement, its excursions, shows and performances, *its intrigues, its gossip.*"[73] Officials quickly learned that one way to remain in the king's good graces was by providing gifts to his favorite consorts, which often devolved into a purchasing competition that left officials in serious debt. In addition, the incessant ceremonies for the king's beloved queens, children, and consorts—who numbered in the hundreds—provided opportunities for officials to "vie with one another to give costly presents and offer their services" and detracted attention and funding away from the public good.[74] As a consequence, nearly all officials were personally indebted, and the Treasury was not treated as distinct from the king's personal coffers. The king was in charge of the money, which had grown under his rule as the various ministries came under his control. By the time he died, he was one of the richest monarchs in the world.[75]

Prisdang's diatribe was not an Orientalist critique of "harem politics" typical for the times, for it had little to do overtly with what most Westerners considered the enervating and depraved sexual practices of "Oriental despots." As noted by the historian Nigel Brailey, Prisdang's memorandum "should not anyhow be viewed as catalogues of scandal, but [as] reflections of deep issues illustrated by the policies of King Chulalongkorn," who "gradually developed a form of despotic authority that he evidently considered his birthright."[76] Only once in the thirty-page memo does Prisdang refer to the king's sexual practices: "The present habits of the King if described in detail would take a volume and read like a story of the Arabian Nights."[77] Instead, he was interested in highlighting the deeply political nature of polygyny in an absolutist system. This "backdoor" form of power enabled endless opportunities for injustice and oppression without providing measures for redress.

Prisdang places the blame squarely on the shoulders of the king. Unlike in the early part of King Chulalongkorn's reign, after the death of the regent in 1883, "the King is absolute, has no fear of and need consult no-one."[78] "The King has hundreds of wives and concubines and proportionate numbers of their relatives, and his own brothers and sisters, and those who have influence and power can, to a greater or less extent, interfere with justice and exercise arbitrary authority and set the law at defiance."[79]

Prisdang's experience was with the more subtle operation of social blacklisting under absolutism, a system in which political institutions and official positions mattered less than one's standing in the eyes of the king. His personal experience of the king's arbitrary favor, impacted by rumors within the palace walls, seeped into his attack on the king.

> The moment the King shews a favour to anyone he is the centre of attraction, everyone smiles on him, talks to him and makes friends with him and the moment the King turns his anger on him, he is the most abject to behold. He loses all, even the friendship of his best of friends who either from motives of fear or selfishness will forsake him and leave him in the lurch to work through all difficulties into the King's favour again which is generally possible only by the help of his wife or female relatives if they are clever enough to work into the favour of one of the favourites of the King. This fact creates an immense amount of intrigues and spirit of jealousy amongst all around the King, and whoever wishes to rise has to sacrifice his self-respect as a man of honour.[80]

He alludes to the 1881 league of sworn friends, which broke apart as its members transformed into sworn enemies: "The reason is not hard to find when one remembers that everything comes from the King."[81] All his former friends denounced him because "they were afraid of the King and dare not acknowledge friendship to a man pronounced by the King to be radical and anti-Palace custom [anti-polygyny]."[82] In an absolutist system, the only thing that mattered was one's connection to the king, which often worked indirectly through a complex but intimate social hierarchy in which most people at the upper levels of rule were related.

> A most vicious custom of the country exists to make honest people discouraged and demoralized. If his superior says a thing is so and so, specially of the subject, a subordinate cannot contradict him and those who are not concerned endorse the opinion and support the superior disputant to gain favour and guard against the displeasure of the superior. If such opinion comes from the King there can be no division except in a whisper amongst intimate friends. Thus a man who is pronounced to have acted or done wrong, notwithstanding the false accusation, if it is pronounced by the King even privately it is accepted and no-one would dare to defend the accused unless he wishes a greater punishment or suffering for himself.[83]

And finally, "The writer [Prisdang] tried to maintain his independence of opinion and not to fall in with some of the present customs and to hold his own, and so gradually fell out of favour and was threatened with danger and disgrace."[84] As noted by one observer of old Siam, "Rank was everything, it permeated every walk of life, it decided the place of everyone at an assembly."[85] Prisdang may have been intellectually brilliant, but socially he failed to observe his proper place in the hierarchy. Had he been a commoner, he no doubt would have been imprisoned. His princely status and former ambassadorial renown protected him from jail but not from the very social system that had empowered him in the first place. Prisdang served as a warning to other elites who upset that hierarchy.[86]

Prisdang's vitriol spilled outside his memo to the British, where one might suspect he would have benefited from exaggerating the faults of Siam's absolutist system. He had no reason to write (in English) in a similar vein to Lanka's Venerable Subhuti in September 1891. "In Siam everyone depends on the favour of the King and therefore everyone tries to please him. Why few fear or no one will waste their time when opportunity occour [sic] to talk to the King on subject which will not give him advantage to himself. . . . There are thousands of affairs which are left in this way and everyone only try [sic] to do what is possible i.e. to carry their object when they see that that object is the King's interest to carry through."[87] Even years later, in 1897, Prisdang expressed disdain about King Chulalongkorn's lack of ethics to Anagarika Dharmapala, a Lankan Buddhist activist.[88]

These harsh denunciations of how influence worked via the inner palace and the moodiness of the king belie Prisdang's voluminous writings expressing his desire to reunite with his king and country. His feelings about his king and country reveal a profound inner conflict that imbue his character and stamp his life journey. He was never allowed to return to Siam in Chulalongkorn's lifetime regardless of how desperately he desired this. It is unclear whether Chulalongkorn ever read Prisdang's damning memo. Prisdang may not have known that Swettenham shared it with Britain's Foreign Office. Swettenham's cover letter to Philip Currie, then permanent undersecretary at the Foreign Office, states, "I did not of course tell him [Prisdang] that I should write to you."

Soon after Swettenham delivered the memo in London in 1892, British officials in Bangkok sent letters to London discrediting Prisdang. A handwritten memo of 1892 by the British consul to Siam, E. H. French, to Lord Salisbury, then British secretary of state (for foreign affairs), summarized Prisdang's fall from grace. He reached far back into Prisdang's history, making claims about the alleged poverty of his family, his father's "weak intellect," Prisdang's embezzlement, his vanity and conceit, and his abandonment of his "wife and children."[89] French retroactively explained that as Siamese ambassador in London and Paris in the 1880s, Prisdang "commenced a life of reckless extravagance and expense which soon got him into difficulties" including debt, which caused his recall to Bangkok, where he was placed in charge of the Post and Telegraph Department.

French continued:

> Before long however he recreated much scandal by his intrigues with a Siamese lady of rank. Last year the King's youngest full brother went to Japan for some few weeks taking Prisdang with him. The journey appears to have offered Prisdang the opportunity he wished for. He persuaded the lady he had been carrying on an intrigue with to desert her family and she, having disguised herself as a boy, collected all her jewelry and that of her family and, going by another steamer, met Prisdang in Hongkong. His own wife and children Prisdang left behind here [Bangkok] quite unprovided for.[90]

Clearly some points in his memo were patently incorrect, which raises the question of who provided French with this particular version explaining Prisdang's departure. Prisdang and his wife, Mom Sadap, had no children. Nor had he any by his alleged minor wives, so far as the historical and genealogical record shows.

A similar memo written in August 1892 by Captain H. M. Jones, British minister and consul general in Siam, to Lord Salisbury states that Prisdang was no political refugee. Instead "the cause of his departure is well and generally known here. He has never gained a reputation but for senseless extravagance and having eloped with a married Siamese lady of high position he feared to return and brave the King's anger. His accounts with the Treasury . . . showed a defalcation of about two thousand Pounds." He then repeats that Prisdang left his "wife and children" without resources.[91]

The British were not unified in their understanding of Prisdang, nor, obviously, was their intelligence correct. Those such as Jones and French, who resided in Siam, had different information than others who resided outside the kingdom's borders. To Frank Swettenham, Prisdang defended himself against each accusation but did not clarify exactly why he had fled. Swettenham then relayed these points to his superiors in London.

> He [Prisdang] did not elope with a married Siamese lady of high rank. He was travelling with one of the Siamese Royal Princes & heard from Bangkok that it would be unsafe for him to return there. Consequently he did not return. The Siamese lady was not married, but a widow, & her husband, who held an official position, was more asiatico [?],[92] charged with certain laches & misappropriations & his widow threatened with

imprisonment if she did not make good the claims. Prisdang assisted her to get away from Bangkok but assures me that she has never been other to him than a sister, and I believe him, I know the lady.[93]

The real reasons, Prisdang explained to Swettenham, were between him and the king of Siam and were political in nature. Even the debts in Europe were "not simply the result of personal extravagance," and the two thousand pounds that went missing from the Post and Telegraph Department were for a contract that Prisdang had made on behalf of the government for running steamers, not for personal use.

"As to Prisdang's wife & children, he has never yet been married, but he has kept concubine's [sic], who by Siamese custom are put on & off as easily as a garment." So Swettenham is not quite right either—Prisdang had married Mom Sadap. Still, he felt Prisdang had been mistreated: "With his record, birth, and intelligence, there must have been some very strong motive to induce him to throw away everything and at his age to begin life again as a nameless pauper."[94]

It is hard to evaluate the impact that the memo had on British foreign policy. It was accompanied by "an elaborate map of the Mekong valley territories already in dispute with the French, [which] may have proved rather overwhelming to the Foreign Office staff who read them."[95] As a consequence, it is difficult in retrospect to assess whether or not Siam's leaders genuinely thought Prisdang capable of threatening the kingdom's independence or whether something else was at stake for them. Prisdang's fluency in English, his personal relationships with European diplomats, and the timing of his exile made him a potentially dangerous man to Siam. He also worked along the indeterminate borders of the kingdom during the most critical years of Siamese sovereignty: the 1890s, when France and Britain essentially carved up the map of mainland Southeast Asia, leaving a shrunken and chastised Siam as a neutral zone in the middle. The Siamese government "wished to obtain his extradition if possible but there being no such treaty between Siam and the Straits Settlements they could not of course obtain it."[96]

In early 1893, while Prisdang assembled a small community of Siamese families in Perak, France laid claim to all of Laos east of the Mekong River, which the Siamese government, relying on principles of international law, refuted. France, in retaliation for the death in battle of a French officer, steered gunboats up the Chao Phraya River and pointed cannons at the king's royal palace in Bangkok.[97] Attempts at negotiation failed, and the British did not, as the Siamese anticipated, interfere on behalf of Siam. The French demanded an indemnity of three million francs, insisted on the punishment of some Siamese officers, and occupied parts of Siam (Chantaburi and Trat) until the Siamese government agreed to these conditions, which it did in October 1893. King Chulalongkorn sent out feelers about traveling to England in November but was discouraged by Lord Rosebery, then foreign secretary, who wanted to prevent a public display of support for Siam.[98] Siam's leaders discovered the limits of British friendship as the British refused to intervene to halt the French or to demonstrate their support in other ways. Confronted with the possibility of colonial occupation, the Siamese government suffered the indignities of imperialism's effrontery, and directly faced its domestic political weaknesses.

King Chulalongkorn, who had fallen ill just before the crisis, withdrew from public affairs in 1893 and suffered a moral and physical collapse. A British official described the king as physically weak: he lost over forty pounds and was covered with boils, even on his eyes.[99] After 1893, he could no longer father children. With the king seriously ill, Siam experienced a vacuum of authority. The British reported that the king's half brothers fought over arrangements for a regency in the event the king died but were wary of presenting their ideas to the king, who was suspicious.[100] Little is heard from the king or Prisdang for a year or two. In the silence, the king gradually recovered, and Prisdang grew increasingly dissatisfied with his exilic existence.

Perhaps the bittersweet thought that he was right all along flitted through his mind as he witnessed Siam's political ordeals from afar. Throughout this most traumatic period for Siam's monarchy and territorial body, he lived in the disputed border areas in French Indochina and British Malaya, working for British colonial authorities. The king's most arduous supporter had become his most damaging defector. It appears that Prisdang went about his work and continued his friendship with Si because they surface together one last time in Siamese government documents before Prisdang left Perak. A letter from June 1894 from Prisdang in Perak to "Jaokhun Thiphakosa" apologizes for not being able to visit Jaokhun Thiphakosa in Phuket because of illness. Si would go in his place and select a variety of fruit trees and flowers for the governor of Perak.[101]

Siam's consul in Penang sent a telegram to Bangkok with news about Si's anticipated travel to Takuathung in Phuket, with a single abrupt question: "Shall I arrest?"[102] Prince Devawongse initially refused to bring the matter to the king's attention because he was still ill, and he thought the telegram had been sent by Prisdang pretending to be Thipkosa. Devawongse pondered the upsides of arresting Si, who was referred to throughout the letters as Prisdang's wife: "When I think about the way Prisdang escaped, it was because of Si. She was the one who persuaded him to go, so it seems appropriate to arrest Si when she enters the kingdom in order to make Prisdang come after her, or in order to clear up and make an official inquiry into the royal funds that remains unresolved. There are also personal debts, such as those valuables of Phraya Surasak."[103]

But the downsides of arresting her proved more significant: the valuables, once returned, were not equal to the trouble of investigating them, and Prisdang might not enter Siam in search of Si if he heard about the arrest or he might be split from her. Finally, if Siam did arrest her, foreign countries could claim Siam acted with brutal vengeance toward a woman. Devawongse decided to let the king know but only after consulting Princes Bidyalabh (Sonabandit) and Damrong. Damrong "thinks that even if we had Prisdang himself [rather than Si], we should not arrest him. It's better to consider him a crazy person."[104] By 1894 Siam's leaders had more pressing concerns. Prisdang was a nuisance but no longer a threat. The king scribbled a final note: "That bastard Chumsai, he won't come. If he did, he'd stir up trouble. I don't think he's too important. Just ignore him, and he will eventually not have enough to eat. We shouldn't create a rift with the British."[105]

The illness that Prisdang mentioned in his 1894 letter to Jaokhun Thiphakosa in Phuket may have been genuine because it motivated him to ask for a leave of absence from the British colonial government in Perak. He never lost sight of his goal to be ordained as a monk in Lanka. In a letter written to Subhuti in late 1891, after the British had hired him as an engineer, Prisdang said he could not yet go to Lanka. "I am not yet able to leave the world . . . because I have not yet completed my arrangement to leave my sister [Si] here and I am now in the service of the Perak Govt in order to facilitate my arrangement and I hope before long to realize my object [of being ordained]."[106]

It took several years before he could realize this goal because of the logistical practicalities impeding his path—ensuring Si's maintenance and obtaining identity papers among them. Prisdang sent letters to several individuals, including Siam's consul in Penang, Neubronner, demanding an identity certificate, the equivalent of a passport, before he boarded a steamer to Ceylon on 19 October 1896. He hoped to be ordained on the Day of Atonement. A small kerfuffle erupted at this resurfacing of Prisdang, who was ultimately denied the travel document because of "the surreptitious leaving of his native country where he found his own bed too hot for him."[107] The internal correspondence between the king and Devawongse criticizes Prisdang for pretending to want to be a monk and for sending letters to the king and others in the hopes of obtaining the king's reply. Devawongse maintained that Prisdang planned to be enrobed simply as a way to get back into Siam. The *Western Argus* (Australia) reported that Prisdang, with his "chequered career," had left Siam under "not altogether favorable" circumstances, had been enrobed, and "will now be able to return to Siam . . . [because] a Buddhist priest is not subject to Siamese law."[108] Scribbled in response to Devawongse's letter is the king's view: "Respond that this prince is no son of this land, thus is no relative of mine. According to rumor, the fact that he left Bangkok was because of some personal shameful incident of his own, that rendered him unable to look his friends in the face."[109]

Prisdang, unaware of Prince Devawongse's and the king's continued vilification of him, sent a letter to King Chulalongkorn on the day he boarded the steamer, begging royal permission to be ordained as a monk.[110] He bid his king farewell with a sense of finality by sending a package of candles and incense on 17 October 1896, requesting the royal secretary to place the items "at the feet of His Majesty, my august sovereign."[111] The package must have been peculiar because Devawongse noted the candles and incense were more "like the candles and incense that someone gives who is taking leave of this world, who dies and goes to another world."[112] For once, Prisdang concurred, for he too notes that this was his fourth life, when he was born again as a Buddhist monk in Ceylon.[113]

BRITISH CEYLON AND INDIA
The Prince Priest

My sole aim and great desire is to devote my whole life to Religious
object . . . in order to make merit and denounce [sic] the world which
has been so unprofitable and cruel to me.

—Letter from Prisdang to High Priest Subhuti of Lanka, 4 December 1890

From the moment his troubles began in the mid-1880s, Prisdang aspired to become
a monk, first in Siam, then Cambodia, and finally in Lanka. He abandoned Si and
his new wife, whose names vanish from the records from this moment on. Despite
his stated desire to lead a life of quiet contemplation, Prisdang led an exceptionally public life as a monk in Lanka. He returned to center stage in an international
Buddhist and colonial drama involving Britain, Siam, and Lanka. He parlayed
his ambassadorial experience into a position of veritable international Buddhist
diplomacy within the first few months of his arrival in Lanka, and when this
failed, he tried again in northern India in a gambit to claim relics of the authentic
Lord Buddha for Siam's king.

Contingency and context played a role as well. In Lanka, the desire of leading
monks to unify and gain the patronage of an Asian Buddhist monarch dovetailed
with Prisdang's personal aspiration to regain an intimate connection with King
Chulalongkorn. From afar, Siam's minister of foreign affairs, Prince Devawongse,
continued to watch Prisdang, whose behavior confirmed his suspicion that Prisdang
had become a monk only because it would provide a way for him to return to Siam.[1]

For Prisdang, one fiasco followed on the heels of another, beginning even
before he arrived on the island in 1896. First, Siamese authorities denied him an
identity card as a Siamese subject, which impeded international travel. Second,
a mix-up in the newspapers reporting on his plans to be ordained confused his
identity with that of a more celebrated and powerful Siamese prince. Third, his
strategy to unite the various fraternities of Lankan monks under the sole remaining sovereign Buddhist king, Chulalongkorn, failed miserably after a visit he

arranged to have King Chulalongkorn see Lanka's most sacred object, the Buddhist Tooth Relic, in 1897 went horribly awry. Fourth, Prisdang's effort to collect sacred relics for the king backfired when he was accused of stealing them. This allegation prevented his anticipated return to Siam in 1899, shattering his dream of coming home to serve his king and country.

The context for that final snub was so egregious that Prisdang contemplated suicide for a second time, drafted an embittered will, considered renouncing the priesthood, and finally surrendered to a quieter life on an equally forsaken island—one teaming with discarded snakes and skeletons. A man of extremes, Prisdang practiced corpse meditation there to remind him of the impermanence of life. However, even at the end of the world on a tiny island he had named after King Chulalongkorn, he attracted attention and fame. It catalyzed his reengagement with politics and diplomacy as the abbot of Dipaduttamarama Temple in Kotahena and the patriarch of Colombo, positions he occupied from 1905 until 1910.

Over the course of his fifteen years in Lanka, Prisdang founded two free schools for impoverished children, acted as guide and interlocutor for many foreign guests, and rubbed shoulders with leading Theosophists, foreign royalty, authors, and political figures from around the world. In his writings from the period, he viewed Lankan Buddhism through the lens of imperialism's patronizing contempt but with a twist. As a native of an independent Asian country, Prisdang felt he had license to condemn Lanka's fractious Buddhist politicking as corrupt *and* British understandings of Lanka as unwarranted arrogance. Endlessly energetic and a showman at heart, he still could not suppress his apparent need to be at the center of politics, let alone exorcise his desire to return to Siam. When he did return home in 1911, the respect and position he had painstakingly reestablished over a fifteen-year period in Lanka were again obliterated.

Prisdang's Ordination as the Monk P.C. Jinawarawansa

Finding a path to ordination had proven arduous, and it was only after five years of exile in French and British colonies that Prisdang was able to be ordained. An illness beset him in 1896, after which he requested a leave of absence from the British government in Perak and arranged his travel to Lanka.[2] He was ordained by the monk Vaskaduve Subhuti, who had long-term personal connections with Siamese royalty, particularly Prisdang and his patron-friend, Prince Phanurangsi (figure 12).[3] Subhuti and Prisdang had first met in about 1880 when Prisdang stopped in Colombo on his way to Europe—even then Prisdang had mentioned being ordained by Subhuti.[4] He returned to visit Subhuti at least once more,

FIGURE 12. Postcard of the Venerable Subhuti, no date. Courtesy of
K. D. Paranavithana.

likely on his way back from Europe in early 1886 with Princes Svasti and Naret, when the small entourage attempted (but failed) to see the famous Tooth Relic of the Buddha in Kandy.[5]

On the basis of the letters they had exchanged, Subhuti expected Prisdang to arrive sometime in late October 1896. Given Prisdang's plan to be ordained by Subhuti, it must have been mystifying to read in the press that Prince Damrong, who was by then Siam's most powerful royal minister helping implement some of the very reforms suggested by Prisdang and others in 1885, would also come to be ordained in Lanka.

> HIS ENROBEMENT TO TAKE PLACE IN COLOMBO. The High Priest W. [V.] Subhuti, well-known about [sic] Oriental Scholars, and the chief of the largest Buddhist sect[6] in Ceylon—the Amarapura—has received a communication from Siam, both officially and privately, that Prince Damrong, who not very long ago visited Ceylon en route to the European courts, will shortly arrive at Colombo, and be ordained as a Buddhist monk by the High Priest Subhuti, and remain in Ceylon as his pupil.[7]

This bit of misinformation was printed in the *Pinang Gazette* and repeated in the *Bangkok Times*. One paper even conjectured Prisdang would return to Europe as a Buddhist missionary.[8] Mysteriously, Subhuti also apparently received a telegram from Singapore informing him of the departure of Prince Damrong, not Prisdang, on a French mail boat called the *Natal*, which would arrive in Colombo on 26 October 1896. The confusion was cleared up in a letter written to Foreign Minister Devawongse in late November by a Lankan named Owen Mendis Obeyesekera.[9]

Obeyesekera explained that he and Subhuti had deduced that Prisdang, not Damrong, would arrive in Colombo but nonetheless arranged for a grand reception. Prisdang arrived unannounced two days earlier, on 24 October, by a different ship (the *Maria Valerie*). He arrived with one attendant, who must have been a servant named Nai Chang.[10] He allegedly "took the High Priest and others by surprise" by showing up without fanfare at the Abhinavaaramaya Temple doors in Waskaduwa, Kalutara, just south of Colombo.[11] Prisdang explained that he had arrived by a different steamship because "he had made up his mind to lead a quiet life and he was not in favour of any public demonstrations in his honour."[12]

Despite this stated desire for solitude, the monks and laypersons arranged for an elaborate, dawn-till-dusk ordination ceremony at the Waskaduwa temple on 5 November 1896 (figure 13). The *Ceylon Independent* reported on the ordination at the "charming," octagonal, two-story temple.[13] The hyperbolic article reports that upwards of five thousand men and women, including some British and elite Ceylonese, congregated to see the prince's transformation from a worldly pleasure-seeking royal prince to a humble Buddhist priest. The more exalted his former

FIGURE 13. The Waskaduwa temple building where Prince Prisdang was ordained in 1896. Author's photo, June 2015.

life, the greater the sacrifice, and the more Prisdang's path was likened to that of Siddhartha Gautama.

More than two hundred priests witnessed it as well on that swelteringly hot, windless day with "nothing to disturb the air except the low chant of the priests."[14] Fruit, flowers, and coconut tree fronds festooned the temple entrance and arches as Prisdang arrived in civilian finery to read an address in English, which no one could hear because of the "hubbub."[15] Obeyesekera relayed in his letter that Prisdang said that "he had during his past life, sought the pleasures of this world, but they afforded him no happiness and that he had come to Ceylon with the resolution to lead a life of peace and seclusion which he could not expect if he had been ordained in the land of his birth."[16]

Prisdang changed out of his civilian attire and into his military uniform (figure 14). In the interlude, two bands played. The *Ceylon Independent* described him as dashingly handsome: "In that uniform with helmet in hand, his breast covered with numerous medals, his raven locks well combed backwards and a small black moustache, well-trimmed and cultivated, the Prince looked the polished man of the world."[17] Crowds rushed in to grab silver coins, fistfuls of which Prisdang tossed in their midst as a symbol of renouncing the material world, a

FIGURE 14.   Prisdang in the same military uniform worn the day he was ordained. Courtesy of the National Archives, Thailand.

gesture unique to Siamese ordination and unusual in Lanka. Some women lost their jewelry in the melee. He broke the sword into pieces, a process that awkwardly required assistance from two additional men.[18] Then High Priest Subhuti began the formal ordination process by cutting off the first lock of hair, all of which was saved as a remembrance and can still be viewed at the temple's museum.[19] "A touching incident at the shaving ceremony was to witness the sorrow of the

"CENTRAL STUDIO."

5. 5th Cross St. Pettah,
Colombo.

FIGURE 15. Jinawarawansa (Prisdang Chumsai), Waskaduwa temple, Lanka,
5 November 1896. Courtesy of the National Archives, Thailand.

Prince's faithful Siamese attendant, who on beholding the locks of his master fast disappearing, with eyes brimful of tears, retired to one of the rooms and was not seen out again the whole of that evening."[20] Prisdang received a ceremonial bathing and at last emerged, robed in white silk, to receive his first offerings from the crowd (figure 15). It was hardly a subdued or secluded beginning for Prisdang, who from that moment on adopted the priestly name P. C. Jinawarawansa, which means "of the great lineage of the Buddha."[21] Notably, he had his pictures taken by an official photographer, who documented the before and after images of his transformation into a monk.

Within a month of his enrobing, Jinawarawansa wrote to King Chulalongkorn to inform His Majesty that he had been ordained under the high priest Subhuti. The notes scribbled across the top and bottom of the letter were telling: "Impermanence is suffering," and "P.S. another thing, I beg to caution Your Majesty to avoid misfortune in responding [to me]. Do not slander me because now that I am a monk, I am no longer Prince Prisdang, therefore it is inappropriate for you to think negatively of me because you hold something against me."[22] His admonishment was meant to protect the monarch and no doubt to make clear that he was no longer a defamed and hounded prince but instead had been reborn as the monk Jinawarawansa. Lankans quickly adopted the shorthand of the Prince Priest, a moniker that stuck.

International Buddhist Politics

Initially the local Lankan papers reported that the king of Siam was well disposed toward the Prince Priest, but then they claimed the opposite, which had prompted Obeyesekera to write the letter apologizing to the king for any offense because of the "very conspicuous part which I took in the public demonstrations devised by me to honour the Prince."[23] In so doing, Obeyesekera believed he was also honoring Siam's king. The confusion about Prisdang and misinformation printed in the press incited Obeyesekera to "humbly" offer his services as Siam's local consul. Clearly, he argued, this incident demonstrated a need for some sort of official representation of Siam in Lanka.

His hand-wringing letter was not the only one issued from Lanka to Siam. H. S. Perera, the manager of *The Buddhist*, a newspaper affiliated with the Buddhist Theosophist Society, also wrote to the king's private secretary about Prisdang's ordination in November 1896. "[W]e have not published anything concerning the affair [the ordination] not knowing who he is, nor, it appears, have any of the highest dignitaries of the Siamese sect [Siyam Nikaya] here participated in it. We are very inquisitive to know the ins and outs of the Prince, and also his connection with the Princes of Siam. He would not tell who his relations are in Siam."[24] If only Siam would appoint a consul in Lanka, then these misunderstandings could be avoided, Perera also suggests. If one was not available, then Perera kindly would offer a suitable Sinhalese Buddhist to appoint. The king scribbled on the letter: "Respond that this prince is no son of this land therefore is not a younger relative of mine as has been rumored. . . . Send the request for a Consul to the Krom Tha [minister of foreign affairs]."[25] Prisdang's arrival catalyzed Siamese authorities to appoint a diplomatic consul in Lanka. Samuel Donnaclift Young, a Scottish banker who had become a successful merchant in Ceylon after he arrived in about 1880, was appointed consul at Colombo for Siam in 1897, likely to facilitate King Chulalongkorn's visit as well as to clarify issues raised by the ordination of Prisdang.[26]

His royal preceptor, the High Priest Subhuti, also wrote a follow-up letter to King Chulalongkorn in early December explaining that Jinawarawansa had been enrobed and was busy studying Pali, Sinhalese, and the Dhamma under Subhuti's guidance. Subhuti did not apologize for ordaining Jinawarawansa but remarked that the prince claimed to have had the king's permission. Subhuti admitted that he was "quite ignorant of the opinion of His Majesty" but that if he hadn't ordained Jinawarawansa, the prince would have found another priest and would have been ordained at a "trifling" temple.[27] "The Buddhists were overjoyed as this was the first time when a Prince was enrobed in Ceylon after the extinction of the Royal Family, and this, I suppose, is a great honor to Buddhism itself."[28] By "extinction," he referred to the British colonization of Lanka that ended Kandyan royal rule. In letters to one foreign scholar, Subhuti called attention to his ordination of this royal pupil.[29]

The Prince Priest's royal and Siamese identity mattered a great deal in Lanka, where Buddhism and politics were fraught with tensions (figure 16). After the British completed colonization of the island in 1815, they replaced the Kandyan monarchy and gradually withdrew government support for Buddhism. As a consequence, the traditional interdependence between the established Buddhist sect, the Siyam Nikaya, and the Kandyan kings broke down.[30] This contributed to disputes and the disestablishment of Buddhist orders that had already begun before the British arrived. Lankan monks looked for royal surrogates such as the kings in Buddhist Siam and Burma rather than alien British authorities to help them settle disputes and establish legitimacy.

By the time Prisdang arrived in Lanka, there were three main Buddhist fraternities that were further segmented along caste, subcaste, regional, and doctrinal lines: the Siyam Nikaya, the Amarapura Nikaya, and the Ramanna Nikaya. The former was affiliated with the Goyigama caste, Lanka's largest and most influential one, and regionally associated with Kandy, the former site of royal power.

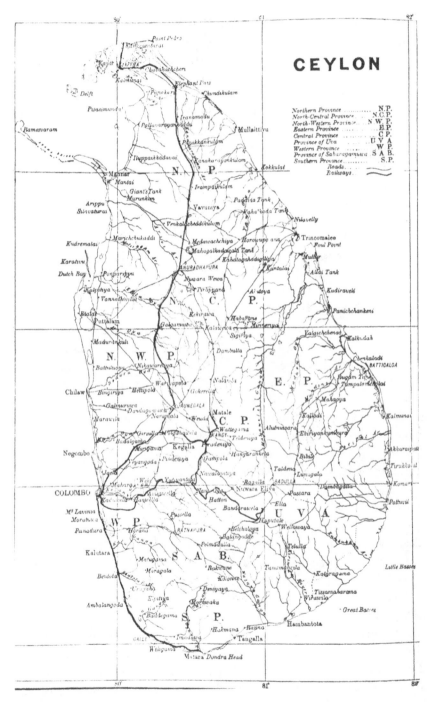

FIGURE 16. Map of Ceylon, 1907, from Wright, *Twentieth Century Impressions of British Ceylon*, 8.

One of Lanka's last reigning monarchs, King Kirti Sri Rajasingha (r. 1747–82), banned men from lower castes from being ordained in the Siyam Nikaya, which still ordains men exclusively of the Goyigama caste.[31] Its namesake reveals its relationship to Siam, or more accurately, to Ayutthaya, from where its ordination lineage was reinitiated in the mid-eighteenth century. A second fraternity was established by 1800 when several dissident monks traveled to Amarapura, then the capital of Burma, to receive ordination as *bhikkhu* (monks). As a consequence, the Amarapura Nikaya was oriented toward Burma, received the patronage of the Burmese king (until the British deposed him in 1886), and was resistant to the caste hegemony of the Siyam Nikaya, based in Kandy.[32]

Significantly, Jinawarawansa's preceptor, Subhuti, led the Amarapura Nikaya, a "fraternity of the traditionally disinherited who [had] challenged the right of the establishment, both religious and political, to keep them permanently excluded."[33] One might wonder why Prisdang was ordained within the Amarapura fraternity rather than the Siyam Nikaya, the sect affiliated with Siam. From the perspective of those in Lanka, it was already peculiar that a Siamese royal prince would be ordained somewhere other than Siam. His selection of the Amarapura sect over that of the Siyam Nikaya required further explanation. Subhuti's scholarly acumen, his understanding and practice of Buddhist principles, and his sect's rejection of caste attracted the exiled prince. According to oral lore, Prince Prisdang was drawn to Subhuti because when he—known among Lankans to be a famous diplomat and member of the Siamese royal family—first arrived in Colombo on his way to Europe in around 1880, an entourage of officials, aristocrats, and monks of various sects greeted him at Colombo's harbor. As Prisdang disembarked, everyone stood, including the monks, who should have remained seated according to the rules of the Buddhist priesthood. The only exception was Subhuti. Prisdang walked directly to him and bowed in veneration because Subhuti alone understood the proper relationship between man and monk.[34] In addition, Prisdang rejected the caste exclusivism of the Siyam Nikaya, a point he made clear in an editorial written in 1897 in which he stated that the "Buddha distinctly ordained the abolition of caste and no priest is a priest of the Order established by Buddha who maintains a caste distinction."[35]

Finally, both Prisdang and Subhuti must also have understood that the Siyam Nikaya, the dominant sect associated with Kandy's former royal ruler, was structurally parallel to Siam's royal Thammayut sect. The high priest who headed the Siyam Nikaya, Hikkaduve Sumangala, would not have wanted to alienate them.[36] For the Siyam Nikaya to harbor a Siamese royal fugitive could have been an offense in the world of Buddhist diplomacy, where particular sects aligned with specific kings and kingdoms for political as well as religious patronage, the two often too complexly intertwined to be effectively distinguished.

Prince Prisdang, as a royal family member from an independent Asian Buddhist kingdom, could not escape politics by becoming a monk in Lanka. Into this fractious context he stepped and immediately became embroiled in the complex politics of Buddhism in British Ceylon. Within months of being ordained, Prisdang—who shall hereafter be referred to as the Prince Priest or Jinawarawansa—discovered his mission: unite the three sects under the ecclesiastic leadership of the sole remaining independent Buddhist monarch, King Chulalongkorn, who was scheduled to stop over in Colombo on his way to Europe in April 1897. This would allow him to gain credit for leading an effort that glorified the monarch at the same time that it gave Lankan priests a "precious opportunity to press for royal resolution to the island's mosaic struggles and divisions."[37] Although Jinawarawansa claimed credit for the idea, it had long been brewing. The Venerable Sumangala of the Siam Nikaya, also considered monastic disunity the most pressing problem impacting Buddhists in Lanka and sought to resolve some of these issues by building Buddhist institutions locally with the patronage of other Asian Buddhists, such as King Chulalongkorn.[38] A cultural space existed in Lanka for a Buddhist monarchy, despite British efforts to divorce secular from religious sources of authority. As "the only remaining Buddhist sovereign of the world,"[39] King Chulalongkorn and his visit provided an appealing reason and opportunity to unify.

To this end, Jinawarawansa attempted to unify Lanka's fractious priesthood. He drafted a letter to the king and asked Lanka's leading monks from the Siyam, Amarapura, and Ramanna Nikayas to sign it.[40] However, his efforts to cajole the various priests into signing were not initially successful. A brazen letter from him to the highly respected Hikkaduve Sumangala chides, "I understand that you object to the other Nayakas [chief monks] signing the letter to the King of Siam with you."[41] "[Y]our objection is quite contrary to my wish" to unify the Siamese and Lankan Buddhist orders. "Unity is strength and respectability, separation is weakness and a source for contempt to the world at large. I do not give you the credit of a narrow-minded and short-sighted policy." The bluntly worded letter ends abruptly, and it is unclear whether Jinawarawansa sent it, though it would not have been out of character. He had a reputation for being "hard" or obdurate to the point of being merciless but also for being a respectable, incorruptible monk.[42]

The Prince Priest encountered enough resistance from the monks that he appealed to the American Theosophist Colonel Henry Steele Olcott, to intercede on his behalf to unify the monks prior to the king's arrival. Olcott had been visiting Lanka since 1880, when he converted to Buddhism, and was closely affiliated with the Buddhist Theosophical Society there. He spent his time between Lanka and the Theosophical Society's international headquarters in Adyar, India. Olcott notes in his "Old Diary Leaves" that on 20 March 1897 Jinawarawansa wrote a long letter appealing to him for assistance. Olcott saw a kindred spirit in the priest who, like him, had come to Lanka "in the hope of finding brotherly unity and religious calm, the very things to soothe his world-beaten spirit. . . . But the Prince-priest, like myself, found himself in an atmosphere of personal bickerings, childish sectarian squabbles, ignorance of the world about them, and incapacity to fit themselves to the ideals which the Lord Buddha had depicted for the government of his Sangha. . . . Jinawarawansa . . . entertained the hope that he might get the leading priests of the Siam, Amarapoora [sic] and Ramanya [sic] sects to agree to a coalition into a single 'United Sect'"[43] under Siam's king.

Olcott continues, "With his natural impetuosity he threw himself into the business with zeal and enthusiasm; wrote to the leading priests of Ceylon and their chief lay supporters, got pledges from many, but soon ran against the awful inertia which pervades all Asiatic countries (Japan now excepted) and bars progress. The personal factor everywhere obtruded itself, and the poor fellow, finding himself at a standstill with the King's visit near at hand, despairingly appealed to me as 'the only man who could awaken the slumbering Sinhalese.'"[44] Both men viewed Lankan Buddhism through the lens of imperialism's patronizing contempt. The Prince Priest's words and actions reveal that he considered himself superior to his Lankan Buddhist brethren. The cultural space conceded to him, as Buddhist royalty and a former diplomat, abetted his occasional condescension. When the Anagarika Dharmapala, a man who eventually championed the Buddhist Revivalist movement in Lanka, met the Prince Priest in late 1897, he described him as "a pleasant looking man; but he is disappointed with [the] Ceylon priesthood. . . . He is impatient and no great reformer should be impatient," a term that surfaces repeatedly in Dharmapala's initial descriptions of the Prince Priest.[45]

In late March, the impetuous, impatient Prince Priest wrote an open letter, published in early April in the *Ceylon Observer*, to his fellow Buddhists entitled "A Religious Manifesto."[46] He deployed the press as well as Olcott's influence to compel Lankan Buddhists to line up behind his plan. "We the undersigned for ourselves and on behalf of the rest of the Buddhist Priesthood in Ceylon beg to tender our deep regard and sincere love to Your Majesty as the only Buddhist Sovereign of the World" it began. In addition to inviting him to visit the various pilgrimage sites on Lanka, the priests also "look forward to the day when all Buddhist Priests and laymen here will recognize, acknowledge and yield implicit obedience to the laws and decisions of your enlightened ecclesiastical Government and Sovereignty."[47]

In addition to the ambitious multipoint scheme to unite the Lankan, Burmese, and Siamese orders under King Chulalongkorn's ecclesiastical (not political) authority, it draws attention to numerous unprincipled Buddhist monks who are more like members of "trade guilds" who "are destroying our religion and respect due to it and its order, and make all the world look down upon us with contempt and disrespect; and as a result the order is laughed at and regarded as being composed of men who, being two [sic] idle to work for their living honestly, not only take refuge on the ignorant but also take advantage of the religion." And, he continues, seemingly without regard for offending at least some Lankan Buddhists, "These bodies of men are under no spiritual or temporal control whatever as regards to their moral conduct.... They are perfectly lawless gangs." Unlike the "English Government," which "is neither competent nor willing to interfere," Siam, as the only independent country under the rule of a Buddhist king, had an ecclesiastic court that could "punish refractory priests."[48]

Jinawarawansa's vision of Buddhist rule demanded that all Buddhists compromise their cultural differences and that King Chulalongkorn "must interest himself more in religious matters and movements. His interests must spread far and wide and benefit all equally and without any preference. He must become one with the Buddhist public opinion of the world, and be the very foundation and part of Buddhism itself and be recognized and accepted as the fountain-head of all that is religious and the temporal head of Buddhist power and *the* Buddhist spiritual authority."[49] One can almost feel the commanding reverberation of his voice coming through the printed page as well as the shame induced by his rebukes. He spoke in the timbre and deployed the discourse of a Buddhist imperialist cum revivalist preacher.

His pride in being a Siamese subject of an independent Asian king is palpable, especially in the private circular sent to the Lankan high priests and to the Ministry of Foreign Affairs in Bangkok. It listed the protocol for appropriately receiving King Chulalongkorn at Colombo and outlined why this was important. "The reasons for honouring him are: (1) he is a Crowned King, and all the civilized nations honour their own as well as foreign sovereigns; (2) he is an Oriental King, and we ought to be proud to be able still to have one in the East; and (3) he is a Buddhist King, and our admirations for him for protecting and cherishing the doctrines of our Lord Buddha and retaining the faith of his ancestors ought to know no bounds."[50] Jinawarawansa makes it clear that he wanted the Buddhists to welcome the king in a way that would upstage the British government there. Lanka's Buddhist community, despite their differences, also wanted to welcome the king of Siam directly, rather than let British authorities alone receive the monarch. Alongside descriptions of the Chakri family colors, the King's "motto," the various sacred and family orders, and description of the "National Flag," he notes imperiously that Siam's kings are really emperors or "Kings of Kings, having as their vassals Kings and Princes of extensive countries tributary to Siam, such as Chiengmai, Luang, [*sic*] Phrabang, (now wrested by the French) among the Shan States, Kedah, Kelantan, etc., amongst the Malay States."[51]

The British and some Lankans regarded with suspicion the "manly manifesto," as one newspaper article referred to Jinawarawansa's political coming-out piece.[52] One editorial asked how the Prince Priest could possibly "get the high-caste Siamese-Ceylonese brethren to fraternize with their Amarapura-Ceylonese brethren." And "As to the king of Siam attempting any protection of Ceylon Buddhists, Her Britannic Majesty's representative here might have something to say to that."[53] In response, Jinawarawansa parried that the King of Siam would offer spiritual guidance to Buddhists, as the pope does for Catholics the world over.[54]

King Chulalongkorn had been forewarned of the petition he would receive upon his arrival in Colombo. He also knew that the exiled prince, dressed in a monk's robes, was behind much of it. At 10:00 a.m. on 21 April 1897, a cheering crowd of thousands and a twenty-one-gun salute greeted the monarch at Colombo's jetty, decorated with flags and greenery.[55] His arrival brought record numbers of visitors to Colombo by train.[56] Lanka's major officials, foreign consuls, monks, and members of the general population joined the Prince-Priest, Olcott, Dr. Perera, O. M. Obeyesekera, and others to witness the king's disembarkation. The king was presented with two written pleas from the Buddhist community, including the Prince Priest's petition.[57] They invited His Majesty to unite the divided sects and "assume the control of our church and its priesthood."[58] As noted by Anne Blackburn, a scholar of Sri Lankan Buddhism, King Chulalongkorn's formal reply, read aloud at the jetty, was "decidedly noncommittal."[59] He merely promised to give the petitions his "fullest consideration."[60]

Early the next morning, the king went by train to Kandy to see the renowned Tooth Relic of the Buddha. A palladium of the former royal court in Kandy, the Tooth Relic "played a central role in the exercise of royal authority and in ritual technologies used to harness auspicious power for kings and kingdoms."[61] As a consequence, the precious object was guarded and could be seen only by prior appointment, which had been made by the king's attendants. All of Kandy prepared for the anticipated royal visit. At the railway station, large crowds of locals arrived early to line up along the side of the road leading to the station. The staff at the Queen's Hotel, where King Chulalongkorn would stay, lit up the structure with Chinese lanterns and retrofitted the reading room to serve as the sitting room for the king's party.[62]

Nearly five hundred monks gathered to chant and witness King Chulalongkorn observe the Tooth Relic housed in the Maligawa Temple, the stone steps of which were covered in colorful cloth leading to the temple entrance. The high priest read an address in Pali, which the king later confessed that he could not understand because he could not tell if it was Pali or Sinhalese.[63] He responded in English and then entered the temple. As offerings, the king had brought with him dozens of silk robes, hundreds of candles, incense, and silver and gold trays and tree-shaped ornaments. He performed his *puja* (prayer ritual) before being shown the Tooth Relic, but first there occurred a "small hitch."[64]

According to an eyewitness, the king asked the Kandyan aristocrat guarding the relic, a Mr. Panabokke, if he could touch the Tooth Relic, which lay under a glass cover. Panabokke denied this request, claiming that only priests could touch it. "'Then, said the King, 'if they can touch it why cannot *I*? You insult me.'" The king then asked to borrow a golden book to have translated, but when Mr. Panabokke asked for how long he might borrow it, the King indignantly retorted, "'I shall not steal it!' He then stood for a moment . . . [and] said, 'I shall make no offerings.'"[65] The majority of the priests witnessing the king's about-face could not understand English. They simply saw him rush from the sacred room and collapse in an "exhausted state on the verandah, surrounded by his Princes, who were vigorously fanning him. His Majesty then rushed out of the place to his carriage" and refused to be placated by Mr. Panabokke or a deputation of Buddhist priests who tried to pacify him.[66]

According to Olcott, "His Majesty, the King of Siam, was naturally anxious to see so far-famed a Buddhist relic, and when he was admitted to the room in the Dalada Maligawa, wanted to take the Relic in his hands, but two Kandyan aristocrats, with the worst possible taste and ignorant fatuity, protested. . . . The King was naturally indignant at so palpable an affront and left the temple; he returned the presents that had been made to him by different High Priests and came back to Colombo."[67] Other Siamese royalty, including Prince Phanurangsi, and nonroyal Christian British officials had been allowed to touch the relic, but the oft-touted sole remaining sovereign Buddhist king was denied. Offended, the king refused to watch the *perahera*, or procession, arranged for him that paraded directly in front of his hotel that evening.[68] "The King before entraining [from Kandy the following morning] expressed thanks for the hearty reception given him and said he would always remember the kind people of Kandy, but would never remember the Dalada Maligawa [Temple of the Tooth Relic]."[69] He left Colombo immediately. On the king's return journey from Europe in November 1897, he refused to stay the night in Colombo, preferring to remain on board his yacht and to leave the next morning.[70]

In the wake of his sudden departure in April, the British press castigated King Chulalongkorn for being "childishly irritable and petty"[71] and offered a self-congratulatory defense of the Ceylonese who denied the king his wishes. "Siam is still where Ceylon was in the past century, in respect of the relations between King and temples and priests: But here, the British Government having freed itself of any connection with Buddhism . . . the trustees [of Buddhist temples] know their independence; they have no fear even of Kings."[72] Rumors spread that King Chulalongkorn had designs on the tooth and that he desired to handle the relic in order to investigate its authenticity as a tooth of the Buddha. Both Olcott and a Belgian legal adviser who had worked for Siam reported that there was good reason to believe that the enormous tooth came from an alligator or was shaped from a deer horn.[73] Aleister Crowley, who arrived in Lanka in 1901, heard about the king's "journey to Kandy with his retinue in great pomp to make the presentation [of a valuable bejeweled casket for the Tooth Relic] in person and the priests refused to allow him to see the tooth! It was a magnificent piece of impudence—and of policy."[74]

Another rumor claimed the king and Jinawarawansa had "improper designs" on the relic—the latter had allegedly asked to weigh and measure it, prompting some to imagine he might steal it or engineer a relic switch.[75] Accordingly, the Prince Priest "was also the subject of controversy after the king's visit. Letters to the newspapers questioned his motives in being ordained on the island, his aspirations to higher status, and his status in the eyes of the Siamese court. He was accused of maligning the character of Lankan monks and of behaving improperly in various ways."[76] Jinawarawansa's open letter to the press in early April that likened Lankan monks to lawless gangs had not earned him friends.

Regardless of the truth, King Chulalongkorn was both disappointed and piqued by the embarrassing public refusal of his request to handle the Tooth Relic. After he left, a committee of Buddhists led by Olcott and two Sinhalese investigated the incident and found the relic's lay custodian, Mr. Panabokke, guilty for his disrespectful handling of the king's request.[77] The committee had no authority to implement punishment beyond this pronouncement. Ultimately and not surprisingly, Siam's ecclesiastical authorities rejected the proposed union of the Buddhist orders for reasons of administrative complexity and fear that any unseemly behavior committed by Lankan monks might reflect negatively on Siam's Buddhist order.[78]

Despite his vigorous efforts, Jinawarawansa had failed to engineer an ideal experience of Lanka for his king. His efforts may have been an opportunistic strategy to inveigle himself into the position of diplomatic go-between who would act as the linchpin in the nexus among Siam, Lanka, and Burma. Regardless, Jinawarawansa took an enormous risk in proposing such a scheme. The idea of uniting Asians under a single Buddhist ecclesiastical court was conceptually bold and not for the faint of heart. It also seemed to stem from a genuine desire to lionize King Chulalongkorn. Jinawarawansa had alchemically transmuted his bitter indignation that fueled the confidential exposé of the king and his administration's failings to the British in 1891 into golden adulation for the monarch, at least in public. His private feelings are harder to discern. An entry from Dharmapala's diary written in November 1897, after King Chulalongkorn's visit, suggests that the Prince Priest still privately critiqued his king. He explained to Dharmapala, "He has seen all the corruptions in Bangkok. The King has nearly 150 children." He also reported to Dharmapala that the mother of the late crown prince was discarded as soon as her son died, causing Dharmapala to exclaim, "Such is the political morality of the reigning King of Siam!!"[79]

Colonel Olcott empathized with the priest, who was in his view simply trying to please King Chulalongkorn and empower him as the monarch reigning over all Buddhists in the region. "Thus an incident [re the Tooth Relic], inexcusable in itself, toppled over the house of cards which Prince Prisdan [sic] and I had so carefully constructed in the matter of the proposed international brotherly union of three Buddhist nations."[80] Olcott and Jinawarawansa also shared an attitude of Orientalist disdain for Lankan Buddhists and Buddhism. They bonded over their bitter disappointment at "not having found in Ceylon the ideal bhikku [sic] . . . I [Olcott] felt very sorry for him for he had thrown up all the luxury, pomp and influence of his worldly position and instead of sitting down to a banquet of spiritual food had found it a sort of a Barmecide [disappointing] religious feast. However, he was not the sort of man to sit down and mourn over his lot, but the very concatenation of affairs seemed to brace him up to perform his monastic duties as best he could."[81]

In his autobiography, Prisdang remains relatively quiet about the Tooth Relic incident, which was not regarded by the king as his fault. For Jinawarawansa, the king's trip to Lanka resulted in one crucial success: it garnered for him an invitation to return to Siam. He noted in his autobiography: "While I was a monk, I took the opportunity to help . . . persuade [Buddhist] patrons—Asiatics of every race in Lanka—and monks, to consider receiving the king when he visited Lanka on the way to his trip to Europe. He was received with honor and so satisfied that in April 1897 he kindly ordered me to return [to Bangkok] to help Prince Wachirayan Warorot [then patriarch of the Thammayut sect] with Buddhist and administrative activities."[82] At last, he had reconciled with his king and could return with personal honor and dignity to Siam.

The Prince Priest and the Buddhist Relics Controversy in British India

Before returning to Siam to work with the revered monk, Prince Wachirayan, Jinawarawansa traveled to India.[83] He wanted to return the favor to the Theosophists and foreign (including Lankan) Buddhists who had supported him and to write a book in Thai on the "Buddhist Holy Land" that would guide Siamese pilgrims.[84] He proposed to do this by taking a pilgrimage to the most important Buddhist sites in India, including the birthplace of Siddhartha Gautama, the Buddha, which had been discovered in Lumbini, Nepal, in 1896. Jinawarawansa hoped Siam would fund his journey to India, where he would collect some of the Buddhist relics then being excavated, tagged, shelved in museums from Lucknow to London, and sometimes traded on the black market. He requested from Siamese officials the documentation and necessities to arrange for his travel from India to Adam's Peak in Lanka, to Yangoon in Burma, to Penang—where he hoped to collect books and documents he had stored there—and then on to Singapore and Bangkok, where he would be ordained in the Thammayut sect.[85] He would remain a monk upon his return home.

A follow-up letter begged again for what appears to be financial and documentary assistance from Siamese consuls in each place he planned to travel because "I do not have a sponsor and object to bothering the Lankan people because my travel is not for their benefit and because I will leave their country" for Siam.[86] In response, the King's royal secretary simply stated, "The fact that His Majesty the King is kind enough to give royal permission to allow you to return to Bangkok is already a great deal, therefore he is unlikely to grant you any of your additional requests."[87] Jinawarawansa sparred back that "leaving the monkhood to earn money to return is inappropriate. Speaking with the Lankan people [about funding] is similarly inappropriate."[88] He needed a Siamese sponsor for a pilgrimage that was undertaken for the benefit of Siam.

In the meantime, the Anagarika Dharmapala, whom Jinawarawansa had met multiple times in 1897, came to his rescue. They both had similar political impulses regarding their Buddhist activism, a "restless love of social organizing . . . and a certain need for adulation and acclaim."[89] Because the Prince Priest had failed to secure the necessary documents and funds from his own government, Dharmapala wrote letters of introduction and arranged to pay the steamer fare for the Prince Priest to travel to India in December 1897.[90] Dharmapala remained in correspondence with Jinawarawansa during this period, sending him funds again in early 1898.[91] Although it is difficult to trace Jinawarawansa's journey precisely, it appears that he used the international headquarters of the Theosophical Society, headed by Colonel Olcott, in Adyar, Madras, as his base from December 1897 until March 1898. He did not return to Lanka until February or March 1899. According to Prisdang's autobiography, he traveled to key Buddhist pilgrimage sites, including the Buddha's birthplace in Nepal and to Bodh Gaya, where the Buddha was enlightened. He visited the northwest province of British India to request relics of the Buddha from the recently excavated Birdpore estate, and in 1899 to Rangoon and Mandalay in Burma with Olcott and Annie Besant of the Theosophical Society to try to convince the monks there to unite under the ecclesiastical authority of King Chulalongkorn.[92]

During those months in India, the Prince Priest became embroiled in an affair of international dimensions. It began in Madras, where he participated in the Theosophical Society's twenty-second annual convention in late 1897. There he responded to the plenary lectures in an open letter that the society's president, Olcott, read aloud on the convention floor. In a move that paralleled his strategic critique of absolutism in the 1885 petition, Jinawarawansa scarcely concealed his critical assessment of the Theosophical Society and efforts to civilize and enlighten: "More anomalous and miraculous to me still [than the division of humans into races and religions, clans and families] is the apparent increase of evils observed throughout the world, as education, civilisation and 'enlightenment' (so called) spread amidst the activity of the teaching of Christianity, Buddhism, Hinduism, Theosophy, &c., and the multiplication of societies that profess to remove these evils and lead men to peace and contentment in the present and to final emancipation from sorrow and misery in the future. I see the increase of crimes and cruelties and no spiritual advancement made anywhere!"[93] Although he praised the Theosophical Society's efforts to promote education, he advocated for Buddhism as the religion that already professed universal brotherhood.

Once the convention ended, Jinawarawansa traveled north, where he had heard about the discovery of authentic relics of the Buddha. Earlier, in December 1896, the Nepalese general Khadga Shamsher Rana and the German archaeologist Dr. Anton Führer, an archaeological surveyor working for the British government in the Northwestern Provinces and Oude, had announced the discovery of Lumbini, the birthplace of the Buddha.[94] Buddhist pilgrims began to trickle into the area to make a pilgrimage to the Sakyamuni Buddha's birthplace and sites of his enlightenment and first sermon. Jinawarawansa too had come to India on such a pilgrimage.

After the discovery of the Buddha's birthplace, many became aware of the possibility that other relics might exist nearby. Noticing an irregular mound on his property suggestive of a man-made site, an English estate owner, Mr. William Peppé, began its excavation in January 1897. The mound, which was located less than twenty miles south of Lumbini, covered a solid brick stupa, which was not broken into until January 1898. In it he discovered jewels, funerary urns, and bone relics of what British authorities determined, based on an inscription, were the Buddha and members of his Sakya clan.[95] As soon as Jinawarawansa heard about the discovery of relics of the Buddha on Peppé's estate, located just across the border from the Buddha's birthplace in Nepal, he rushed there and arrived before the end of January, just days after the discovery. Presenting himself as sponsored by his Lankan preceptor, the Venerable Subhuti, Jinawarawansa asked if he could view the relics and collect some as well.

Having no official form of identification as a consequence of the refusal of Siamese authorities to issue him one, Jinawarawansa used the photos taken before and after his ordination to prove his identity as a relative of King Chulalongkorn and grandson of King Rama III. He also had "visiting cards" produced with his photo as a monk (figure 17).[96] His standing as a royal prince continued to open doors for Jinawarawansa. His fluency in English, "commanding presence and impeccable manners" kept the door ajar.[97]

In late January, Peppé and a British official, Vincent A. Smith, traveled north to Lumbini to meet with Dr. Führer. There they conferred about the authenticity of the relics and the inscription found at Piprahwa. By early February, Führer invited Jinawarawansa to his camp in Nepal, after Jinawarawansa had finished working on Peppé's find. The Prince Priest had impressed them to the extent that they had invited him to join them. Peppé's letters suggest not only that he had become well acquainted with Jinawarawansa but that he warmly welcomed the monk to stay at his estate. In a letter to Subhuti, who desired information about and a portion of the relics for Lanka,[98] Peppé wrote, "I also expected to have the Rev. Jinavaravansa [sic] with me again and I wished to discuss your letter with him. He came but having been very much disappointed at the arrangements made for him by the Nepalese he very suddenly left."[99]

Jinawarawansa returned to Peppé's estate at Birdpore in April. Letters written from there reveal that he had sent the Piprahwa inscription to Subhuti, a renowned Pali scholar, to decipher. Subhuti translated its significance to the British: he explained the relics were from the Buddha and the kith and kin of the Sakya race.[100] The significance of the discovery at Piprahwa was not lost on any of the men, least of all the monks. Jinawarawansa continued to promote his campaign on behalf of (and perhaps unbeknownst to) King Chulalongkorn. In addition to his personal visits to the Peppé estate, the Prince Priest also wrote a lengthy memorandum in which he argued that since Europeans attached little importance to bones and ash relics, they might keep the vessels and jewels but pass on the contents to the king of Siam, who, for all the reasons rehearsed earlier in Lanka, was the rightful and legitimate custodian of such sacred items. The king would then distribute portions to those who had a legitimate claim on the relics. It also would ensure that the king would "be induced to take a more active interest" in the conservation of Buddhist monuments.[101] Once the Prince Priest could "obtain the consent of the [British colonial] Government to hand over the whole of the relics to the King of Siam," he would personally deliver them to the king on his return home.[102] He would not leave India until he had successfully concluded what he considered his mission.

FIGURE 17. Visiting card of Jinawarawansa presented to W. C. Peppé in April 1898. Courtesy of Chris Peppé.

Although Peppé respected Jinawarawansa's efforts, he followed British colonial law and handed the contents of the find over to the government to decide what should be done. He also forwarded the letters of both monks to the authorities to decide what to do with them.[103] A great deal had occurred, however, since the discovery of the Buddhist relics in British India, where other religious groups demanded attention. Jinawarawansa's colleague, Anagarika Dharmapala (1864–1933), had catalyzed unrest a few years earlier between Buddhists and Hindus over the ownership of a temple in Bodh Gaya, the place where the Buddha became enlightened. Buddhists thus considered the temple part of their heritage, but Hindus had occupied it for generations. The Maha Bodhi Society (1891), founded by Dharmapala, was dedicated in part to reclaiming for Buddhists and from Hindus the site of the Sakyamuni Buddha's enlightenment.[104]

In addition, it had been discovered that Dr. Führer had repeatedly committed plagiarism and fraud, including the sale of counterfeit Buddha relics to a Burmese monk.[105] Problematically, he had been connected to the authentication of the relics found on William Peppé's estate. Jinawarawansa, on his Buddhist pilgrimage, had unwittingly arrived at the heart of another controversy. No one but high-ranking British India officials who dealt with archaeological finds was at the time aware of Führer's shady reputation and the long shadow it would cast over the Piprahwa relics.[106] The relevant governmental authorities kept the scandal from becoming public knowledge. They confronted Dr. Führer and accepted his immediate resignation in September 1898.[107] The British press in Singapore also publicized the fact that Führer had resigned because he forged relics that he sold to Burma.[108] Although today evidence strongly supports the authenticity of the Piprahwa relics and their inscription, at the time, British colonial authorities in India sought to quietly resolve this political and religious outrage.[109]

They found their resolution in Jinawarawansa. He had spearheaded the effort to take the relics personally to King Chulalongkorn, who would distribute them to Buddhists in other countries. However, some British officials were "not prepared to recommend that the gift should be made to him [Jinawarawansa]. It is a matter of common knowledge that Buddhists are not satisfied because the Budh-Gya [sic] temple is in the possession of Hindus. . . . At the same time the connection of the British Government with Buddhist countries renders it desirable that if an incidental opportunity to evince its consideration for Buddhists should arise, advantage should be taken of it to manifest its good will." In other words, the letter continued, the British government should give the "coveted relics" to the king of Siam directly, not through the Prince Priest, so as to take credit for the idea that was originally Jinawarawansa's.[110]

Not only could the British manifest their good will toward Buddhist countries in Asia by gifting the relics of potentially inauthentic provenance to King

Chulalongkorn, but they could also thereby avoid a public imperial and archaeological scandal.[111] Lord Curzon, who formally took over as viceroy of British
India in January 1899, sent experts to Nepal to get to the bottom of the issue, but
the idea of gifting the relics to Siam's king had already been publicly floated. If his
experts discovered the relics were indeed false, the ensuing scandal would cause
him and British India to lose face. It might have been easier to quietly cover up
the investigation. Regardless of the debate about authenticity, the relics were in
high demand among Buddhists, as seen by the illegal trade engaged in by Führer
and the numerous letters penned by the Venerable Subhuti to British authorities in India and to Siam's king. He urged them to deposit the relics in Buddhist
stupas, including those in Lanka, where they would be worshipped.[112] They could
hardly be quietly disappeared.

In July 1898, Jinawarawansa wrote again to Siamese authorities, this time from
Patna, southeast of the Peppé estate and north of Bodh Gaya. He provided an
update on his activities since he had left Olcott's residence in Madras that March.
He had lived off the generosity of scattered groups of Ceylonese and other Bud-
dhists as he traveled to Bodh Gaya and to the district of Kapilavastu, where the
Buddha had grown up.

Excitedly, he listed the relics disinterred and scriptures being deciphered at
Lumbini. At least ten boxes of sacred images and relics had been collected, including some stone Buddha images more than two thousand years old. His efforts to
collect the items had exhausted him because the jungle had long grown over the
ruins.

> I had decided that I would bring these to present [to Your Majesty]. Now,
> I do not have the strength to keep going or to bring these important
> things to present to you personally. I have come all the way here only to
> exert myself in the search of important items that were found with great
> difficulty. This has taken an enormous physical toll on me because I had
> to walk through jungles and cross over mountains. This was not for
> my own benefit. I determined to take these items along with my broad
> local knowledge and place them in Siam. . . . Therefore by sending this
> diplomatic letter, I am entreating Your Majesty to have faith in [these
> items] and be pleased to receive them, should they be placed in Siam.[113]

If not, then the items could be given to the devout in Lanka. Jinawarawansa suggested sending them through the consul in Singapore. He requested one thousand rupees to cover his costs, which could be sent to the Maha Bodhi Society
in Calcutta.

In a characteristically long postscript, Jinawarawansa mentions the generosity of locals who housed him and arranged for his transport through these

localities as he collected the relics. He lists and describes the amazing discoveries and ends his letter with the final point that "if these invaluable items do not end up in Siam, it will be a great shame."[114] King Chulalongkorn passed this information to Prince Phanurangsi, who gave a check in August 1898 for 1149.43 baht/ 1,000 rupees made out to the Maha Bodhi Society to support the costs incurred by the collection of these relics and their delivery to Siam.[115]

In contrast to the Prince Priest's letters, which reveal that he alone engineered the gifting of the relics to his monarch, Lankan, British and Siamese published histories all but ignore his role in the process. Correspondence between Siam's minister of foreign affairs, Prince Devawongse, and the British minister in Bangkok do not mention Jinawarawansa.[116] Devawongse agrees with the suggestion to send an official deputation to receive the relics in a ceremony performed at the Peppé estate in early 1899.

Upon learning from Peppé that another would deliver the relics to the king, Jinawarawansa wrote magnanimously, "'To me it matters not in the least who takes the relics to Siam . . . so long as the King is recognized as having claim to them as the head of the Buddhist religion.'"[117] "I am satisfied with the result of my mission, and can now leave India with satisfaction."[118] But first, he requested to keep a few of the jewels and other items from the Piprahwa dig himself and in exchange sent to Peppé an album or two of Siamese postage stamps that he had collected while director of Siam's Post and Telegraph Department. It appeared that Jinawarawansa had successfully accomplished his mission. He had personally obtained one of the Buddhist crosses, some of the flower jewels, and a trident that came from the Piprahwa stupa; he had ensured that King Chulalongkorn would receive the bone relics; and he had guaranteed that his patrons in Lanka would have a portion as well. Siam's king not only acknowledged this, but it was made clear that he desired the relics and even arranged to offset some of Jinawarawansa's expenses.

Just before he left India in 1899, the Prince Priest met in Calcutta with Siam's deputed representative, Phya Sukhom (Pan Sukhum). The two men had met years earlier, in 1885, when Phya Sukhom, an erudite Buddhist who had tutored several royal princes in England, escorted Prince Rabi (Ratburi Direkrit) through Paris on their way to London.[119] On 15 February 1899, the British hosted a ceremony during which they imparted the relics, seals intact, to Phya Sukhom in Gorakhpur.[120] The officials broke the seals and transferred the charred bone shards and pottery to two gold-plated pagodas, which Phya Sukhom accepted on behalf of the king.[121] Jinawarawansa then began to make his way back to Lanka in preparation for his journey home to Siam. By late February, a letter from the king of Siam's private secretary to Subhuti makes it clear that "Prince Prisdanga [sic] himself" is expected in Bangkok, that his servant Nai Chang had already arrived in the capital, and that Phya Sukhom was on his way back from India with relics and was expected in March.[122] Everyone, including the king, anticipated the Prince Priest's arrival home after a decade in exile.

However, Jinawarawansa had barely disembarked in Colombo before he received the shocking news that he would be stripped of his monk's robe should he dare set foot on Siamese soil. This, in effect, amounted to a prohibition against his return home since taking off his priestly garb would render Jinawarawansa vulnerable to arrest for past and present offenses. On 2 March 1899, Prince Devawongse sent a telegram to Siam's consul Young, commanding him to "Inform Jinavaravansa [sic] that owing to his action concerning Sacred relic which he declared to Royal Commissioner [Pan Sukhum] at Calcutta he cannot be recognized in Siam as member of Holy Order."[123]

The news stunned Jinawarawansa, whose jaw must have dropped as he read the cryptic telegram. The same day, he fired off a letter in response. "I see that it is a prompt decision and a public denounciation [sic] of my country against the action which I have taken on its behalf out of patriotic feeling to secure the Sacred Relic of Lord Buddha for its blessing at all cost[s]." He closes with "So long as there is still a delusion in us we shall so long continue to struggle against shadows and fantoms [sic] created by our own thoughts[,] and the battle of life will continue as we see around us everywhere. I thank your Royal Highness for this timely warning."[124]

This missive in turn prompted Devawongse to send a longer note to Young explaining the specifics of Jinawarawansa's crime. Upon his return to Siam, Phya Sukhom told Prince Devawongse that when he had met with the Prince Priest in Calcutta, Jinawarawansa told him that he had obtained three pieces of the bone relics "without the consent of the gentleman [presumably Peppé] who possesses them. This shocking fact is clearly an offense of 'Addinadana Parajika' [theft] according to Buddhist Law." Moreover, as a consequence of the alleged theft, Jinawarawansa could not be considered a priest in Siam; otherwise "bad faith will be imputed to His Majesty the King in recognizing him as a member of the Holy Order."[125] Devawongse also hints vaguely at the rumors from a decade earlier that had catapulted him out of Siam and into Ceylon, thereby casting doubt on the integrity of Jinawarawansa's status as a monk in Lanka.

Prince Devawongse and Phya Sukhom seem to have conspired to prevent Jinawarawansa from returning to Siam, though the truth remains a matter of speculation. What is clear is that Prince Devawongse considered the Prince Priest, when he was a diplomat in Europe, arrogant for using an inappropriate pronoun in his interactions with the more highly ranked Devawongse. He also shared with the king Jinawarawansa's private letters regarding his views of polygyny. He, of all officials, most intensely kept tabs on the Prince Priest in exile as he groped for a way to make a living in French Indochina and British Malaya—he received copies of his letters from Phra Satja in Penang and news about his employment by Swettenham. All along Devawongse considered his decision to be enrobed in Lanka a fraudulent act and a gambit designed to enable him to sneak back into Siam. The king also no longer wanted the Prince Priest back in Siam. He had been informed of the allegations of Jinawarawansa's theft, read the priest's letters of protest in response, and gave permission to Devawongse to send the telegrams.[126]

In response, a despondent Jinawarawansa wrote one last desperate missive to King Chulalongkorn in May 1899 in which he reminded the king that he had agreed to allow him to return to Siam as a monk, that Jinawarawansa had traveled and collected Buddhist relics on his pilgrimage, and that contrary to these plans, Prince Devawongse's telegram banned his reentry. He ended the letter: "Because of this, I am sorry that I still cannot return to serve Your Majesty, for whatever reason which Your Majesty already fully knows in your heart."[127] Jinawarawansa attached a list describing the relics that he had planned to carry personally to Siam, including rubbings from the inscription on Ashoka's stone pillars in Lumbini and three genuine Buddha relics, ashes, and other items from the Priprahwa site at Peppé's estate. These, presumably, were the same relics he had exchanged, legally, for the postage stamp albums.

When Prisdang reflected on this confusing moment decades later in his autobiography, he wrote, "The relics were given to the commissioner [Pan Sukhum] who came out to [India to] collect the relics and deposit them at Wat Saket where they remain to this day. The commissioner also made up some story, the success of which is apparent in that clever man's life, and Prince Prisdang was the fool."[128] Jinawarawansa watched as Pan Sukhum took credit for obtaining the relics, while he was unjustly maligned and banned from returning home. Jinawarawansa certainly owned many Buddhist relics and statues, as did many of his Lankan priestly brethren, but there is no proof anywhere that he "stole" relics. It mattered little to Prince Devawongse, who rebuffed him under the guise of protecting the monarch's reputation.

In early 1900, King Chulalongkorn hosted a grand public ceremony at which he ostentatiously presented portions of the Piprahwa relics to representatives from Burma and Lanka and enshrined the Siamese portion in the Golden Mount (Wat Saket) Temple in Bangkok.[129] Unfazed by his part in disparaging Jinawarawansa for stealing relics and thereby preventing his homecoming, Pan Sukhum allegedly kept a bone shard of the Buddha for himself.[130] Priestly deputations from Burma and Lanka accepted their portions of the relics. The Venerable Subhuti was not listed among those who received a portion, and it remains unclear where these relics were eventually deposited in Lanka.[131]

Meanwhile, Jinawarawansa suffered a genuine psychological blow that sent him reeling. Dharmapala noted in his diary in November 1899 that the "Prince

Priest came here [this] afternoon. Had a long chat. He wishes to put off the robe. At present his . . . life is made miserable."[132] For unknown reasons, he did not carry through with this desire. Jinawarawansa fell ill: "I became sick with pain in my joints. I couldn't write with my right arm." He was hospitalized for two weeks, being treated for rheumatism and hemorrhoids. The press even reported on his rheumatism in November 1900.[133] During that time, he felt poorly enough that he drafted his will and hoped to die in peace.[134] The will, handwritten in English from his hospital bed in December requested that "my flesh while fresh should be given to birds and beasts of prey for a feast," and that his bones, stripped of flesh, be reconstructed to form a complete skeleton that he would like to donate to Siam's Buddhist university for students to use for meditation and study. He bequeathed most of his Buddhist relics, papers, and manuscripts to Prince Pha-nurangsi, "my friend and benefactor," "the only friend who in helping me to build did not destroy what he had helped [to build]" or invent "stories to justify his action, to make an efforts [*sic*] to restore the Piprahwa stupa in Mr. Peppé's Estate in India."[135]

News of his illness was relayed to an official working in the ever-watchful Ministry of Foreign Affairs, still run by Prince Devawongse, who further snubbed Jinawarawansa. In late December 1900, the acting Siamese consul in Lanka reported that "the Rev'd Jinawarawansa is in poor health and badly in need of change. He wishes to leave the Island for Burmah [*sic*] returning to Ceylon later on. Before, however, he can move it is necessary that he should be in funds."[136] Funds had been raised within Siam and collected by Phraya Phiphatkosa, an official in Siam's Ministry of Foreign Affairs, to pay for Jinawarawansa's planned but thwarted return to Siam in 1899. When the Prince Priest asked to use the funds instead for a restorative trip to Burma, he was denied the money. According to the Prince Priest, Phraya Phiphatkosa "collected the money, but never sent it to me (because he knew that I wouldn't return to Siam if I had to leave the monkhood, thus he understood that I might not dispute this [])]. He repeatedly told ministers and people who trusted him that he had sent the money to me but that I had spent all of it on my trips in India."[137] Jinawarawansa, denied this one last request, may have reached a turning point in his life. Siam and its king barely rate a mention for the next decade.

The Prince Priest Commits to Lanka

For about two years, Jinawarawansa nursed his health and psyche. Hint finally taken, he appears to have abandoned hopes of returning to Siam and instead turned his attention to Lanka. Initially, after the final denial of any mercy from Siam, he sought a quiet place to recover. He and Aleister Crowley were both seen at Anuradhapura in October 1901.[138] Crowley—a British occultist, self-styled Satanist, author, and mountaineer—traveled to Lanka in 1901 and 1903, likely meeting with Jinawarawansa both times. He dedicated the play *Why Jesus Wept*, written in Kandy in 1903, "to you, Eastern of the Easterns, who have respectively given up all to find Truth; you, Jinwaravansa [*sic*], a Siamese prince who became a Buddhist monk, who esteemed the Yellow Robe more than your Princedom . . . by sticking manfully to your Work in the World, yet no more allowing it to touch your Purpose than waters may wet the lotus leaf . . . , must I dedicate this strange drama."[139] In Crowley's own words, the play offered "an allegory of the corrupting influence of society" a description that could have described the Prince Priest's experiences with members of Siamese high society and officialdom.[140]

Jinawarawansa briefly retired to a small island he named Chulalanka in honor of King Chulalongkorn, which served as a bittersweet reminder that he was linked to both his former king and his new home, Lanka.[141] This abandoned port, south of the southern tip of Lanka, had no bridge to the mainland, making it an ideal depository for snakes, which Lankans refused to kill, and a burial place for individuals who died sudden, unnatural, or violent deaths. There, finally, the Prince Priest found peace: he could hear "the faint sound of the waves because the reefs were scattered near the shore." His supporters wanted to build him a temple and have other monks join him, but Jinawarawansa claimed to want solitude.[142] As his lay supporters dug into the earth to build him a hut, they found two skeletons— allegedly the remains of dead Buddhists buried rather than cremated because of their calamitous deaths. Jinawarawansa had his supporters hang the skeletons on his wall so he could use them to meditate on the transitory nature of existence.[143] The tradition of corpse meditation typically involves monks observing corpses as they decompose into skeletons, suggesting that Jinawarawansa was unfamiliar with the tradition.[144] Or, as likely, the photos he had taken of him meditating in front of skeletons suggest that his desire for celebrity had not been fully extinguished.

His supporters had to wade across the shallow shelf from the mainland to the Prince Priest's island to offer him food and make merit, so eventually they built a bridge, despite his alleged protests. From there, Jinawarawansa continued to attract domestic and international attention, such that over the next year or two a stupa and facilities for visitors were built on the island. In 1904, the governor of British Ceylon, Sir Henry Blake, and his wife, Lady Blake, became Jinawarawansa's supporters and visited him on the island, as did Queen Victoria's granddaughter, Her Highness Princess Louise of Schleswig-Holstein, and others.[145] One visitor couldn't help but notice a photograph that Jinawarawansa had attached to the door of his room of "a young man, apparently well dressed and smoking a cigar, walking stick in hand and bottle of liquor by the side," underneath which the Prince Priest had written "'the result of modern education of young Ceylon.'"[146] His years on the little island had done little to attenuate Jinawarawansa's strong opinions about the potential impact of a modern, presumably Western, education.

His secluded life hardly seems isolated in retrospect, given the company he kept. Nearly every European seeking enlightenment in the fabled East found him. Olcott and Crowley were just two of many. A German, a Dutchman, and an Austrian were ordained with him on Chulalanka Island in 1905,[147] the same year that the Venerable Subhuti sent him to Colombo to take the position of abbot of Dipaduttamarama Temple in Kotahena.[148] Reginald Farrer, the disaffected son of a British politician who was an avid writer and gardener more comfortable with plants than with people, sought out the Prince Priest at the Kotahena temple in 1907.[149] Referring to him as the incumbent, Farrer said he "is a man of energy, and bent on doing many things."[150] Farrer's otherwise caustic references to Colombo—"a modern ugly mushroom, a convenience, an invention of modern ugly races that were ravening in blue woad when Asoka ruled the East, that were jabbering inarticulate jargon when the Most Perfect One was incarnate for the last time on earth"[151]—soften considerably when describing the Kotahena temple grounds. Jinawarawansa's temple room "looked out upon a dappled gloom of green, every plumy fern and trailing liane kindled to emerald here and there, and pierced in places by the sun's rays, that fell, slating solid lances of light, on the flagged stones of the courtyard before that long low house." In the room where he waited for the Prince Priest, Farrer noticed "above a crowded bookcase, a ballet-girl of tissue paper, with full crinkly skirts, [who] sat coquettishly balancing on the horns of a cardboard new moon, fitted up with a waggish face. How so indecorous a decoration had come into the precincts so learned and pious I am at a loss to guess."[152]

F. F. Martinus put Prisdang on the tourist map and pilgrimage itinerary by writing a book that promoted the Prince Priest and his temple. In his 1907 *Guide to Buddhist Temples*, he advised visitors who might have time to see only one temple to visit that of the Prince Priest: "His kindness in acting as guide is invaluable. ... There is much that will require explanation to be thoroughly appreciated and the Prince Priest makes it his business to give every assistance."[153]

Once he had left Chulalanka, Jinawarawansa created a respectable reputation for himself as abbot at the Kotahena temple. Oral history maintains that he was in great demand by patrons as a preacher at local ceremonies. He never became proficient in Sinhala, so he preached in Pali and in English, utilizing translators when necessary. He protected and developed the temple grounds and buildings, he provided opportunities for the education of children, and he attracted patrons and donors to the temple, solidly fulfilling the duties of abbot.[154] Wealthy Lankans and South Asians, including a "Parsee Lady Millionaire," visited him at the temple.[155] Even so, he refused to kowtow to Lankan elites on the basis of their status or wealth alone. In a private letter to Subhuti, Jinawarawansa deployed shockingly impolite language, switching the official title of the "Mudaliar [a colonial title] of the Governor's Gate" to read instead as "Mudaliar of the Governor's Toilet."[156]

The Prince Priest worked closely with the Blake family to open a free and nonsectarian school for indigent boys in Colombo in 1905. He donated funds to the school collected from contributions made by the many foreign visitors to his temple and to his "sacred Museum," from which he donated and "labeled with gummed tags of paper" his books, Buddha images and relics, uniforms, insignias, and certificates.[157] He wrote speeches for the inauguration of the "first free and nonsectarian" schools for boys (March 1905) and girls (August 1906), which the local press published.[158] Sir Henry Blake attended the opening of the boys' school, and his wife was present at the inauguration of the girls' school.[159]

His short years on the secluded island had done little to temper the Prince Priest's flair for simultaneous self-promotion and support for progressive causes. "I may add also the fact that for nearly seven years that I have been connected with this temple [Dipaduttamarama], every attempt at its improvement failed continually till I took the management of its temporal affairs into my own hand. Since then I was able to introduce reform, effect repairs and improvement and turn this Temple, which had become a notorious place of refuge for undesirable characters, into a respectable public institution which we now see."[160] The two schools constructed on temple grounds were, according to him, Lanka's first free and nonsectarian schools for the poor that taught both Sinhalese and English, thereby decoupling the teaching of English and Christianity.

Never shy of controversy, the Prince Priest used the opening of the girls' school as an opportunity to rant, eloquently, about the poor state of so-called civilization engineered by Westerners, many of whom counted among his audience. "A period of unrest and struggle for existence has come . . . giving birth to a new doctrine as its fruition, which the modern sage of a matter-of-fact world pronounces in these terrible words, '*survival of the fittest?*'"[161] For Jinawarawansa, the influence of the West threatened to homogenize the world along Western lines, eradicating cultural difference. "[T]he Civilisation of a go-ahead-quick world demands for its rapid progress [that] . . . we should live as one man with one view and speak the same language which, in Ceylon, *should be English*."[162] The best way to counter this "undue and indiscreet Western influence of a low order" and "moulding the future to *a world of monotony*" was to promote the education of girls "who are the backbone and sinews of the nation[.] Begin education at home, *in the nursery*, in which character is formed, by educating the future mothers. . . . Aim at home life and comfort and industrious habits that they may get rice and curry, and *not* bread and butter, that they may *not* have to resort to *questionable* means of livelihood."[163] The school would teach English, Sinhala, cooking, needlework, math, and agriculture ("kitchen gardening"), all of which would be imbued with an unspecified moral essence, one "*without* the aid of the *figment* of a particular dogma or creed."[164]

Lady Blake balked at some of what Jinawarawansa said. "I must say that I totally disagree with the Prince Priest that the doctrine of 'The Survival of the Fittest' is a terrible one. It seems to me that the terrible thing would be if the unfittest were to survive. I trust that this school will prove itself 'the fittest' and will survive."[165] Indeed, both schools thrived in Colombo in the twenty-first century. The girls' school was named after the Kotahena temple's famous abbot, Mohottivatte Gunananda, and the boys' school, which initially faltered but later was revived under Jinawarawansa's pupil, Jinanan, was named Prince College, in honor of the Prince Priest.

From Kotahena, Jinawarawansa entertained visitors every year, and sometimes every month. The temple became a regular stop where royal family members, politicians, and businessmen from around the world came to see his museum, plant a tree, and make a donation to the schools attached to the temple. Prince Arisugawa of Japan, Siamese royalty, Cambodia's Prince Suttarassa, and the crown prince of Germany visited him.[166] The press reported on Jinawarawansa's attendance at funerals of major British officials in Ceylon, the departure of the Blakes, the state ball in honor of the king of England's birthday in Colombo in 1907, and his one-on-one meetings with a diverse array of colonial officials and British politicians who visited the island.[167] Among them were Hugh Clifford, future high commissioner of the Federated Malay States and governor general of the Straits Settlements, and Sir William Wedderburn, a Scottish civil servant who cofounded the Indian National Congress Party.[168] Apparently Jinawarawansa and James Keir Hardie, a Scottish socialist and pacifist who had led the British Labour Party, "enjoyed a long conversation" at the temple in 1907.[169]

Jinawarawansa, known also to be an artist, worked with Dr. Ananda Coomaraswamy, a British Lankan who became the first curator of South and Southeast Asian art at Boston's Museum of Fine Art. Coomaraswamy cites the Prince Priest as an expert on the mechanics of Indian puppetry and Siamese shadow puppets, and he included a chapter about Siamese craftsmen by Jinawarawansa in a book on *The Indian Craftsmen*.[170] Coomaraswamy purchased a wooden bracket from the Prince Priest, which is now housed in the Boston museum's collection.[171] His drawings continue to circulate, including one of a mythical vine that grew flowers in the shape of women (figure 18).

Jinawarawansa engaged in Lankan politics. He sat on a committee to preserve Lankan shrines and was vocal at meetings among Buddhists about political

FIGURE 18.   Drawing of Sri Lankan mythical vines with flowers in the form of women called *nari-lata-vela* made by Jinawarawansa. In Ananda Coomaraswamy, *Mediaeval Sinhalese Art* (Campden: Essex House Press, 1908), 92.

events, including the Anuradhapura riot of 1903 in Lanka.[172] Tension had been building as a consequence of attempts by the Maha Bodhi Society, still under Dharmapala's leadership, to preserve access by Buddhist pilgrims to ancient Buddhist sites in Lanka such as Anuradhaphura. There conflict existed between Lankan Buddhists and British colonial authorities over the preservation of Buddhist sites. Leaders of the Maha Bodhi Society desired to make Anuradhaphura exclusively a Buddhist area, ousting Christians and their institutional presence. In 1903, Buddhists in Anuradhaphura violently rioted in response to the accidental death of a Buddhist woman during pilgrimage season, damaging a Roman Catholic church and school in the process.[173] Soon thereafter the Prince Priest "raised such a hubbub" about an uncarved stone at Anuradhapura in 1905, suggesting that he stayed abreast of pertinent conflicts involving Buddhism in Lanka.[174]

In early 1911, he attended public meetings and wrote against the illicit sale of liquors then debated in an excise commission report. One attendee announced that he agreed with the Prince Priest "that the natives of Ceylon should band themselves together and do all that they can to check the use of intoxicating liquors which in recent years has been spreading octopus-like through-out the length and breath [sic] of the Island, to their moral and physical degradation."[175]

The Prince Priest's reputation as an educational reformer and institution builder outlasted other failed experiments, such as his 1897 attempt to unite Buddhists across the region under King Chulalongkorn. His final effort to meet with King Chulalongkorn occurred in 1907, when the king passed through Colombo on his second trip to Europe. It ended in disappointment as well. Prisdang prepared for the monarch's arrival with enthusiasm in the hopes of obtaining a donation from the king to help build a monumental stupa at Dipaduttamarama. "I waited impatiently, longing for an opportunity of getting some distinguished person whose liberality and ability to help might justify my aspirations, till the return of H.M. the King of Siam from his second visit to Europe. . . . I was justified . . . in expecting a visit of His Majesty. . . . It was, however, a great disappointment to me, that he did not pay a visit to this Arama [temple] as I had been led to expect that he would."[176]

Among his many admirers, he had attracted a wealthy Penang woman of Sino-Thai descent, Mrs. L. L. Cheak, who arrived soon after King Chulalongkorn left Lanka. Upon hearing the Prince Priest lament about the king's failure to appear, she offered five thousand rupees to the temple and was honored with laying the foundation stone in 1908 for the construction of the stupa where his Buddha relics from Piprahwa, sacred items, gems, and gold images were enshrined (figure 19).

Jinawarawansa's health faltered several times as he oversaw the construction and fund-raising for the stupa. News about King Chulalongkorn's death in October 1910 shocked the frail Prince Priest, who perhaps imagined he would someday reconcile with his former monarch. "The news made me faint, pensive, rendered me unconscious, and I could not sleep . . . for several months."[177] After recovering, he performed a ceremony with twenty-five monks before a large gathering meant to accrue merit for his deceased liege.[178]

Jinawarawansa never forgot his link to the king, nor did he allow others to forget that he had once belonged to royalty. It heightened his reputation as a Buddhist, one who like Prince Siddhartha, had it all but gave it up to pursue enlightenment. Despite his diplomatic cunning, his acute and biting intelligence, and his artistic inclinations, Jinawarawansa remained naive in his loyalty to his king and country. A short month after learning of King Chulalongkorn's death,

FIGURE 19.   The Ratna Chetiya at Dipaduttamarama Temple, Colombo, 2015. Author's photo.

he wrote to Siam's new king, Vajiravudh (Rama VI, r. 1910–25), expressing his condolences and regrets. King Chulalongkorn's death

> is a great calamity to our nation at this juncture, and to all Your Majesty's subjects, high and low, far and near, to be deprived of a good King, a wise commander and the best of friends. Remorseness [*sic*] has completely overcome me, Your Majesty, weak foolish and wrong that I am, in that I have left His late Majesty's service and my country so that I am unable to express my own personal feeling of sorrow and grief and great loss; for His late Majesty had been to me a second father greater than my own, in that He gave me a new birth to a higher sphere of usefulness; to whom I was indebted for all the good things I ever enjoy in this fleeting world, which were beyond my birth and rank, for which I could never repay, even with my life.[179]

The Prince Priest wrote that it was unbearable to think about the fact that he could have given up the robe earlier and returned to implore the late king's forgiveness and to serve him again. "Alas! It is now too late, impossibility which I had not the remotest thought that it could ever come to pass." But King

Chulalongkorn was not immortal. Jinawarawansa begged King Vajiravudh for permission to return to Siam to "unburden my grief and perform my intended act of retribution at Your Majesty's feet instead, and to pay my last respects to His late Majesty's remains and do my duty at his funeral." The king must have consented, for Jinawarawansa decided to return to Bangkok to attend the late king's funeral, scheduled for March 1911. The last press report featuring him is curious and creates the impression that he had a personal enemy who wanted him out of the Kotahena temple. In early February, a man named G. M. Abeyesekera barged into Jinawarawansa's room at his temple in Kotahena and "threatened to pull him out."[180] This was a personal rather than an anonymous crime: Abeyesekera did not steal from or vandalize the temple: he grabbed the Prince Priest and tried to

FIGURE 20.   Jinawarawansa as he boarded a ship from Colombo on his journey back to Bangkok, February 1911. Courtesy of the National Archives, Thailand.

drag him out of his room. The Prince Priest charged Abeyesekera with criminal trespassing for which the accused had to post bail of one thousand rupees and promise "to keep the peace for six months," by which time Jinawarawansa was long gone. He had quietly boarded a ship to Siam within days after the attack in February to pay his respects to his dead king (figure 20). His Lankan supporters allegedly cried at his farewell and begged him to return quickly, which many believed he planned to do after the funeral. Unbeknownst to them and to the Prince Priest, he would be stripped of everything that remained dear to him after his bare monk's feet touched earth in Bangkok.

BANGKOK

Home without Quarter

Reborn. When I came back and left the monkhood in Bangkok, waiting to die, from the age of 60 years and one month.

—Prisdang, *Prawat yo*, 82

The Prince-Priest Jinawarawansa embarked on his final journey home in February 1911. On board the ship from Colombo, he shared the deck with Prince Henry of Prussia and some unnamed members of the Rothschild family, who found Prisdang's description of the stupa he was constructing in Colombo so compelling that they wrote him a check for twenty pounds. In Lanka, Prisdang had rebuilt his life and regained a high social status and sense of purpose. As a renowned monk and abbot, he hosted royal family members and iconoclastic Western spiritualists from around the world. He made an impression on them sufficient to have plays dedicated to him by the likes of Aleister Crowley and donations gifted to his temple by commercial and royal elites in Europe and Asia. However, Bangkok's ruling officials obliterated within weeks fifteen years' worth of effort to resurface from social ignominy, to reconstruct his identity, and to rebuild his self-worth. Prisdang had just turned sixty years old when he disembarked with a heavy but hopeful heart in Bangkok in March 1911. There, Siam's grandest cremation ceremony for the death of the (by then) longest-reigning Chakri monarch had begun.

After three days in a coma, King Chulalongkorn succumbed to chronic nephritis, an infection related to the kidneys.[1] He died on 23 October 1910 after reigning for forty-two long years—so long in fact that few remembered the proper funeral rites for a monarch. A small procession, which according to one observer "was one of the most moving spectacles that I have ever witnessed," brought the king's body from his Dusit Park Palace, where he had died, to the Grand Palace (figure 21).[2] For the six months between the king's death and his cremation, the

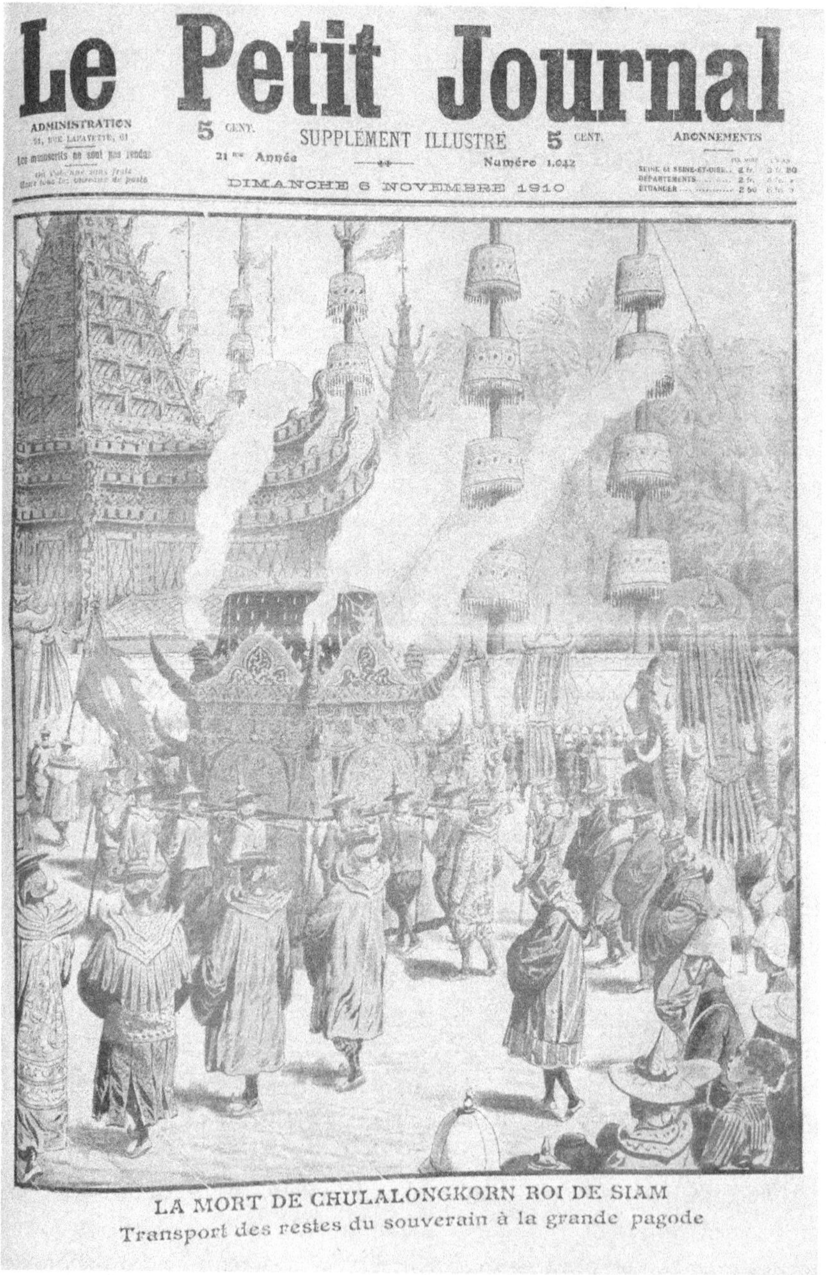

Le Petit Journal

ADMINISTRATION
61, RUE LAFAYETTE, 61
Les manuscrits ne sont pas rendus

5 CENT. SUPPLÉMENT ILLUSTRÉ 5 CENT.

21me Année — Numéro 1.042

DIMANCHE 6 NOVEMBRE 1910

ABONNEMENTS
SEINE et SEINE-ET-OISE
DÉPARTEMENTS
ÉTRANGER

LA MORT DE CHULALONGKORN ROI DE SIAM
Transport des restes du souverain à la grande pagode

FIGURE 21. "The Death of King Chulalongkorn, King of Siam," *Le Petit journal*, Supplément illustrée, no. 1042, November 6, 1910.

population mourned and foreign diplomats sent their condolences. In Lanka, Prisdang had performed a merit-making ceremony with twenty-five monks for the deceased king's spiritual benefit. King Chulalongkorn's apotheosis had begun while he still lived. It was based on the longevity of his reign and the credit given to him for maintaining Siamese independence, qualified though it was, during an era of imperial treachery. Siam's administrative reforms had, in the end, created an absolute monarchy where one had previously existed only in theory, and had justified its creation through reference to the threat of impending imperial domination. Royal authority reached its peak of power under King Chulalongkorn and the image of him as Siam's savior. Into this context returned Prince Prisdang, ready to surrender to royal hierarchical authority so long as he could work for his king and country once again and receive protection within it.

First, however, he would attend the funeral events. Hamilton King, the US minister plenipotentiary in Siam, and his wife quietly paid their respects to the late king in the Grand Palace. Mrs. King's eyewitness account describes the weeks leading up to the official cremation in mid-March 1911, during which she observed increasingly grand ceremonies. Protocol determined not just who could attend but where they stood in line in the procession to the cremation grounds.[3] The official cremation began at dawn on 13 March. Guns boomed across Bangkok. Thousands of Siamese dressed in funereal white slowly wended their way, like a river of milk, to the area in front of the Grand Palace where architects had constructed an enormous and elaborate cremation pyre.[4]

At the center of the platform stood a symbolic Mt. Meru, out of the top of which arose an immense nine-tiered umbrella latticed with white flowers. Resting in its penumbra, the late king's body lay folded in the diamond-studded golden urn.[5] On March 16, the last day of the grand ceremonies, a procession of Bangkok's royalty, officials, and dignitaries commenced. They included a scarlet-clad police band; a golden car carrying the Buddhist patriarch, who read scripture as he passed by; and the state funeral car drawn by more than two hundred men. Seated at each of the four corners of the crematorium platform, monks chanted.

Everyone central to Prince Prisdang's former life marched in the procession, "carrying great jeweled swords, long silver spears, golden vessel [sic], and the insignia of state," which passed in front of the decorated state car carrying the bejeweled urn.[6] Once the urn ascended the flanks of the makeshift Mt. Meru, King Vajiravudh had a moment of silence behind a curtain with the remains of his deceased father. He then lit the pyre. A trumpet announced this final farewell. Prisdang's royal relatives and friends, still in service to the state and monarch, paid their respects by depositing a lit candle and wreath made of imitation flowers upon the pyre.[7] Prince Devawongse still headed the Ministry of Foreign Affairs, Prince Damrong led the powerful Ministry of the Interior,

Prince Svasti translated for the American ambassador and his wife,[8] Prince Phanurangsi was the Minister of War, Jao Phraya Surasak served as the king's chief aide-de-camp, and Jao Phraya Yommarat (Pan Sukhum) was the minister of the capital.[9] Like Prisdang, most of these men had sworn an oath of loyalty and friendship three decades earlier to serve King Chulalongkorn until the day he died. That day had come and gone. This band of brothers came together to pay their respects to the deceased monarch, even though their bonds to one another had long been broken.

Once prominent among them, Prisdang now was refused a place alongside his former comrades, in painful contrast to his deepest wishes. He had arrived in Bangkok in March 1911, just in time for the cremation ceremony but was barred from seeing his once-dear friends or paying respects to King Chulalongkorn until he threw off the protection of the priestly robes.[10] In Siamese Buddhism, all men regardless of rank must pay respect by bowing in veneration to monks. This would have been anathema to the princes who ordered Prisdang's disrobing, an act that reasserted their superior rank and ensured that Prisdang would instead pay obeisance to them. The prince priest removed his robe at Wat Suan Phlu in Bangrak district, where he had been staying with a distant relative since he arrived.[11] The authorities allowed him to lay candles and incense at the pyre but not to light a candle or add it to the fire, as other relatives and high officials were able to do. These seemingly insignificant slights set Prisdang apart from these others: they did not consider him one of them. Instead of lighting a candle to add to the fire and smoke that would float the king's essence into the afterlife, Prisdang wrote a note that he wrapped around the offering stating that "in all future lives, I wish to be Your Majesty's servant and I wish that no enemies come between us as [occurred] in this life."[12]

Bangkok's ruling elite made Prisdang pay for his resignation and escape in 1890, even though he had initially hoped for a happier homecoming. Prince Devawongse, who for so long and unbeknownst to Prisdang had kept tabs on the errant prince and thwarted his efforts to return home, became emotional when he met with Prisdang. According to Prisdang, "Prince Devawongse was very sad. He cried as he lamented that the king gave me such great opportunity, but I ran away. Had I stayed, I would likely hold a high position in the government."[13] His former friend and patron, Prince Phanurangsi, to whom Prisdang had willed his most personal possessions, denied him an audience until he took off his robe. Prince Damrong, by then Siam's most powerful prince minister, also refused to see him until he reverted to his status as a layman.

Once the ceremonies for King Chulalongkorn ended, Prisdang asked to be reordained in Siam, but the supreme patriarch of the Buddhist order, Prince Wachirayan, refused to allow this. He asked his former comrades for the funds to return to Lanka, where he could resume his position as the Buddhist patriarch of Colombo. Unlike in Bangkok, where he had no money and few friends, in Lanka laypersons and monks had, according to Prisdang, cried at his departure and begged for his speedy return. He was denied this as well. Inexplicably, given his past attempts to keep Prisdang out of Siam, Devawongse refused to speak with him unless he committed to staying in Siam. Phanurangsi, upon hearing Prisdang's request to return to Lanka, "shook his head and said that he wished I had come to see him while the king still lived, so he could help me out, but now it is out of his hands. He feared there would be danger and he heard a rumor that Jao Phraya Yomarat [Pan Sukhum] was waiting to arrest me."[14] Yomarat was the commissioner sent to India to pick up the Buddha's bone relics who had allegedly double-crossed Prisdang in 1899 by accusing him of stealing relics. In the meantime, King Chulalongkorn had promoted Yomarat to the position of the minister of the capital, in charge of the police among other governmental departments. Prisdang, who had returned to Siam only to be denied his proper place in the funeral ceremony and had been forced to remove his robe, now found himself threatened with imprisonment.

Fearing arrest, Prisdang again asked Prince Devawongse for help. The irony, lost on Prisdang, was that Devawongse had been party to so many of the decisions that ensured Prisdang could not easily return to or remain in Siam. Yet, Prisdang notes, pointedly, that Devawongse "hugged" him and promised to take care of him.[15] Devawongse may have been deeply conflicted about how to handle him, both while in exile and when back "home" in Siam. Prisdang provoked intense reactions, even after twenty years in exile.

Having been a monk for the last fifteen years, he had no personal funds to support himself. Even if he had found the money to pay for a journey back to Colombo, leaving Bangkok in 1911 would have amounted to another self-exile, one for which Prisdang, now in his sixties and frail, had insufficient energy. Instead he fell back on his former friends, whose commitment to him was ambivalent at best. He had violated the unspoken cultural conventions supporting Siam's status hierarchy in an era when that hierarchy was most threatened—republics were toppling emperors and monarchs across the globe. Those who benefited from Siam's existing social ranking system punished him to ensure that others continued to abide by the suffocating norms of royal-elite politesse.

In ways that parallel his recall to Siam in the mid-1880s, Prisdang's return in 1911 delivered him into an unforgiving and vindictive social, material, and professional context. He had no place to live and no position to fill regardless of his qualifications. By the age of sixty, he had served as Siam's diplomat to the West, a civil engineer, an artist, an author, an abbot, a fund-raiser, and a rabble rouser who had established schools for the poor in Lanka, but in Bangkok he remained

persona non grata even after King Chulalongkorn, the one person at the crux
of his predicament and the only one in a position to have redeemed him, had
passed away.

As a consequence, Prisdang spent his first years in Bangkok entreating others for a place to reside and a job that would enable him to live independently.
He moved repeatedly the first year: a couple of months with Mom Rachawong
Suphan in Bangrak, an area in Bangkok;[16] briefly in Bangkok's Si Phraya area as
arranged by Devawongse; several months with Jao Phraya Surasak; another location for a month; and so on. Finally Prince Rabi, one of King Chulalongkorn's
sons, who had studied law in England, allowed Prisdang to reside in a building
he owned on Captain Bush Lane in Bangrak from late 1911 until around 1920.[17]
Prince Rabi, then minister of agriculture, promised that Prisdang could stay in
this house "for life," but the former died at the young age of forty-seven in 1920.
Prisdang lamented that Prince Rabi "allowed me to stay as long as he lived, not
as long as I lived, which is what I thought he promised. I tried to send requests
asking the king [Vajiravudh] to give me a tiny place to stay so I won't be bothered,
but the officials didn't process the request for me. . . . Together, throughout my
life, I have stayed in thirty-five places. In fact, none of them belonged to me. None
of them is the house I had settled my family in. Am I considered anagariya?[18]
What caused this to happen to me?"[19]

Those who inherited Prince Rabi's properties tried to eject Prisdang after 1920,
when he began to request government housing, in vain, from King Vajiravudh.[20]
As late as 1924, letters from Prisdang beg the king to provide him with "government housing in any empty place anywhere." But the king's royal secretary
responded that Prisdang "has made this sort of request for domicile many times
already and His Majesty has not granted it, therefore this time, His Majesty sees
no reason to command otherwise."[21]

Curiously, Prisdang never mentions his natal family, Si, his wives (Mom Sadap
or his wife in Penang), or the younger consorts he allegedly obtained. Over
twenty years had passed since he left Bangkok in 1890, so it is possible that they
had passed away or otherwise disavowed their connection to him. Some relatives
were still alive, including at least one brother, Mom Jao Prawit. Yet for unknown
reasons that likely have to do with the conflict over family assets, Prisdang did
not reach out to his siblings. He had no place to live and was not allowed to be
reordained, which would have allowed him to reside on temple grounds, supported by his lay community. Perhaps Prisdang felt he had few alternatives to
redress his dire financial situation but to initiate a legal battle against the estate
of older sister, Mom Jao Ying Prapha, over the family inheritance that was in the
possession of his siblings when he fled into exile.[22]

He rarely mentions it in his autobiography, but the inheritance case surfaces incidentally in some official correspondence. In one letter to the king in
1915 in which he asks for a position in the government, Prisdang swears he has
impeccable personal integrity: "If I ever misbehave, am extremely intoxicated,
cheat relatives, friends or anyone, as Mom Jao Prawit [his brother] has alleged
in his court petition over the inheritance of Mom Jao Ying Prapha [their older
sister], then do not support me any longer, and punish me severely. I have never
behaved with bullying corruption as accused and have taken care of every one
of my relatives and siblings. The petition of Mom Jao Prawit in which he accuses
me thusly is completely false."[23] The courts did not resolve the case until 1921,
when they found against him. "I lost everything. . . . I lost because it was a special
case, a special court, not under the law."[24] Despite the royal family's disavowal
of him, Prisdang still belonged to the royal lineage, and this meant that his case
could not be tried in Siam's newly established court system. Instead, it went
to a special court for royal family members. Indirectly, Prisdang critiqued the
continued special privileges belonging to royal family members: had he been
tried in a regular court, he imagined he would have won. Given his pariah status
among royal elites—even his own family members disavowed him—he may
have been right. His critique of elite privilege stemmed more from his sense that
it worked against him than from an unambiguous belief that all Siamese should
share equal rights.

Prisdang despaired: "I became so ill that I vomited blood for two years because
of the estate case."[25] The caption below a photograph taken of him in 1921 and
included in his autobiography reads, "Prince Prisdang, taken after he recovered
from over two years of heartbreak, awaiting the Lord of Death, when inheritance
was confiscated, 1921."[26] He claimed the inheritance was worth forty thousand
baht, though it came in the form of land rather than liquid assets. His oldest full
sister, Mom Jao Ying Prapha, had made a will in which she bequeathed the family
land to Prince Lopburi Ramet, who was serving as viceroy in southern Siam.[27]
Prisdang had obtained a title deed to the land as well (allegedly illegally); hence
the court case. Prince Lopburi relinquished the inheritance to Mom Jao Ying
Prapha's relatives to decide how to deal with the land. The case reached an
impasse in the courts until 1920 or 1921.[28]

Prisdang continued to pay a heavy social and financial price for his past
actions—what they were precisely did not seem to matter—which permanently
placed him at odds with Bangkok officialdom and royalty. Housing and family
property were only parts of the problem: finding employment proved just as
arduous. For the first couple of years, he scrambled to find reasonable employment that would enable him to maintain a lifestyle worthy of his status as a

royal prince. Initially he taught English to Siamese and foreigners, found a variety of translation jobs, and worked briefly for the *Siam Observer* and the *National Review.*

The *Siam Observer*, a daily English and Thai language newspaper established in 1893, hired him to edit the Thai section in about 1912 but fired him within a month because, according to Prisdang, "I had too much love for my country and condemned Westerners and the Burmese for not respecting the king, the laws, or Thai culture when the king traveled along the river."[29] Prisdang also worked for the *National Review*, which may be the publication that King Vajiravudh closed for defamation and whose printing press he had chained up to prevent its further use.[30] Irrepressible Prisdang failed to hold back his opinion, which proved inflammatory even when in defense of his king and country.

It is difficult to know, without accessing the original article, what his political views were in the 1910s and 1920s. Few Siamese, except the older generation of princely and aristocratic bureaucrats, knew who he was. Some contemporaries alluded to shadowy rumors about his alleged offenses that earned him the enmity of the former king and royal family members, but they never described the rumors with precision.[31] Phraya Anuman Rachathon (1888–1969), who became one of Siam's foremost scholars of Thai culture, studied English with Prisdang when he first returned from Lanka. Anuman learned from his father that Prisdang had once been an ambassador in London but that he came to loggerheads with a high-ranking royal family member under Rama V, so he decided to resign and was forbidden from returning to Siam during King Chulalongkorn's reign. The truth of the story, however, remained elusive to Anuman's father.

Anuman responded to an ad Prisdang placed in the paper in 1911 or 1912 offering to teach English. He was Prisdang's only Siamese pupil, which hardly netted much income. Although their lessons lasted only a few months, Prisdang made a lasting impression on the young scholar. Anuman remembers him as "misanthropic," giving the example of his posting a sign on his gate that read, "Prohibited from Entry: Dogs and Humans."[32]

By mid-1912, just a year after he arrived in Bangkok, it became clear to Prince Prisdang that he could not earn a living informally, teaching English and translating. He needed government work and perhaps even a pension for his past service: anything to make ends meet in early twentieth-century Bangkok. "Ever since I returned to Bangkok," he pleaded to King Vajiravudh, "I hoped that I would receive your royal pardon because I thought that my past offenses against the King had been settled, and that Your Majesty might forgive me. I am forever hopeful about this. . . . It has come to the point now that I have no way at all to follow my wishes. Destitution and limitations have increased doubly with poverty and being deprived of a way to make a living. It is impossible to maintain myself. There is no way to be self-sufficient, so I find it necessary to write the letter to Your Majesty, begging you, upon whom I am dependent, to support me until I die."[33] Prisdang was under the impression that he could not have a personal audience with the king because it would violate a royal decree and that this restriction was a result of his past transgressions, so he begged the king's secretary to ensure the letter reached the king. King Vajiravudh consented to paying Prisdang a monthly income of eighty baht from the royal privy purse, an amount so low that Prisdang was unable to survive without borrowing from others.[34] Prior to World War I, the exchange rate was thirteen baht per pound sterling, which meant Prisdang received a bit more than six pounds per month, or US$29 per month, the equivalent of about $493 per month by 2014 standards.[35]

Prisdang followed up with multiple letters to the king and other government officials asking for work or an increase in the stipend or both. He expected the government or the royal coffers to help provision him, it appears. In 1916, a lengthy letter from Prisdang to the king that may well have served as a rough outline for what became his autobiography summarized in typical point-by-point fashion his history of government service, his connections with royalty at home and abroad, his honors and insignia of rank, and his salary and royal stipend at each juncture. The petition ends with his efforts in Lanka, particularly his attempt to unite Burmese, Siamese, and Lankan Buddhists under the sovereign ecclesiastical rule of Siam's king, which he claims would have worked except that King Chulalongkorn rejected it.

Notably, Prisdang not only references but boasts about leading the effort in 1885 to report views to King Chulalongkorn about how to reform the administration to avoid the peril of colonization. But he does not mention why he left in 1890 except to admit he contravened royal authority by respectfully submitting his resignation from the government before being ordained in a foreign country. "My crime deserved to be condemned and that was a grave punishment. By now I have been punished for more than 25 years, until I am over 65 years old. I beg Your Majesty to free me from the denunciation that has kept me from belonging to the group, release me from the disdain of Your Majesty, the royal family, and government officials high and low. I beg Your Majesty to kindly give me my freedom from punishment and allow me serve at your feet according to my aptitudes and duty. . . . I beg Your Majesty only this one additional thing, to grant me these important wishes while I am still alive, so I can face my friends, fellow Thai nationals."[36] In response, he was told that he should be satisfied with the king's support of eighty baht per month.

Not able to live on this amount, Prisdang tried a new approach. On 23 July 1917, one day after Siam declared war on Germany and Austria-Hungary, Prisdang wrote to King Vajiravudh: "In this era when the Thai wage war with global enemies, I beg to work for Your Majesty's war, as suits my strength and abilities. Even though my body is old and crippled, my heart is still young like that befitting my warrior lineage. . . . I beg to volunteer to be alongside the soldiers as one of them." Parroting King Vajiravudh's own nationalist propaganda, Prisdang asked for "a part in the duty of protecting our nation, religion, and king, and land of my birth, my fatherland that produced warriors as well. This time it is befitting that I had once held the position of Special Colonel under Rama 5."[37] The king politely declined this request. Meanwhile, more than one thousand Siamese expeditionary troops were sent to the western front, and the nineteen (noncombat) casualties were commemorated in the Volunteer Soldiers' Monument in Bangkok. Prisdang's brother, Mom Jao Prawit Chumsai, who at the time was still locked in a legal battle over family inheritance with Prisdang, supervised its construction.[38]

In late 1917, Prisdang selected another auspicious occasion to appeal to the king for assistance: the king's upcoming birthday. Prisdang explains that while he awaited a government posting, he made ends meet through various translations and teaching jobs and lived quietly. However, after the war began, Siamese students with foreign language skills increased to the point that he could not find additional employment, and the eighty-baht stipend was insufficient on its own to support him. "I am indigent and in debt to relatives and friends in the effort to preserve my noble rank that was conferred upon me, to prevent anyone from looking down on me."[39] No response is recorded.

One year later, in December 1918, Prisdang tried another tack, which exposed his desperation. He wrote to the king: "I am aware that by now I am over the hill and crippled by my age, too old to perform my duty as Your Majesty's subject. I must only lie in the position of a sleeper waiting, in the posture of death. I have no value, I have no opportunity. All my wishes to do something of use for the country, even including searching for personal happiness in this life, are lost. Thus, I desire to receive Your Majesty's kindness and mercy and permission to return to be ordained in Lanka."[40] First, however, he had to settle his estate and pay outstanding debts and costs associated with being reordained. He proposed to donate to the king his assets, which comprised land worth forty thousand baht, if the king would pay his personal debts of roughly seven thousand to eleven thousand baht. The remainder, "I humbly offer Your Majesty to use in whatever way you consider appropriate to be of value to the country, nation, religion and king." He promised he had no wives or children or forebears alive to whom he would allegedly have had to give the land. "If anyone contests my inheritance, claiming that these are not my assets, I beg Your Majesty to appoint a special committee of legal experts to investigate fairly this case according to royal law, validly with clear and complete evidence and all documents. If it is found that these really are not my assets as I have informed Your Majesty, I beg Your Majesty to punish me gravely for audaciously bringing groundless facts before Your Majesty, causing him to naively believe in them."[41]

This must have given King Vajiravudh pause. The minister of the palace, Jao Phraya Thammathikoranathibodi, investigated and found that the land assets allegedly worth forty thousand baht were not exactly Prisdang's to hand over because in 1918 the court battle with his siblings was still at an impasse. The minister politely suggested that Prisdang might have a hidden agenda to have the king pay off his debts by accepting this gift of land, and it would be a source of "unending irritation" to the king, especially because the king already had "generously" provided the eighty-baht-per-month stipend. The minister also cautioned against permitting Prisdang to be ordained in Lanka because "it was too far outside the boundaries of His Majesty's territory."[42] The king, through his royal secretary, ordered the minister of the palace to tell Prisdang that he would not grant his requests to donate his land to the king or to be ordained in Lanka. "The king thinks that Prisdang is difficult to deal with in every respect. However, if the king does not respond, then Prisdang will go around spreading the rumor that he already gave the letter to the king but the king is ignoring him. So the king wants you [Jao Phraya Thammathikoranathibodi] to call on Prisdang and explain the matter (or at least make sure he knows) that the king does not agree to grant him his wish for various reasons."[43]

Prisdang was prevented in 1918 from leaving Siam, where he had exhausted his options and hope to contribute to his country, and also from returning to Lanka, where he imagined he might still have an impact. At some point between 1920 and 1921, the court decided against his claims in the inheritance case, which provided another stinging blow from which Prisdang found it hard to recover. The same year, his benefactor, Prince Rabi, died, and his relatives reclaimed the property where Prisdang lived, which sent him out in search of affordable housing. Poor, unable to be ordained in Bangkok, and prevented from going to Lanka, Prisdang found himself in an impossible situation. He appealed directly to Prince Devawongse, one member of Prisdang's generation who was still in a position of power in the 1920s.

Just before he died in June 1923, Devawongse arranged to have Prince Prisdang hired under his son, Prince Traidos Prabandh (Traithot Praphan), who replaced Devawongse after his nearly forty years of leading the Ministry of Foreign Affairs. Devawongse convinced King Vajiravudh that Prisdang could help translate documents, which the king allowed so long as the ministry, instead of the king's privy purse, would pay Prisdang a salary.[44] Prisdang finally began to earn a living wage of three hundred baht per month, which had increased to five hundred baht by the time he was laid off from government service in 1925.[45] He credited Prince Devawongse's kindness for this act of charity and the king, "who allowed me to be reborn as a Thai and gave me an opportunity to serve him as a government officer in the ministry. Unfortunately, my time [then] was like the setting sun. I couldn't contribute much to the country, unlike in the past."[46]

Frequent illnesses kept Prisdang from coming to work regularly, so when the government began to tighten its fiscal belt, Foreign Minister Traidos proposed to the king that he be laid off.[47] Ineligible for a pension, Prisdang once again began to petition the king for a royal stipend or a position in any ministry willing to take him except the Ministry of Foreign Affairs "because I feel, according to my observations, that some people despise me, we don't get along, so I have no desire to return, even temporarily, because I'll be obstructed in that ministry."[48] Ultimately, no ministry would hire him. The king, who died a few months later in November 1925, refused to press the issue.[49] The next king, Prajadhipok (Rama VII, r. 1925–35) reinstated Prisdang's royal stipend, increasing it to 150 baht, for the remainder of his life.[50]

The frequent unemployment and instability of his housing situation may have contributed to an almost nihilistic sense of impudence for Prisdang in his seventies and eighties. This attitude is reflected in the memoirs of Khun Ying Mani Siriworasan, who, as a little girl in the early 1920s, recalls hearing Prisdang holler to her father, always about politics, across their neighboring balconies at the end of an alley near Mahaphrutaram (then called Wat Takhian) Temple in Bangrak, Bangkok.[51] Everyone on the street could hear her father, Phraya Rachanuphan (Pia Bunnag), chat with Prisdang, whom she recalls as peculiar, unlike anyone else.[52] She would watch him leave home to go about his business, agile and strong in his seventies. When he went out, he wore a cream-colored "universal" (Western style) suit and a Panama hat, always with his cane. This might explain his indebtedness to stores like Harry Badman and Company, a "Naval, Military & Civil Tailors, Court Dressmakers and General Stores" to the tune of forty or fifty baht.[53] Mani recalled that wherever Prisdang walked—whether to the import store, B. Grimm & Company, where he also owed money, or to the Siam Society, which he frequented as a member—everyone would stare at him because of his unusual appearance.[54]

Mani, who wrote her memoirs in 1990, remembers Prisdang as having strong prodemocracy, antiauthoritarian political views. He considered odious those who expressed power or asserted privilege over others. Prisdang wrote, printed, and posted in front of his home pronouncements severely critiquing particular high-ranking royal and nonroyal officials. Crowds of people, she recalls, gathered around to read the proclamations, some of which constituted lèse majesté, but no one took him seriously, not even those he denounced. They considered him demented (fanfuen).

Mani's heart would race every time she and her parents, who respected Prisdang for his intelligence and progressive politics, stepped foot in his home, which they did a couple of times a month. He had a large foyer with a balcony and a room with a long table, covered with Buddha statues, heads, and figures from many Asian countries. But he did his work in a small room at the top of the stairs to the right, full of books of all sizes, floor covered in scraps of paper, and a small table full of photographs of royalty flipped upside down, an illegal act because it showed disrespect to the royal family. He would explain at length how these men did not wish the nation well and had committed crimes that were ruinous to the country. Her parents praised him as knowledgeable and intelligent with ultramodern (*lamyut*) and progressive views. Mani recalls that he "was a genuine prodemocracy advocate because he wished that the poor and the commoners had the same opportunities as everyone. He condemned every kind of privilege. Accordingly, he disdained ruling officials and those with power, and he was an enemy of all those in charge at that time."[55]

Prisdang stopped writing about the events in his life in the early 1920s. As a consequence, his voice surfaces only in the letters he wrote to various government officials. Friends, officials, and a few distant observers such as Mani fill in some of the gaps in his final years in Bangkok. One example is the view of Prisdang provided in the biography of a German monk, Nyanatiloka Thera, who had been ordained with him on the small island off the southern coast of Lanka in 1905–6. Nyanatiloka Thera visited him in Bangkok in early 1921.[56] He claimed that the police had arrested Prisdang during World War I for publishing an antigovernment newspaper called *The Truth*. No record of this paper or his arrest has surfaced, and it's possible that Nyanatiloka misremembered the details of the conversations he shared with Prisdang in 1921. Nyanatiloka and his entourage received poor treatment by Bangkok authorities: they were temporarily jailed as spies, perhaps because he was German. When they called on the Supreme Patriarch Prince Wachirayan for help, that "malevolent monk" who headed Siam's monkhood "showed little compassion for our suffering."[57]

In the 1920s, Prisdang futilely vented against the establishment, and his personal eccentricities were increasingly apparent. He entered his photo in and won an international contest held in Japan for the most beautiful and longest beard, which in Siam symbolized mourning.[58] In a similar photo, Prisdang scribbled notes all around the picture (figure 22). As if to explain the origins of the photograph, he wrote, "Photographed on the loss of his only true friend and adopted second father, Prince Rabi of RajaBuri, the friend of true men and true Patriot of Siam."

What occasioned the notation was a visit in 1922 by another former pupil and monk, Jinanan, to whom Prisdang had passed on responsibilities for the upkeep of Dipaduttamarama Temple and the two schools for indigent children he helped found in Colombo, Lanka. Given to Jinanan on 28 July 1921, the picture's

FIGURE 22. Prince Prisdang in Bangkok in 1920. Courtesy of the National Archives, Thailand.

annotations provide a bold narrative about Prisdang's predicament. "Forced by necessity to disrobe on 11–3–1911 [March 11] and refused permission to be re-ordained by the Patriarch of Siam (The Maha Samana), and to go back to be ordained in Ceylon by Rama the King of Siam."

Jinanan had gone to the French protectorate of Cambodia to meet with the minister of the interior and public worship, Prince Phanuvong, and to have an audience with Cambodia's King Sisowath in the hopes of raising funds for the temple and schools in Colombo.[59] To this end, Prisdang wrote a letter of intro-duction for Jinanan to present to Phanuvong, whom Prisdang had met while in Lanka. However, he supplemented the letter with unrelated personal information that alarmed French Legation officials in Bangkok. The letter suggested that the current king of Siam was prohibiting Prisdang from being ordained or return-ing to Lanka, reducing him instead to a pointless life of poverty. "A regrettable fatality," presumably a reference to King Chulalongkorn's death, had prevented Prisdang from his "wishes to follow my religious life." He related that he had returned to Siam in order to pay his final respects to his former king. "[A]s proof of my gratitude toward Him, His Majesty the King [Vajiravudh] has ordered on my arrival in the country to leave off the frock, which should give me the oppor-tunity to take part in the ceremonies of incineration of the body of the Somdech [King Chulalongkorn] aforementioned. Later, His Majesty would not authorize me to resume my frock, or to permit me to return to Ceylon to resume the vows there, as before. Since then, I only live waiting for my end, as I have lost all oppor-tunity to be useful to myself and to others."[60]

The purpose of the letter was to enable Jinanan to meet with Cambodian royalty to raise money for the Colombo temple, yet Prisdang linked the priest's visit with his own immobility and lack of opportunity to complete the work he had begun and felt he rightfully should continue.

> For the motives above related, I have not been able up to present to real-ize my desire to come to salute Cambodia. . . . As I have lost also the hope to return to Ceylon to complete the work undertaken and projected, I have sent my pupil to Ceylon to pass his period of abstinence in my pagoda and to execute in my place the work projected on the part of this pagoda. I have charged him also to bring to Cambodia the merits acquired and to make known the works realized as well as those to be accomplished. . . . My pupil is entrusted moreover to bring the relics of Our Seigneur Bouddha [the Buddha] and other objects to be offered to His Majesty Sisowath, King of Cambodia, in my place.[61]

The relics of Piprahwa were used, once again, to create a connection between Prisdang and ruling Buddhist royalty. He suggested that the King of Cambodia send an emissary to pick up the additional relics since Prisdang could not bring them to His Majesty.

The French minister plenipotentiary in Bangkok, Fernand Pila, wrote to Siam's minister of foreign affairs "to be good enough to let me know what you think of the character of the application made to King Sisowath and of the significance of the attached. I take this occasion, Mr. Minister, to reassure you this matter receives my very highest consideration."[62] In other words, Pila found the letter disturbing and requested immediate advice about whether Prisdang had secreted other motives within it. Devawongse ordered his son, who by then ran the Ministry of Foreign Affairs, to follow up with Prisdang about the intent behind his letter. Prisdang replied that he had searched everywhere but could not find nor would he have kept a copy because it was of no significance beyond his chatting with an old acquaintance (Phanuvong) in an effort to enable Jinanan to present Buddha relics to King Sisowath as a way to raise funds for the temple. He produced a draft version of the letter of introduction, which also included a similar narrative of being forced against his will to remain a layperson.[63] Devawongse reassured the French diplomat that Prisdang's letter was harmless and that he should not be taken seriously: "Prince Prisdang is rather an eccentric man, it is evident that not too much importance must be attached, nor too much heed given, to any uncouthness of expression that he may have used in his letter to Prince Bhanuwong [Phanuvong]."[64]

Jinanan, with Prisdang's hand-annotated picture in one hand and his sad narrative of being held against his will in the other, may have described Prisdang's situation to fellow Buddhists once he returned to Lanka. A couple of years later, in September 1925, the members of the Southern Buddhist Association in Galle, Ceylon, sent a petition to the King of Siam, politely asking for the release of Prince Prisdang.[65] They had learned that Prisdang was "in a state of isolation" in Bangkok but

> had played an active and prominent part in the cause of Buddhism in this part of the Globe [Lanka], which invaluable and inestimable works, are still fresh in the minds of every Buddhist as they were of yesterday's or today's and that such willing conduct of his remains in the annals of Ceylon for ages and ages to come. The petitioners further submit that the Buddhists and the said association in special have missed to an alarming extent the absense [sic] of the said Royal personage and that since he has much more to be done here for the Blessed One's Faith, the voice of the association would be to secure the presence of the said Royal personage once again among them.

They asked the king "to cause such measures enabling" Prisdang to come to Lanka.

The king, who died within a month of reading this letter, had Minister of Foreign Affairs Traithos reply that "a command from His Majesty that His Highness [Prisdang] should leave Siam for Ceylon does not only seem unnecessary but might be misunderstanding [*sic*] construed as an act of unjustified expulsion."[66] Prince Prisdang may have found it impossible to return to Lanka without being financially supported, but it was hardly up to him alone to make the decision to go. He had learned that without his king's permission, he should not take leave of his country. Rama VI had previously, when Prisdang was physically able, refused to grant him permission to be ordained in Ceylon.

Perhaps it no longer mattered where he lived. Prince Prisdang's health was faltering. Still, he had managed to outlive nearly all his contemporaries: Prince Devawongse died in 1923, King Vajiravudh in 1925, and Surasak in 1930. Si's whereabouts at the time remain unknown. Maybe the death of Surasak liberated Prisdang to publish in 1930 his autobiography, a work he had drafted by 1924. At that point he noted that "I have lived my life into my 73rd year. The order of life events is as I depicted them. Prince Prisdang is still alive today. . . . I have recalled my memories as best I can. . . . Please forgive this old man if there are mistakes. I hope all who read this biography are enlightened and learn lessons from it. I wish everyone happiness and growth in the right direction of Buddhism. Signed, Prisdang, the Backbone."[67]

For unknown reasons, Prisdang did not publish his account until he turned seventy-nine. He dedicated it to his country and king but had a different message for those who judged him. He invited royalty, family, the supreme patriarch of the Buddhist Sangha and others to his mock death-rebirth ceremony, where he distributed copies of his autobiography—one at a time so he could watch each recipient sign above his own signature. It ensured that Prisdang had the last word about his version of his life story.

> I have written and published [my own biography] so that anyone who reads it can either condemn, laugh, think it serves me right, find it pitiful, or even praise it. [I write] because there are people who consider themselves to be soldiers, students, scholars, politicians, and philosophers, who [think they] know it all and have seen it all, who condemn me as dangerous, turbulent, crazy, and so on—whatever they can come up with. I don't mind [if] they accuse me of being crazy; it gives me an advantage over being normal. As for the ones who don't know who Prince Prisdang is, they will have a chance to get to know me before I die.[68]

Prisdang reclaimed his place in Siam's history while he still lived, so he could see their reaction and have the chance to remark on its absurdity: "Oh my! What a pity!"[69]

Even though Prisdang's body grew frail and he wrote far less frequently—or at least far fewer of his letters surface—in the last decades of his life, his storyline and perspective remained remarkably consistent, in word and in image. Prisdang never found a way out of Bangkok, where he witnessed World War I, the Depression, and an attempted coup in 1912 by Siamese soldiers against King Vajiravudh (1912). He was there for a successful, nonviolent coup in 1932 that a group of midlevel nonroyal military and civilian men carried out. They stripped the king of political power and placed him under a constitution. Despite Prisdang's reputation for political and social iconoclasm and for having first voiced as essential to Siam's political survival the creation of a constitutional monarchy, his views of the 1932 overthrow of the absolute monarchy and establishment of a constitutional one are unknown. It may not have been so important to this black sheep after all—not nearly as significant as his desire to return to the flock. Prisdang also never published his proposed second and third autobiographical volumes in which he promised to tell "the truth" about why he had had to resign and be ordained, about Si, about the Piprahwa Buddha relics, about "giving my views to King Chulalongkorn about Western belligerence," or about his "stoic coming to terms with his great sins."[70]

Newspapers around the world announced his death at the age of eighty-three on 16 March 1935.[71] His funeral ceremony was held at Khuruhabodi Temple, built under the auspices of his maternal grandfather. His descendants—the Chumsai and Sanitwong families—and other royal family members came to participate in the funeral and perhaps pay their final respects to one of the most provocative iconoclasts of the era.[72]

Prince Damrong, who moved to Penang in self-exile in 1933 in reaction to the antimonarchical leanings of the new government, imposed the royal social hierarchy upon Prisdang even after he died. A 1937 letter by Damrong states that because of Prisdang's dubious past, his remains were placed in an urn wrapped in white cloth rather than in a properly ornate urn used for a royal family member.[73] Prisdang was denied his place as a royal family member and lifelong patriot and supporter of King Chulalongkorn by this one last postmortem insult. Despite his energetic efforts within his own lifetime to reclaim his place in Siam's history, Prisdang died a quiet death. He took his secrets with him to the grave.

AFTERLIFE

The Uses of Prince Prisdang

Prince Prisdang made a lasting impression on those he met, including Reginald Farrer, a British gentleman who encountered Prisdang in 1908 in Lanka. Farrer delighted in jotting down a story he had heard in Colombo about

> a [British] planter who, with his friends, was in a 1st Class Railway Carriage. He was leaning out to keep it for himself, when, to his horror, up comes an old yellow Buddhist monk, and tries to get in. Planter, in vulgarest coolie Cinhalese, tells him he has made a mistake and can go to Hell. 3rd Class. To which the monk, in perfect English, blandly replies, "It is probably far more unpleasant for me to travel with you, than it is for you to travel with me: however, I have paid for a first Class Ticket, and I mean to use it. Kindly get out of the way!"—Utter Collapse of the planter.[1]

The monk was, unsurprisingly, Prisdang. His barbed wit, unflappable cool, and inversion of power dynamics appealed to many—Siamese, Lankans, British, and Americans—who were critical of imperialism and the excesses it enabled. Prisdang's linguistic and cultural fluencies offered a bridge across racial and imperial divides. The emotional expression of sarcasm, suffering, and resentment he voiced in his letters also traveled smoothly across time. In this sense, his mobility was not just geographic but cultural, racial, and historical. The narrative about his life reveals his impact on people, places, and histories within and beyond the boundaries of Thailand.

Writing about colonial-era Asia through a narrative about his extraordinary existence enables the telling of history from the vantage point of an individual. It makes the historical abstractions of imperialism, resistance, Buddhist universalism, and the transformation of Siam into a modern state approachable and intelligible by describing them on a human scale. A narrative account also allows for the incorporation of intimate and subjective experiences of Siam's diplomacy abroad and domestic politicking. Prisdang's emotions and the atypical sources preserved about them reveal how vital the maintenance of social norms was to political life in turn-of-the-century Siam, a period of radical flux. His story offers insights into the operation of power, particularly the extrainstitutional forms of disciplining witnessed most clearly through reference to emotions and rumors. In fact, the meaning of emotions crystallizes only in the process of reconstructing them within a narrative, especially when trying to explain how rumor and gossip become catalysts for action: in this case, for exile. No emotional refuge existed for Prisdang within Siamese elite culture.[2] He had to leave Siam to obtain respite. Remarkably, even in exile he was hunted down for offenses of behavioral and emotional impropriety.

We cannot access Prisdang's full life as he lived it. Even he omitted, reinterpreted, embellished, and misremembered bits of his own history. As a consequence, this is not his biography, nor is it a microhistory, though it steals from both genres. It is more selective than a biography, which would include details about the individual's life regardless of their relevance to broader issues. And it tells a more expansive story about imperialism, Buddhist activism within the British Empire, Siamese state power, and the role of emotions in history than most microhistories provide. Prisdang, by offering so much chatter yet remaining mute about a pivotal moment in his life, challenges us to follow his footsteps to discern, through telling his story, what was at stake for him, Siam, and his international affiliates.

Prisdang was an astute political critic when alive and remains so in his afterlife, though he exerts less control over his legacy. During his lifetime, he expended seemingly endless energy on behalf of several political causes: Siam's political equality, King Chulalongkorn's status as a royal sovereign, and the religious entitlements of Theravada Buddhist communities in Asia. Politics animated Prisdang: both the formal type of mediation required of him as a diplomat and an activist monk and the informal social maneuvering necessary to navigate high society in each place he resided. A review of his accomplishments reveals his zeal for high-profile international and national politics. Prisdang did not sit passively in his ambassadorial office in London. Instead, he took advantage of his posting to position himself and Siam in front of the world's political leaders and social elite. He noted this in his autobiography when describing his endless travels and engagements in Europe as a diplomat, tennis player, royalist, stamp designer, student adviser, surveyor, architect, and political maverick: "I am an active person, never pausing for leisure. If there is something to do, I do it."[3] He proactively brokered Siam's relationship to the world.

When King Chulalongkorn asked for Prisdang's views about how to avoid colonization, Prisdang did not shrink from the task, nor did he limit his response to Siam's international relations. Instead, he led a group of Siamese princes and officials who drafted a comprehensive blueprint to reform Siam's domestic system of governance. He was a creative interlocutor between imperialist notions of what makes a "modern" state and how Siam might reform its administration in ways palatable to its ruling elite. It may not have been his place to do this and his motivations may have been tinged by egoism, but it reveals minimally that Prisdang desired to make history, not passively observe it.

Once exiled, Prisdang continued to lead a public life despite his stated desire to live in disguise as a commoner. In Indochina, he attempted to work with Cambodia's King Norodom as his royal secretary, which hardly signified a desire to lead a quiet existence. The French chased him and Si out of their colonial possession for fear they would incite King Norodom against French rule. In British Malaya, he built roads that edged along Siam's borders, almost as a taunt to his former countrymen, and wrote a damning evaluation of the Siamese government for the British. British colonial officials were wary of Prisdang's energetic zeal and shrewd intelligence, evidenced by their declaration that no matter what, he should be kept busy or he would presumably stir up trouble.

Even when Prisdang paid his debts; ensured that the woman, Si, whom he considered his responsibility, had a secure future; and was ordained as a monk in Lanka, he could not contain his political drive. Sitting still too long on 22 February 1897, three short months after his ordination, Prisdang spent twelve obsessive hours, from 9:30 a.m. until 9:30 p.m., sketching his version of the Abhidhamma Wheel of Life (figure 23).[4] It was the day before his birthday, and he must have been pondering his life's meaning. The involuted, elaborate wheel he drew included the usual images of birth, suffering, and death but added a flashing bulb of "electricity," which may as well have represented his own charged energy. Within a month of his ordination, Prisdang spearheaded an effort to unify all Theravada Buddhists, from Lanka's factionalized Buddhist fraternities to those in British Burma and Siam, under King Chulalongkorn, who visited Colombo in April 1897.

When that endeavor failed, Prisdang took a Buddhist pilgrimage through British India where sacred relics of the Buddha had recently been discovered. With stunning speed and ingenuity, he then campaigned to have the British imperial government in India place the relics under the guardianship of the world's

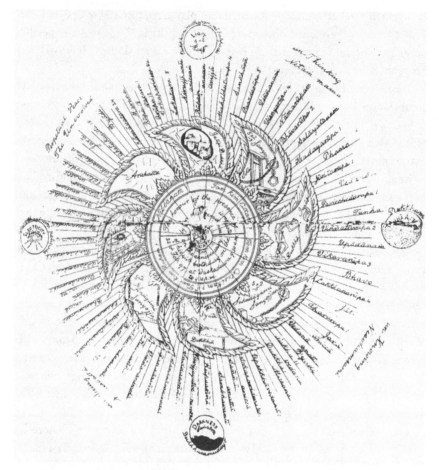

FIGURE 23. Sketch by Jinawarawansa, 22 February 1897, hanging in Waskaduwe Temple, Colombo, Sri Lanka. Photo by author.

only remaining sovereign Buddhist monarch, King Chulalongkorn. Despite his efforts, Prisdang received notice from the Siamese government that he remained persona non grata within Siam and would be stripped of his robe and arrested for theft if he tried to return. Demoralized, he turned his attention to Lanka, where over the next decade he built a vibrant social and political life, established schools for indigent children, and entertained literary, political, and royal figures from around the world. The earliest tourist guides to temples in Colombo insist upon a visit to that of the Prince Priest. Prisdang's activism ceased only after he returned to Siam in 1911, when Siamese authorities finally contained his energies and muffled his voice. He was forced to give up his robe, was blacklisted from all but the lowest-paid government positions, and became dependent on others for housing. His family, the Siamese public, and his government disavowed him. Yet, even at the end of his life when he no longer could muster an audience or obtain an official position, Prisdang refused to let his fellow Siamese forget him. He wrote an autobiography to tell his version of his story and to manage how he would be remembered.

Prisdang, were he alive today, might smirk defiantly at the fact that he is enjoying a comeback in twenty-first-century Thailand. Contrary to his fear that history would forget him, he has resurfaced in the press and scholarship. Individuals deploy particular moments of Prisdang's life for diverse purposes. This happened within his lifetime but often to the disadvantage of Prisdang. When members of the ruling elite and his former friends swarmed to attack him in the 1880s, they used his flaws as an opportunity to express their comparatively obeisant loyalty to Siam's monarch. The British colonial official Frank Swettenham used Prisdang's insights into the opaque ways power and influence moved within Siam's royal palace walls to help the British formulate more advantageous policies regarding Siam. The Sri Lankan Owen Mendis Obeyesekera utilized the moment of Prisdang's confusing arrival in Colombo in 1896 as an occasion to offer his services to the king of Siam as the local Siamese consul in British Lanka. Leaders of the conflicting Buddhist sects in Lanka arguably saw in Prisdang's royal Siamese status a risk-free chance both to unify and to request patronage by Siam's king. The British in India sought to gain diplomatic capital with Buddhists throughout Asia by conveniently agreeing to the Prince Priest's idea of gifting the relics to the sole remaining sovereign Buddhist monarch in the world, hoping it would divert attention away from the fallout of politically explosive issues surrounding Bodh Gaya and Dr. Führer.

In his afterlife, Prisdang continues to be harnessed to several causes—international Buddhist diplomacy, monarchism, and democracy. Paradoxically, conservative royalists, antiestablishment politicians, and political progressives have appropriated him, but for divergent purposes. By refusing to explicate why he fled Siam, he invited interested parties to speculate about and to project onto that silence. The story of his life demonstrates that it is not so easy to encapsulate Prince Prisdang and his multiple political loyalties. All the reclamation projects have it partly right. And partly wrong. And that is likely the real impetus behind Prisdang's defiant grin.

Prisdang's Appropriation by Buddhists, Royalists, and Nonroyalists

The final impoverished and embittering decades of Prisdang's life in Bangkok starkly contrast with the positive assessments of him after he died in 1935. No one knows what he thought about the 1932 bloodless coup in which a group of military and civilian commoners overthrew the absolute monarchy and established a constitutional monarchy. At that time, Prisdang was in his eighties and often hospitalized for ill health. Politics may finally have taken a secondary role to survival for him. In the aftermath of the coup and the failed royalist countercoup in 1933, many royal family members and their supporters went into self-imposed exile abroad, as Prisdang had done decades earlier. King Prajadhipok (Rama VII) abdicated on 2 March 1935, a mere two weeks before Prisdang passed away, and moved with his wife to London.

In 1937 another royal family member living in exile, Prince Prem Purachat, a grandson of King Chulalongkorn, traveled to British Ceylon. There he had the honor of unveiling a portrait of Prince Prisdang at the Dipaduttamarama Temple in Kotahena, Colombo.[5] Almost immediately after his death, Prisdang was welcomed back into the fold as a royal family member and Buddhist monk. The context had changed quite radically: the Chakri dynasty was under siege rather than in power, and many of its members had relocated outside the boundaries of Siam. They considered it worth celebrating their affiliation with Prisdang during the Lankan phase of his life. The press cited his praiseworthy diplomatic career, highlighting the degree to which he had given up worldly attachments when he renounced his princely status in 1896. The article was among the first of many that reclaimed Prince Prisdang as a Siamese royal family member and as a Buddhist abbot-cum-diplomat.

Those most interested in his life as a monk effortlessly claim Prisdang's fifteen years in the Lankan monkhood and his successful appeal to the British Raj to have the Buddha's relics sent to Siam but conveniently ignore the years he worked for the British imperial government in Perak, when he wrote a blasphemous confidential memo about corrupt forms of power and influence within the royal palace and court circles. To this day, Prisdang is still affirmed as part of a shared Buddhist and royal heritage in diplomatic relations between Thailand and Sri Lanka. In Sri Lanka, his reputation as an advocate for education continues at Prince College, which one of his disciples reestablished in his name.[6] In the same compound as Prince College, one can also pay homage to a life-size wax figure of the Prince Priest (figure 24).

In another reversal that would have tickled Prisdang and infuriated his enemies, monks from the Kotahena temple presented the Prince Priest's hair and personal effects to the supreme patriarch of the Buddhist Monkhood at Bowonniwet Temple in 1993 in Bangkok.[7] Wat Bowonniwet is intimately associated with the Chakri royal family. King Mongkut was the royal temple's first abbot, King Chulalongkorn was ordained there, and the Supreme Patriarch (Prince Wachirayan) was the abbot of Wat Bowonniwet when he refused to allow Prisdang to be reordained in Siam after 1911.

FIGURE 24.   Life-size wax figure of Jinawarawansa at Dipaduttamarama Temple, Colombo, 2015. Author's photo.

Thais of every political persuasion readily appropriate Prisdang's period as a monk in Sri Lanka. Thai tourists, dignitaries, and royal family members who travel to Sri Lanka invariably visit the "Thai temple," which is now also considered the "official temple of Thai royalty."[8] Officials in Thailand and Sri Lanka symbolically deploy Prisdang's Thai temple to strengthen their diplomatic connection by emphasizing a shared history of Buddhism and monarchism, even if that comes at the expense of adherents of other religions, political creeds, and ethnic backgrounds.[9] Thai visitors to Sri Lanka take a pilgrimage that includes minimally the Temple of the Sacred Tooth Relic in Kandy and Prisdang's temple in Kotahena. Rama VIII (King Ananda), Rama IX (King Bhumibol Adulyadet), his queen Sirikit, Crown Prince Vajiralongkorn, Princess Sirinthon, Princess Chulabhorn, and many other royal family members from Thailand, Germany, Cambodia, and elsewhere have paid their respects to the Prince Priest's temple (figure 25).[10]

This has not prevented purported nonroyalists from gracing the temple. In her status as elected prime minister, Yingluck Shinawatra visited in 2012, following her brother, Thaksin Shinawatra, who had visited in 2003 when he was prime minister.[11] The Shinawatra visits trace the footsteps of previous Thai royalty but may also represent an attempt to claim Prisdang as the multivalent political

FIGURE 25.   "Siam's young King [Ananda] (right), with his Mother, sister and brother [Prince Bhumibol], and a Court Official, aboard the liner Meonia in Colombo Harbour on his way to Bangkok. Extraordinary precautions were taken to safeguard him during the liner's brief stay in port." Photographer: Peter Batten, *Times of Ceylon* (1936), Sri Lankan National Archives, photograph 1151/09.

symbol he has come to represent. Prisdang remains an ambivalent figure. Some interpret him as a critic of monarchical absolutism, and others see him as a royal Buddhist nationalist.

Prisdang's Political Lineages in Scholarship

Those who claim Prisdang as setting a precedent for an indigenous political critique of absolutism highlight his role in drafting the 1885 proposal to reform the government as an attempt to curtail the power of the king. Their interpretations also reflect the historical contexts within which interest in Prisdang is piqued. The late 1920s was the first such context. In 1927, the Siamese government published King Chulalongkorn's 1888 speech on reforming the Siamese government, which implemented many of the 1885 proposal's suggestions. Siam's embattled last absolutist monarch, King Prajadhipok (r. 1926–35), wrote the foreword to the publication of the 1888 document. He emphasized King Chulalongkorn's "proper" timing and the gradual nature of the changes he introduced.[12] In other words, King Prajadhipok published the speech written by his more popular predecessor in order to convince his subjects that now—1927—was not yet the time to abolish the absolute monarchical system and replace it with a constitutional monarchy. The politically edgy 1885 proposal that catalyzed King Chulalongkorn's 1888 speech was not published until decades later.

Sumet Jumsai reminds us that Prisdang and the 1885 proposal for government reform sank deep into the folds of history for eighty-two silent years until the Thai National Archives decided to "liberate" the 1885 petition in March 1967, when the public first gained access to the document.[13] In 1970, the head of the National Library enabled the republication of Prisdang's autobiography. The near simultaneous republication of the documents could not have been coincidental. The politically vibrant context of Thailand in the 1960s and 1970s made Thais hungry for domestic precedents to their political aspirations for a more open political playing field.

In the late 1960s and '70s, Thailand's economic growth had enabled the development of an educated middle class and a concomitant increase in the numbers of Thai students receiving a tertiary education. They began to demonstrate against the flagrant corruption within the military, exploitation by business interests, the government's slavish subordination to American policy and its war in Indochina, inequitable land policies, and miserable working conditions for the lower classes in Bangkok. Despite the paternalist authoritarianism of military rule, supported by big business and the monarchy, Thais—like many peoples the world over at that time—experienced an unprecedented moment of political openness.

In this context, Prisdang's 1885 proposal found fertile soil. It enabled a serious critique of the military dictatorship through the historical study of what soon was touted as Thailand's first attempt at constitutionalism and democracy. Academics promptly consumed the proposal, churning out conferences and scholarship that drew incisive parallels between Prisdang's era and that of Thailand in the 1960s and '70s. The political scientist Chai-anan Sumudavanija (Chai-anan Sumutthawanit) plucked the proposal out of its context to serve his political critique of military authoritarianism afflicting Thailand in the 1970s.[14] He did not single out Prisdang, except as the one prince with the most experience in Europe among those who signed the 1885 proposal.[15] What mattered most to scholars and activists was not Prisdang's involvement but the incisive political critique embodied in the proposal.

Even after a brutal military crackdown on dissenters in 1976, which King Bhumibol (Rama IV, r. 1946–present) supported, the 1885 proposal continued to have an academic life of its own, though with greater attention paid to Prisdang and his autobiography. Once the proposal and autobiography found their way to the Thai public, scholarly interest in Prisdang surged, and he really did avenge history. Still, it was not his version of history.

Interest in Prisdang has revived again in the early twenty-first century, as Thailand experiences the most tumultuous political upheaval since the 1970s and imprisonment for lèse majesté is at an unprecedented high.[16] More than a dozen scholars have written about Prisdang, whom they locate among other early progressive political thinkers who refused to be co-opted by absolutism. In their separate 2014 reviews of the literature on Prisdang published after the 1970s, both Pirasri Povatong (Phirasri Phowathong) and Bunphisit Srihong (Bunphisit Sihong) argue that most scholars are interested in Prisdang's connection to the 1885 petition for what it enables them to say about Thai politics, historically and in the contemporaneous context.[17] Bunphisit and Phirasri point out a gap in this narrative of Prisdang's life—the anomalies in the record about why King Chulalongkorn and Prisdang had a bitter and permanent falling out. As rehearsed in the previous chapters, Prisdang resigned for any of a number of reasons, including some that revolved around the 1885 petition: it arguably threatened the king's power and provoked his disfavor, and by including other princes in drafting the proposal, Prisdang breached the protocol of his private conversation with the king. Yet these rationales for his exile do not always square with Prisdang's understanding of his role in drafting the proposal. Sometimes he proudly cites it as proof of his commitment to the king and his vision for Siam, while at other moments he deploys it as proof that he deserves status as a political refugee. When he mentions in his autobiography that he might have broken protocol by including other princes in drafting the document, he says this tentatively, as if he is still groping to understand what happened.

Some authors argue that the proposal not only suggested limiting the king's power but also threatened that of many established elites, who were envious of Prisdang and therefore jealously pounced upon every opportunity to ruin his reputation in the eyes of the king. This too may well be true. However, many of the elites who destroyed him with their vicious attacks included his fellow reformers and former sworn oath brothers. Prince Sonabandit allegedly spied on him in London, Prince Svasti turned on him because of the Mom Jao Pan incident, Surasak may have wanted to murder Prisdang for his relationship with Si, and Prince Devawongse offered mercurial support at best. All these men rose in the ranks of government power even though most of them also signed the 1885 petition or, as in Sursasak's case, submitted a more radical proposal.

Three of Prisdang's oath brothers shared their private letters from Prisdang with the king. In them, Prisdang may well have penned his critique of polygyny as an outdated custom. Some scholars believe these anti-polygynous views aroused the king's deepest ire.[18] Indeed, Prisdang did author a sophisticated critique of polygynous ties as an informal network through which power operated unjustly in his 1891 confidential memo to Swettenham. He argued that polygyny was an invidious, noninstitutionalized form of influence that lacked transparency. Yet he too admits to having practiced polygyny—so it wasn't the custom of obtaining multiple wives per se that he saw as problematic but how it could undermine the careers of otherwise capable and devoted officials.

Another reason why Prisdang fled Siam may have been his inability to pay personal debts. He admits he owed money to stores in London and in Siam, and it is possible he married into a wealthy family in Penang to pay off his debts. He never explains what the debts were for, but he does not appear to have had a gambling, sex, alcohol, or drug addiction. Yet Prisdang sheds doubt on this rationale as well. He argues that his debts stemmed from purchases he made for the king and Siam while he served as a government official. He explained that "officials vie with one another to give costly presents and offer their services [to the King and his favorite wife or child] in various ways. . . . The expenditure thus incurred by the Treasury as well as [by] individual officers is enormous every year and many of them get into debt by competition. . . . All the ministers are poor and mostly indebted."[19]

In the end, Prisdang believes he was framed: that people with influence exploited the misunderstanding about Mom Jao Pan to build a case against him; that his relationship with Si was purely platonic but that his enemies twisted it ruinously into vulgar adultery; that his debts were for king and country, not personal opulence; that he did not steal and hoard Buddha relics but collected them for the glory of Siam's king, and so on. Perhaps the entire series of accusations combined to build an irrefutable case against Prisdang as a dangerous nuisance no longer worth the risk in the eyes of the king and his former friends.

But this long list of possible explanations demonstrates that his exile and permanent ouster from Siam's ruling circle were a consequence of more than the 1885 proposal to reform the government.[20] When the proposal alone is continually underscored as Prisdang's main historical contribution and also the cause of his falling out of favor with King Chulalongkorn, it accomplishes two objectives. First, Prisdang's petition is cited to prove that Thailand has an indigenous history of progressive political thought, which is in itself laudable. By focusing on the petition as the ultimate reason for Prisdang's demise, scholars lament the outcome of what happens to those who articulate the need to limit the monarch's power. Prisdang becomes a hero, and his example provides a cautionary tale about dissent and injustice at the hands of the state. However, this simultaneously forecloses a more profound critique by Prisdang of the opaque ways that power worked within Siam's polygynous monarchical system and obscures his deeply felt monarchism.

Second, this narrative about the 1885 petition as the cause of Prisdang's ouster recenters the monarchy at the heart of power and history.[21] Despite the intentions of scholars, an emphasis on King Chulalongkorn's reaction to the petition reinforces the royal nationalist discourse that dominates much of Thai history, even if it is an oblique critique of the monarch. Moreover, it co-opts Prisdang into the Thai royalist narrative of history as yet another "brilliant prince who proposed what would have become the Kingdom's first constitution."[22] His face now graces a stamp that commemorates the 125th (in 2010) anniversary of Thailand's membership in the Universal Postal Union (figure 26).[23]

The state, royalists, and progressives can safely claim him because royal blood flowed through his veins *and* he heroically advocated for a decrease in the king's power. While all this is, in a way, true and supportable, it is only a partial explanation for his excommunication from the kingdom.

Prisdang's confusion about what led to his expulsion from ruling society reveals his position on the edge of belonging. While in Europe, his ability to traverse racial boundaries and express himself with dignity triggered an occasional negative response, such as when one British official called him a "coxcombical little puppy" who needed a good snubbing, or when a London periodical referred to him as "monkey" who made "advances" on female dancers. These were stereotypical efforts to denigrate a social and racial upstart: by likening Prisdang to a jungle beast, evolutionarily one step below humankind, and implying that he, as a brown man, had an obsession with white women. In Siam, the accusations against him were far more specific and damaging. Even before the king recalled Prisdang from his post in Paris, he faced some troubling accusations that he had

วันสื่อสารแห่งชาติ ๒๕๕๓ NATIONAL COMMUNICATIONS DAY 2010

THAILAND

H.H. Prince Prisdang who led Siam to be a member of Universal Postal Union

FIGURE 26.   Stamp with Prince Prisdang's portrait issued in 2010 on the 125th anniversary of Siam's entry into the Universal Postal Union.

behaved in ways and used language that was above his social station. Once he was recalled to Bangkok, the trickle of rumors and accusations swelled into a deluge that nearly ended with a self-inflicted gunshot to the head.

The preceding chapters have revealed that no single truth exists behind the rumors that catapulted Prisdang out of Siam. However, the investigation of the accusations has exposed some certainties about the local context within which they were found credible. The rumors concerned two themes: sexual and financial improprieties, which were precisely the kinds of accusations leveled by imperialists against Siam's ruling elite. During the same era that foreigners rebuked King Chulalongkorn for his extensive "harem," Prisdang was accused of adultery with an unmarried widow—an accusation that was culturally unintelligible in polygynous Siam. Financially, he was accused of malfeasance, or the use of public funds for private purposes. Yet there was little distinction historically between Siam's royal family and the state, let alone between royal and government coffers. Prisdang arguably served as a communal scapegoat, excommunicated for the fiscal and sexual offenses most commonly committed by his regal and social betters.

The attempt to reconstruct Prisdang's life story still leaves us with uncertainty. We search frantically for the singular truth, weighing the relative significance of the evidence. We open a space in the historical record for otherwise ephemeral rumors and social snubs that fail to meet the standards of historical evidence yet make their presence known nonetheless. Prisdang had his reasons and motivations, which he simultaneously divulged and concealed by ripping out pages of his autobiography before he published it. As a consequence, his deafening silence and overt signposting of the omitted pages in his narrative catalyzed a search into Prisdang's long and circuitous life. The formerly monochromatic understanding of him from the limited perspective of his role in the 1885 petition instead opens onto a view of him as a multihued, vibrant individual: quick-witted, opportunistic, sharp-tongued, and impetuous. An investigation into his life also reveals him as a complex political being who was critical of Siam's political and social system in the late nineteenth century but not of the king, which makes it harder to discern his actual politic beliefs and their consistency. After their falling out, Prisdang spent his life trying to regain the king's favor. For him, the king and Siam were inseparable. Even at his most critical, he blamed the social system supporting the king as much as or more than he blamed the king for failing to commit to reforms he suggested. He forces us to consider the deeply entangled personal networks through which power moved and shifted under the sometimes-oblivious nose of King Chulalongkorn. His example shows that royal families were not a monolithic group and their expressions of dissent were sometimes policed with ferocity.

Prisdang valued his status as a royal elite. He did not mingle with commoners except for the purpose of noblesse oblige, such as his opening of schools for poor Lankan children, or to sermonize to lay Buddhists. Instead he used his regal status to open doors and position himself in ways beneficial to his diplomatic career and religious vocation. His critique of the ruling system was broader and less progressive than what scholars have argued. It makes him redeemable by the left (for his work on the petition) and the right (for his less threatening life as a monk). But it also raises the question, If he, a devoted patriot and royalist, could not offer a critique of Siam's political and social system, then who could?

Prisdang and Lèse Majesté

Prisdang's resurgence in early twenty-first-century Thailand offers an alternative history of the construction of royal power: one that provides insights into the politics of lèse majesté that rankle Thailand in the twenty-first century. The mystery behind his expulsion from Siam exposes the cultural practices bolstering Siam's power structure at the turn of the century. Prisdang's refusal to submit to cultural norms about proper speech and deference to hierarchy triggered his communal ousting, a form of punishment that set a precedent for rigid, codified laws that served *not* to democratize power or protect the truth or the population but instead to reify a particular political and social hierarchy. Certain speech acts and behaviors became not just blasphemous but treasonous in this new discourse of subversion regarding monarchical power and Thai nationalism. Like many others then and now, Prisdang in the autobiography he handed out to royal elites in 1930 very publicly highlighted his act of self-censorship of the incident that had catapulted him out of Siam forty years earlier.

His conflict with the monarch goes to the heart of problems that continue to beset Thailand today regarding the sacred cultural authority of the king and the forms of self-policing it necessitates. Support for the institution of the monarchy, as it is currently constituted as outside yet central to Thai politics, began to crumble in the early 2000s. To buttress it, Thai authorities—from the military and the police on down to university officials and even family members—enforce the country's draconian lèse majesté law, known as Article 112 of the Criminal Code. Article 112 criminalizes the act of defaming, insulting, or threatening the king, queen, heir apparent, or regent, with a penalty of three to fifteen years in jail. This includes most defamation laws that prohibit anyone, anywhere—even in the privacy of their own home or outside Thailand's national boundaries—from making defaming statements about the king, queen, or heir apparent. Ironically, what constitutes defamation cannot be specified without repeating the criminalized speech or writing.

Prisdang's decision to flee the country is a mystery, but his blacklisting by elite society was caused in part by behaviors and speech acts that he failed to censor. He broke a cultural taboo against critiquing monarchical authority, broadly construed, that was soon thereafter transformed into the codified criminal law on defamation.[24] His exile, self-imposed, may have been the first of many in Thailand's history where one can find a pattern in which deeply nationalistic individuals flee the country because of social and quasi-legal persecution.[25] Regardless of their political leanings, these patriots—typically middle- and upper-class men invested in their relatively privileged place in the nation[26]—chose to live abroad for significant periods of their lives rather than face the consequences of their political beliefs; they were deeply patriotic but in opposition to the existing government, which was most frequently backed by royal authority. Prisdang may have been the first to experience social and political blacklisting that made life within Siam unbearable.[27] He was not the last.

In the first decades of the 2000s, techniques of intimidation such as arbitrary detention, torture, surveillance of social media, martial law, blockage of websites, imprisonment for lèse majesté, the erasure of Thaksin Shinawatra from history books, and other violations of rights have created a climate of fear. The coup in 2006 that ousted the government of Prime Minister Thaksin, the coup in

2014 that ousted his sister, Prime Minister Yingluck Shinawatra (Yinglak Chinawat), and the arrest and detention of thousands of Thais since then has heightened the stakes for committing any act that can be construed as anti-monarchical. The establishment, when threatened, enforces silence. The political and cultural context demands demonstrative promonarchical expression.

Many proud patriots were similarly expelled from Thailand after these coups because no safe space exists in their country for the expression of anything except promilitary, proroyalist sentiments or silence. Even after the formal abolishment of absolutism and polygyny and the introduction of constitutions and democratic political institutions, a lack of transparency and extrainstitutional forms of power have continued to characterize Thai politics.[28]

Perhaps the similarities end here. Prisdang lived in a very different era. Siam had a weaker military and a stronger monarchy in his lifetime, and republics were relatively new inventions. Imperialism loomed large then in ways quite distinct from the transnational forms that capitalism takes today. Yet his story offers one final undeniable parallel. It draws critical attention to acts of self-censorship. Prisdang decided it was safer to censor parts of his autobiography when he downplayed and removed details regarding his falling out with the monarch. He continued to self-censor even after he returned to an inhospitable situation in Siam. Prisdang was a royalist till the end of his days but a political critic and social maverick as well. His regal contemporaries ensured his political and social demise.

Thus Prisdang's example forces us to consider the invisible acts of self-censorship that many Thai nationals exercise to avoid prosecution for breaking lèse majesté laws. Problematically, their self-silencing might also indicate support of the status quo. As a form of intentional silencing, self-censorship does not necessarily mean powerlessness. Silence can function as a potent political act: a form of resistance, a signal of complicity, or a sign of oppression. Silence's power lies in its malleable interpretation. It allows others to project meaning onto it. By pointing out his self-censorship but refusing to tell us the intent behind it, Prisdang offered an enduring and generative silence.

Acknowledgments

This book stemmed from a desire to write a history of Thailand that would appeal to general readers who might not otherwise read about the country I have studied for over twenty-five years. Using biography as a vehicle for writing history occurred to me when I took a trip with my older brother to climb Mt. Kilimanjaro, where I was inspired to find an individual who strove to make history, who was intensely alive to life's possibilities, and who was fully conscious of his or her place in the world. Luckily I stumbled across Prisdang Chumsai, to whom I am most grateful.

I owe thanks to many others, including those who generously invited me to share my progress on this project, even at its earliest stages. They include the Kyoto Center for Southeast Asian Studies and Caroline Hau in particular; Sara Friedman, Gardner Bovingdon, Susan Williams, David Williams, Fred Aman, and the Center for Constitutional Democracy at Indiana University; Siobhan Somerville, Kenneth Cuno, Feisal Mohamed, and the Center for Advanced Study series on the Cultures of Law in Global Contexts; Ben Schonthal, Angela Wanhalla, the Centre for the Study of Colonial Cultures, the Centre for the Study of Islam and Muslim Cultures, and the Department of Theology and Religion at the University of Otago in Dunedin; and my colleagues in the Cornell History Department who read portions of the book for the Comparative History Colloquium. In particular, I am grateful to Sherm Cochran, Ray Craib, Oren Falk, Maria Cristina Garcia, Itsie Hull, Aaron Sachs, Victor Seow, Eric Tagliacozzo, and Rachel Weil, who took extra time out of their full lives to consult with me or read some chapters closely and offer me superb feedback.

Thanks also to my many colleagues in Cornell's Southeast Asia Program. Anne Blackburn provided riveting archival sources from Colombo, helped me set up my research trip to temples and archives in Sri Lanka, and read the relevant chapter. Kaja McGowan gave me the talismanic black sheep figurines that encouraged me to work on "baa-aad" boys who helped shape Thai history. Other colleagues, friends, and graduate students have read portions of the manuscript, helped with research, or otherwise offered essential forms of encouragement: Thak Chaloemtiarana, Lawrence Chua, Chantal Croteau, Alexandra Dalferro, Drew Dolgert, Hugh Egan, David Elliott, Sara Friedman, Tyrell Haberkorn, Deborah Homsher, Michael Kidd, Sarosh Kuruvilla, Samson Lim, Moodchalin Sudcharoen, Natasha Pairaudea, Lorraine Paterson, Trais Pearson, Maurizio

Peleggi, Chairat Pholmuk, Anissa Rahadiningtyas, Matt Reeder, Ben Schonthal, Rebecca Townsend, Chris and Ding Xiang Warner, and Susan Wiser. Credit for the jacket image goes to the artistry of Anissa Rahadiningtyas, who sketched Prisdang's image, and Alexandra Dalferro, who colored it in.

Translating Prisdang often proved trying but always worth the effort. I owe a great debt to Apikanya McCarty and Ida Aroonwong, who both helped enormously with the translations. All remaining errors are my own. I am also grateful to Chris Baker, Penny Edwards, Bonnie Loos, James Loos, Craig Reynolds, and an anonymous reader for the press for reading the entire manuscript carefully, with enthusiasm, and with a critical eye. Thanks also to the many individuals at Cornell University Press who have helped improve the manuscript and have supported me throughout the process: Jamie Fuller, Ange Romeo-Hall, Karen Hwa, Mahinder Kingra, Michael McGandy, Michael Morris, Peter Potter, and Dean Smith. I am most grateful to Roger Haydon, my editor at Cornell University Press, whom I respect enormously. He took on my first book and crazily consented to helping the second one find its way to publication. It has been a great pleasure working with him.

Portions of the research were supported by Cornell's Southeast Asia Program, the history department's Walt and Sandy LaFeber Fund, and the Society for the Humanities. Their funding enabled me to conduct research in London, Colombo, and Bangkok. My research trip to Sri Lanka yielded unanticipated riches. I am grateful to John Rogers and Ira Unamboowe, the US director and Colombo executive director, respectively, of the American Institute of Sri Lankan Studies in 2015. They generously facilitated my trip to Colombo and the Sri Lankan National Archives. Thanks also to Krishantha Fredricks, my research assistant in Colombo; Urane Atukorala of the Sri Lankan National Archives; and Dr. K. D. Paranavitana, historian and preservationist extraordinaire, who not only found and cataloged for future historians letters by and about Prisdang from Buddhist temples in Colombo but shared with me his vast knowledge of Sri Lankan history. I am grateful to the Venerable Mahindawansa, who spoke with me at length and with warmth about the Thai Prince Priest and showed me the temple and museum where Prisdang once presided. On my last evening in Colombo, I met fellow researchers Michael Charlesworth and Janice Leoshko, whose research on and stories about the fabulously sardonic Reginald Farrer and ubiquitous Ananda Coomaraswamy enriched Prisdang's story and my life. I am also thankful for Chris Peppé, a descendant of W. C. Peppé, who conversed with me over the phone and e-mail about the complex story surrounding the Piprahwa relics. He was an insightful and humorous interlocutor who shared stories, documents, and photographs that have proven essential for the Sri Lanka and India chapter.

In Bangkok, I am grateful to Thanet Aphornsuvan, Coeli Barry, and their two fabulous daughters, Maya and Saran, who comprise my family there. Absolutely essential to the project was Ida (B) Aroonwong, who came to Ithaca in exile, briefly, after one of the more recent coups. She and I have spent many evenings together in Ithaca and Thonburi, where we hashed out the details of Prisdang's words and intentions. She shared much of this journey with me. We are both grateful to the late Ben Anderson for introducing us. Chusak Pattarakulvanit would occasionally join B and me and provide his interpretations of Prisdang. I also am grateful to Prisdang's descendants: Professor Sumet Jumsai; his wife, Suthini; Maymay; and Wen. They warmly and generously opened their home and archives to me. I also thank Pramin Kreuthong, Phirasri Phowathong, Bunphisit Srihong, and Supapij Bee Xoomsai na Ayudhya for generously sharing their sources, articles, and insights.

Closer to home in Freeville, Kim Sneddon, Sandy Fitterer, and Lorrie Tiley ran with me every Thursday at predawn, when in the dark they were my captives, forced to listen to me talk about the project. I think they ran faster as a consequence. My mom and brother, James, shouted encouragement from the other side of the continent. My dog, Kobi, who died unexpectedly just as I finished the book, was my constant companion. I miss her immensely.

Out of this long list, I am most grateful to Dave Vernon, my haven. He listened to me conceptualize the project and then read every single draft. He discovered the most unusual materials about Prisdang that have found their way into each chapter. And along the way, he introduced me to members of his family, who have become part of my own: Lisa, Diane, Dianne, and Annali.

Thai Naming Conventions, Dating Systems, Transcription, and Translation

Naming Conventions

Thai naming conventions regarding personal names make it difficult to trace most individuals, even those officials and royal family members who are deemed important enough to leave a paper trail. There are several reasons for this. First, Thailand did not adopt family surnames until 1913, and even then, the transliteration into English of family names was not always consistent. When Prince Prisdang registered for school in England in the 1870s, he did not have a last name and was required to claim one. He took the name of his father, Prince Choomsai, as his surname. Descendants now transliterate their names in multiple ways: Chumsai, Jumsai, Xoomsai, and so on. Second, the name by which an individual is referred to can change several times over the course of his life, such as when that individual passes through certain life stages (puberty, marriage), or after major events such as traumatic accidents, ordination as a monk, or promotion in rank or office (mostly for men). Third, government officials were often referred to by the title of the office they held, so when they changed positions, they obtained a new title. Into their former position stepped a different individual who then obtained that title. As a consequence, a single individual can be known by numerous names, making it difficult to trace a specific individual over time. To help clarify this complexity for naming of officials, Thai scholarly conventions refer to persons by their titles and then provide their given names in parentheses. For example, when the individual with the personal name of Joem Saeng-Xuto appears in Prisdang's story in 1882, he was then titled and referred to as Jamuen Wai (Joem Saeng-Xuto). However, by 1886 he had been promoted to Phraya Surasakmontri (Joem Saeng-Xuto), and later to Jao Phraya Surasakmontri (Joem Saeng-Xuto). While this reveals that the Thai cultural system valued making overt one's social status over his or her personal identity, it is in practice unwieldy and difficult for those unfamiliar with Thai conventions to follow. To make Prisdang's story more accessible to non-Thai readers and specialists, I have referred to individuals by a single name dictated by Prisdang's usage. Titles and honorifics are given in the footnotes when relevant.

Dating Systems

No fewer than four calendar dating systems were deployed in the documents used to tell Prisdang's story: the Julasakharat, Ratanakosin, Phutthasakharat, and Christian-era calendars. All three of the Thai calendar systems began their year with the month of April rather than January until 1941, when Prime Minister Phibun Songkhram issued a decree that began the calendrical new year in January. To convert Buddhist era (P.S.) dates to CE dates from January through March prior to 1941, subtract 542. For dates from April through December, subtract 543. The Rattanakosin Era (R.S.) began with the first reign of the Chakri dynasty, in 1782, so one adds 1782 or 1781 to the R.S. dates depending on the month to arrive at the appropriate CE translation. And to convert the Julasakharat (J.S.) dates, one adds either 638 or 637 to the J.S. year depending on the month.

Transcription

For pragmatic reasons having to do with publishing in the United States, I have transcribed all uses of Thai terms rather than using Thai script. The transcription guide I use largely follows that outlined by the Royal Institute's 1982 *Romanization Guide for the Thai Script* with a few exceptions. Instead of transliterating จ as "ch," I use "j" when possible. There are notable exceptions, such as the convention of using "ch" to transliterate certain place names that have become common usage, such as the Chao Phraya River, and surnames and titles conferred by the king. I use the spellings of family and personal names preferred by those individuals when known even though these transliterations are not phonetically accurate or consistent.

Translation

Translating from one language into another is never a direct process. It becomes even more complicated across historical and cultural divides. Prince Prisdang's expressive style is unusual and provides a special challenge even to educated native Thai speakers, likely because of his unique education abroad in English, which affected not just the content of his writing but his prose and grammar as well. In addition, most of the documents are handwritten: Prisdang scribbled by hasty, frantic hand hundreds of pages of letters that have been poorly copied multiple times over the years. Some portions are frustratingly illegible. To help clarify his sentiments, Apikanya McCarty and Ida Aroonwong graciously assisted me in checking my translations and helping translate Prisdang's distinctive and sometimes unwieldy use of language. All potential remaining imperfections are my responsibility. I invite other scholars to return to the original sources penned by Prisdang and help us perfect them.

Notes

In the endnotes, Thailand's National Archive sources are cited as "NA," followed by the reign number, the ministry or department from which the source comes, and numbers that refer to a division and subdivision in the ministry or department. For example, NA R5 R B 3/4 refers to the National Archives, reign of Rama V, and the Department of the Royal Secretariat (Rachalekhanukan). The B refers to Bettalet, the section of collected documents called "miscellaneous." The number 3 refers to the collection of files about Prisdang within "Miscellaneous," and the number 4 refers to the fourth set of files in the Prisdang collection.

1. STAGING SECRETS

1. The information about the ceremony comes from the looseleaf insert in Prince Prisdang's autobiography, *Prawat yo naiphan ek phiset phra worawongthoe phra 'ong jao pritsdang tae prasut pho. so. 2392 thung 2472* [Abbreviated History of Special Colonel Prince Prisdang, from 1850–1930], reprinted in the cremation volume for Luang Aneknaiwathi (M. R. W. Narot Chumsai) (Bangkok, 1930; repr., Bangkok, 1970). The actual dates of Prisdang's life are 1852–1935. The one copy of the autobiography that exists in the public domain belongs in Prince Damrong's collection. It was reprinted as a cremation volume for M. R. W. Narot Chumsai, one of Prisdang's descendants, who died in 1970.

2. "Bangkok Fire Season Wanes," *Singapore Free Press and Mercantile Advertiser*, February 19, 1930, 6.

3. I refer to Thailand and Thai subjects as Siam and Siamese unless referring to the period after 1939. For an analysis of Prisdang's autobiography as the first Western-style version within Thai autobiographical and biographical genres, see Tamara Loos, "Renegade Royalist: Autobiography and Siam's Disavowed Prince Prisdang," in *Clio in a Phanung: Ten Essays on the Cultural and Intellectual History of Thailand*, ed. Maurizio Peleggi, (Ithaca: SEAP Publications, 2015), 63–77.

4. Far from being static sources of tradition and morality, these tales underwent change, particularly during the reign of King Chulalongkorn, who revised and marginalized the Jatakas. See Patrick Jory, "Thai and Western Buddhist Scholarship in the Age of Colonialism: King Chulalongkorn Redefines the Jatakas," *Journal of Asian Studies* 61, no. 3 (August 2002): 891–918. Craig Reynolds has translated one of the first autobiographies written by a Siamese, Prince-Patriarch Vajiranana (Wachirayan Warorot), which was published posthumously in 1924. It was of the Buddhist didactic variety. Prince-Patriarch Vajiranana, *Autobiography: The Life of Prince Patriarch Vajiranana*, ed. and trans. Craig J. Reynolds (Athens: Ohio University Press, 1979).

5. It is possible that a draft of volume 2 might be interred in the chedi of the Dipaduttamarama Temple in Kotahena, Sri Lanka. Sumet Jumsai, personal communication, 19 October 2015.

6. There may be additional copies held in private. For example, in Sumet Jumsai's collection, I saw a photocopy of the signature page of number 26 signed by Kromamun

Devawongse (Traidos Prabandh), who took his father's (Prince Devawongse Waropakan) place as minister of foreign affairs in 1924.

7. He planned to use the proceeds earned from donations at his ceremony to purchase a new set of dentures. The dates in his autobiography are confusing—the publication page states it was 1930, but the signature page lists 1928, and the concluding page is dated 1924. Like layers of sediment, his story slowly accreted until he forced its publication in 1930. It is clear from the context that the birthday ceremony was held in 1930 but that he had hoped to publish it earlier. Prisdang, *Prawat yo*, 37, 41–42.

8. Ibid., 41.

9. Patrick Jory, "Republicanism in Thai History," in *A Sarong for Clio: Essays on the Intellectual and Cultural History of Thailand*, ed. Maurizio Peleggi (Ithaca: SEAP Publications, 2015), 97–117.

10. Simon Schaffer et al., *The Brokered World: Go-Betweens and Global Intelligence, 1770–1820* (Sagamore Beach, MA: Science History Publications, 2009), xxix.

11. For an in-depth treatment of Siam's internal factions in the late nineteenth century, see David Wyatt, *The Politics of Reform in Thailand* (New Haven: Yale University Press, 1969).

12. Ibid., 86–87nn7–8.

13. Although the term did not appear in dictionaries until the 1940s, the cultural concept seems to have been in practice by elites much earlier as part of polite, upper-status "manners." A social superior may then have said to an inferior, "mai ru thi tam thi sung." See also Penny Van Esterik, *Materializing Thailand* (New York: Berg, 2000), 36–41.

14. Rosalind Morris has discussed the dualistic conservative-liberating aspects of this ideology (though she makes no reference to the term *kalathesa*) in the context of sexuality—how one practices it privately (which is the space of relative freedom) versus how one externalizes one's sexuality identity. "Three Sexes and Four Sexualities: Redressing the Discourses on Gender and Sexuality in Contemporary Thailand, *Positions* 2, no. 1 (1994): 15–43.

15. Many scholars differentiate between gossip, rumor, and scandal. For example, Sally Engle Merry summarizes the anthropological literature on gossip. She notes that gossip is informal and private, whereas scandal is gossip that has been introduced into the public arena. "Rethinking Gossip and Scandal," in *Toward a General Theory of Social Control*, vol. 1, *Fundamentals*, ed. Donald Black (Orlando: Academic Press, 1984), 275. Luis White, a historian, makes a distinction between gossip, rumor, and scandal but then suggests that such a taxonomy is not particularly helpful. See "Historicizing Rumor and Gossip," in *Speaking with Vampires: Rumor and History in Colonial Africa* (Berkeley: University of California Press, 2000), 56–86.

16. White, *Speaking with Vampires*, 58.

17. The second time Siam faced such a challenge was in 1893 when the French sent gunboats up the Chao Phraya River to Bangkok and demanded territories and indemnities.

18. Ann Stoler, "Matters of Intimacy as Matters of State: A Response," *Journal of American History* 88, no. 3 (December 2001): 896.

19. His closest friend, Surasakmontri, mentions Prisdang very briefly only once in his four-volume reminiscence, *Prawatikan khong jomphon jaophraya surasakmontri* [The History of Army Field Marshal Jao Phraya Surasakmontri] (Bangkok: Khuru Sapha, 1961). He notes that Prisdang served as an interpreter on one of Surasak's diplomatic missions in Europe, which occurred before Prisdang became Siam's minister plenipotentiary. Prince Damrong briefly mentions sending Prisdang as a young man to study English in Singapore. See Prince Damrong Rajanubhap [Rachanuphap], *Khwamsongjam* [Memories] (Bangkok: Khlang Withaya, 1963), 173–74.

20. Prisdang, *Prawat Yo*, 39.

2. GULF OF SIAM

1. King Mongkut reigned from 1851 to 1868.

2. Samuel J. Smith, "Events in Siam Connected with the Eclipse of 1868," *Siam Repository* 1 (January 1869): 2.

3. Prince Chula Chakrabongse, *Lords of Life: A History of the Kings of Thailand* (1960; repr., London: Alvin Redman, 1967), 212.

4. Damrong Rajanubhab, *Khwamsongjam* [Memoirs] (Bangkok: Khlang Withaya Publications, 1951), 56–57, 60. He wrote his memoirs in 1933, more than fifty years after the eclipse. Ibid., 1.

5. King Mongkut to Sir Henry Ord, 8 July 1868, http://www.siamese-heritage.org/jsspdf/1921/JSS_022_1b_EnglishCorrespondenceOfKingMongkutContinued.pdf.

6. David Aubin, "Eclipse Politics in France and Thailand, 1868," in *The Heavens on Earth: Observatories in Nineteenth-Century Science and Culture*, ed. David Aubin, Charlotte Bigg, and H. Otto Sibum (Durham, NC: Duke University Press, 2010), 92–94. This otherwise excellent article mistakenly identifies a photograph of the glassblower and goldsmith Prince Kromkhun Worajaktharanuphap (Prince Pramot) as that of King Mongkut. Ibid., 97. For more on Prince Pramot, see Joti Kalayanamitra, *Phon ngan 6 sattawat khong chang thai* [Six Hundred Years of Work by Thai Artists and Architects] (Bangkok: Fine Arts Commission, 1977), 60.

7. Chula Chakrabongse, *Lords of Life*, 212.

8. Smith, "Events in Siam Connected with the Eclipse of 1868," 2.

9. As noted by Thongchai Winichakul, recent attempts to discover the location of Wako Beach have ended in controversy. Chaen Patchusanon, "Suriyupparakha temkhrat ph.s. 2411" [The Full Solar Eclipse of 1868], *Nawikkasat* 62, no. 11 (November 1979): 124–41, cited in Thongchai, *Siam Mapped* (Honolulu: University of Hawai'i Press, 1994), 183–84n47. However, since 1989, there has been a restoration of the place where now there exists the King Mongkut Memorial Park of Science and Technology. See http://www.waghor.go.th.

10. Malcolm Smith, *A Physician at the Court of Siam* (1947; repr., Kuala Lumpur: Oxford University Press, 1982), 45–46. He describes the layout of the community that was built along the coast.

11. He later was given the noble title of Somdet Jao Phraya Si Suriyawong, but his personal and family name was Chuang Bunnag. I refer to him throughout as Si Suriyawong. He was born 23 December 1808 and died 19 January 1883. He was the most powerful minister during Mongkut's reign and was appointed regent to King Chulalongkorn in 1868 until Chulalongkorn came of age in 1873.

12. Chula Chakrabongse, *Lords of Life*, 212.

13. B. J. Terwiel, *Thailand's Political History: From the Fall of Ayutthaya in 1767 to Recent Times* (Bangkok: River Books, 2005), 169.

14. Chula Chakrabongse, *Lords of Life*, 213.

15. Damrong, *Khwamsongjam*, 62. The word means to disappear (and reappear) quickly into something, as when a tortoise retracts its head into its shell.

16. Chula Chakrabongse, *Lords of Life*, 213.

17. This memory stems most likely from Queen Saowapha, who was Dr. Malcolm Smith's interlocutor for his book *A Physician at the Court of Siam*, 47, 49. He also read the reports by French lead scientist at the scene, Édouard Stéphan.

18. Thongchai Winichakul, *Siam Mapped*, 43, 46. The reference to the distribution of gifts to celebrate the accuracy of his prediction comes from Aubin, "Eclipse Politics," 87.

19. Abbot Low Moffat, *Mongkut the King of Siam* (Ithaca: Cornell University Press, 1961), 171.

20. Chula Chakrabongse, *Lords of Life*, 212–13. Regarding champagne, see Nerida Cook, "Tale of Two City Pillars: Mongkut and Thai Astrology on the Eve of Modernization," in *Patterns and Illusions: Thai History and Thought*, ed. Gehan Wijeyewardene and E. C. Chapman (Singapore: ISEAS, 1992), 298.

21. Aubin, "Eclipse Politics," 93. Aubin explains that the significance of the 1868 eclipse in Western science resided in the use of spectroscopes for the first time to determine the chemical constitution of the sun by focusing on the pinkish flames around the moon during the eclipse. Ibid., 88.

22. Ibid., 94.

23. Ibid., 101.

24. Cook, "Tale of Two City Pillars," 300–301.

25. At least nine people died, and dozens fell ill, including most of the French astronomers. Terwiel, *Thailand's Political History*, 171.

26. David K. Wyatt, "Family Politics in Seventeenth and Eighteenth Century Siam," in *Studies in Thai History* (Chiang Mai: Silkworm Books 1994), 127.

27. David K. Wyatt, *Thailand: A Short History*, 2nd ed. (New Haven: Yale University Press, 2003), 177.

28. Smith, *A Physician*, 87, mentions the death of Prince Chulalongkorn's mother. Chulalongkorn, born on 20 September 1853, was the ninth of King Mongkut's children. See *Rachasakunwong* (Bangkok: Department of Fine Arts 2512/1969), 46.

29. David K. Wyatt's translation in "King Chulalongkorn the Great," in *Studies in Thai History*, 277–78. For the original, see King Chulalongkorn, "Phraboromaratchowat nai ratchakan thi 5 chapab thi 2," in *Ekkasan kan muang kanpokkhrong thai* [Documents on Thai Politics and Administration], ed. Chai-anan Samudavanija and Khattiya Kannasutra (Bangkok: The Social Association of Thailand, 1975), 103–4.

30. Cholera came to England in 1831 and began the first of a few murderous sprees, killing more than fifty thousand in 1849. According to a public web source, the infant mortality rate was high as well: 437 out of 1,000 children died before they reached the age of two. Marjorie Bloy, "A Web of English History," http://www.historyhome.co.uk/peel/p-health/pubheal.htm.

31. Smith, *A Physician*, 16–19. Prisdang's mother, Noi, died of cholera around 1886.

32. Ibid., 137.

33. Ibid., 19.

34. Memo by E. H. French, The National Archives (UK): Public Records Office, Foreign Office 628/15/209 (hereafter TNA: PRO, FO); Captain H. M. Jones to Lord Salisbury, 24 August 1892, TNA: PRO, FO 69/146. This is a handwritten memo with some sections cut off and portions illegible. Even so, the legible portions are full of enormous errors that suggest the entire document may have been fabricated to irreparably tarnish Prisdang's reputation so that no one would trust his opinion as expressed in the 1891 confidential memo that arrived at about the same moment as the letter. The most obvious errors in the note: Prisdang's father was the half nephew of the "late king," not the half brother. Prince Chumsai was the son of a consort (not a full queen) and Rama III, who was the half brother of Rama IV (King Mongkut).

35. Prince Chumsai was known by his princely rank and title, Krom Khun Ratchasihawikrom. For ease, I refer to him as Prince Chumsai, but in nearly all accounts he is referred to only by his more formal name. He was a prince of the second rank (Phra Ong Jao).

36. Wyatt, "Family Politics." This is a remarkable article for its ability to map out the degree to which Siamese administration and politics were run by relationships among a few powerful families who had intermarried prior to the beginning of the Chakri dynasty.

37. Chris Baker suggests that the status system was in the process of being created during this era, as King Chulalongkorn's power strengthened after the death of the former

regent. He explains that the "elaborate hierarchy was an attempt to discipline the royal clan, probably with an eye on the 'krom wars' of the Ban Phlu Luang era, which figure so prominently in the chronicles compiled in this era. Mongkut's proclamations show he was obsessed with managing (and financing) the royal clan." Baker, personal communication, 12 June 2015.

38. Wyatt, "Family Politics," 109. The five ranks were (1) Jao Fa, the child of a king by one of his queens; (2) Phra Ong Jao, the child of a king by a lesser wife; (3) Mom Jao, the grandchild of a king; (4) Mom Rachawong, the great-grandchild of a king; and (5) Mom Luang, the great-great-grandchild of a king.

39. Robert B. Jones, *Thai Titles and Ranks, Including a Translation of Traditions of Royal Lineage in Siam by King Chulalongkorn* (Ithaca: Cornell Southeast Asia Program Data Paper 81, 1971). He explains that King Chulalongkorn wrote the essay in 1878 to reassert the traditional legitimacy of royal power vis-à-vis powerful nobles. Ibid., 5.

40. These were, in order, Somdet Jao Phraya, Jao Phraya, Phraya, Luang, and Khun.

41. Phraya Ratchamontri's personal name is Phu. Walter Vella, *Chaiyo! King Vajiravudh and the Development of Thai Nationalism* (Honolulu: University of Hawai'i Press, 1978), 6 and n21.

42. K. S. R. Kulap, "Prawat Phraya Ratchamontri (Phu)" [The History of Phraya Ratchamontri (Phu)], *Sayam Praphet* 4, no. 16 (27 March 119 [1901]): 545–55. Several sources describe Phraya Ratchamontri as head of the Royal Treasury—both Kulap and Prisdang make this claim. However, the minister of the Phra Khlang was Dit Bunnag, who had been appointed as such in 1822 and held that position well into the reign of Rama III.

43. Kulap does not provide a number but deploys hyperbole: he claims that Phraya Ratchamontri had too many children to name in his article because the list would be longer than pages of paper in his possession.

44. *Rachasakunwong*, 34.

45. Sumet, *Wang tha phra* [Tha Phra Palace] (Bangkok: Krung Siam, 1971), 46. Sumet and his wife compiled and distributed this book privately after they were married in the Tha Phra Palace in 1971. It was, by the 1970s, the home of Silpakon University, which was founded in 1939.

46. Noi had two children from her previous marriage to Prince Matayaphithak and eight children with Chumsai.

47. Cook, "Tale of Two City Pillars," 290. For treatment of Prince Chumsai as the architect in charge of the construction of the clock tower, see Joti Kalyanamitra, *Phon ngan 6 sattawat khong chang thai*, 42 and 45. Rama V had the clock tower dismantled.

48. With his appointment he received a raise in salary and increase in the numbers of attendants who worked for him. Rama IV appointed him Krom Khun Ratchasiha-wikrom with a *sakdina* (status marker typically representing rights to possession of land and attendants) ranking of 15,000 and gave him a personal *krom*, or department, with a *jaokrom* (department director), a *palat krom* (department deputy), and a *samutbanchi* (accountant) who held sakdina rankings between 600 and 300. Constance Wilson, "State and Society in the Reign of Mongkut, 1851–1868: Thailand on the Eve of Modernization" (PhD diss., Cornell University, 1970), 320–21, 328.

49. This would make Prisdang the cousin of the queen mother of Chulalongkorn, who had passed away when Chulalongkorn was nine.

50. He was also known as the Front Palace King. His name was Phra Pinklao (Itsaret). He was close to Mongkut, studied English with missionaries, and was interested in Western technologies, particularly clocks, Western artillery, and the steamboat. Wilson, "State and Society," 228–29. As second king, he had the same honors as the king, but these were less elaborate in scale.

51. These stories come from Narot Chumsai, a nephew of Prisdang, and Sumet Chumsai's grandmother. Sumet, *Wang tha phra*, 19–20.

52. Ibid., 45. This is Sumet's translation into English of a statement by Prince Prisdang that exists at Wang Khlong Toey.

53. During the reign of Rama V, Prince Narisranuwatiwong lived in Ban Tha Chang. Ibid., 21, 47.

54. Prisdang, *Prawat yo*, 43.

55. Wyatt, *Politics of Reform*, 36.

56. Wyatt, "Family Politics," 124.

57. Joti covers several of them and their contributions. Mom Jao Rabiap, the oldest son, was a goldsmith and artist who painted china. *Phon ngan 6 sattawat khong chang thai*, 79. Mom Jao Jamroen, the third child, went to India in 1871 with King Chulalongkorn as a sketch artist. Ibid. Mom Jao Prawit, who lived until 1925, yet curiously is not mentioned by Prisdang in his autobiography, was very active under Rama V as an architect, designer, sculptor, and painter. Ibid., 83–85.

58. *Jotmaihaet sadet phraphat tang prathet nai ratchakan thi 5 sadet muang singapo lae muang batawia krang raek lae sadet praphat india*, 2nd ed., cremation volume for Phra Jao Boromawongthoe kromaluang adison udomdet (Bangkok, 2468/1925), 54–55. Depending on which book one consults, it was either Jamroen or Prawit who came as the official sketch artist. Joti mentions Jamroen. *Phon ngan 6 sattawat khong chang thai*, 79. See also Narisaranuvattiwongse and Damrong Rajanubhab, *Prawat sawek-ek mom jao prawit* [History of Court Official Mom Jao Prawit] (Bangkok, 1926).

59. *Jotmaihaet sadet phraphat*, 56n2. The footnote lists fourteen names, but oddly, Prisdang is not listed. Prince Damrong in his memoirs lists Prisdang as one of these students in Singapore who excelled and was consequently selected to study in London. Damrong, *Khwamsongjam*, 172–73.

60. Prisdang, *Prawat yo*, 44.

61. The other two were Mom Jao Jek Nophawong, the son of Prince Mahesuan Siwilat, and Mom Rachawong Thewanung Siriwong (Phraya Chaisurin). They were put in the care of Jao Phraya Surawong Watanasak (To Bunnag), the grandson of the regent. He studied military sciences in England with private funding. Udom Pramuanwithaya, "Jaonai nakkanthut khon raek khong sayam thung 13 prathet" [The First Siamese Prince Diplomat to 13 Countries], in *Nung roi jaofa lae senabodi* [100 Jaofa Princes and Ministers] (Bangkok: Khlang Withaya, 1962), 448–49.

62. Prisdang, *Prawat yo*, 44–45.

63. Ibid., 47.

64. M. L. Manich Jumsai, *Prince Prisdang's Files on His Diplomatic Activities in Europe 1880–1886* (Bangkok: Chalermnit, 1977), 5–7. Prisdang was the great uncle of Manich Jumsai. Manich's father was Mom Jao Rabiap, the eldest brother of Prince Prisdang.

65. Aubin, "Eclipse Politics," 86–87.

66. Damrong noted this unfortunate selection of a viewing site in his memoirs, *Khwamsongjam*, 60.

3. EUROPE

1. There existed radical critics outside government circles, but their heyday came a bit later and the degree of their radicalism varies. Examples include K. S. R. Kulap Kritsananon, Thianwan (T. W. S. Wannapho), and Narin Phasit. Notably, Siamese political history is replete with men and bereft of women, at least in the public record.

2. The Thai for "backbone of the king" is *kraduk sanlang phrapiyamaharat*. Prisdang, *Prawat yo*, 84. See also Supot Jaengrew, "Phra ong jao prisdang 'kraduksanlang' khong

ongsomdet phrapiyamaharat" [Prince Prisdang, "Backbone" of His Majesty], *Sinlapa Watanatham* 14, no. 12 (October 1993): 156.

3. For an in-depth discussion of these factions, see Wyatt, *Politics of Reform*, and Kullada Kesboonchoo Mead, *The Rise and Decline of Thai Absolutism* (London: Routledge-Curzon, 2004), esp. chapter 4.

4. Prisdang, *Prawat yo*, 48.

5. King Mongkut's seventeenth child, born as Phra Ong Jao Kritsadaphinihan on 7 May 2398/1855 to Jao Jommanda Klin. He was promoted to Kromamuen Naret Worarit in 1875, then to Kromaluang in 1899. He became the ambassador to England and the United States, then later served as head of the Ministries of the Capital and Public Works. Under Rama VI he was promoted to the princely rank of Krom Phra and was given other accolades. He died 10 August 2468/1925. *Rachasakunwong*, 48.

6. Prisdang, *Prawat yo*, 48–49.

7. Ibid.

8. Prisdang's appointment to Kabinburi is mentioned ibid., 48, and in Udom, "*Jaochai*," 449.

9. Prisdang, *Prawat yo*, 49; see also Nigel Brailey, *Two Views of Siam on the Eve of the Chakri Reformation: Comments by Robert Laurie Morant and Prince Pritsdang* (Whiting Bay, Scot.: Kiscadale Publications, 1989), 13.

10. Chris Baker and Pasuk Phongpaichit, *The Palace Law of Ayutthaya and the Thammasat: Translation and Commentary* (Ithaca: SEAP Publications, forthcoming).

11. Phra Pricha's family was at odds with the powerful Bunnag family and the former regent, Si Suriyawong, in particular, whose own potentially shady fiscal interests in opium were being scrutinized by Phra Pricha's father, Phraya Krasapkitkoson. Pricha's father sat on Chulalongkorn's council of state and was in charge of drafting new legislation on opium farms, "a delicate task because the farms were an important financial resource under the control of Somdet Chaophraya" (Si Suriyawong). According to Kullada, Phraya Krasap's role in drafting this legislation made his family, the Amatyakul, a target of political attack and eventually caused their disgrace. Kullada, *The Rise and Decline*, 48.

12. Wyatt, *The Politics of Reform*, 88–89; Kullada, *Rise and Decline*, 48; Manich, *Prince Prisdang's Files*, 236–37.

13. Manich, *Prince Prisdang's Files*, 236–45.

14. Udom, "*Jaochai*," 450; Terwiel, *Thailand's Political History*, 192–93.

15. He was later known as Jao Phraya Surasakmontri (Joem Saeng-Chuto).

16. Wichitwong na Pomphet, *Rachathut haeng krung sayam* [Siam's Diplomatic Envoys] (Bangkok: Saengdao, 2004), 119. Phraya Phatsakorawong (Phon Bunnag) was the son of Dit Bunnag and younger half brother of Si Suriyawong. Dit Bunnag had forty-four children by twenty-four wives and consorts, thus contributing to what became a massive Bunnag progeny. (The regent and Phraya Phatsakorawong were both uncles of a woman named Si, who was accused later of having an affair with Prisdang.) Phraya Phatasakorawong was an outspoken member of the Young Siam faction and a prolific and controversial contributor to *Darunowat*, Young Siam's short-lived magazine. See Kullada, *Rise and Decline*, 48–49.

17. This was a difficult situation for Chulalongkorn to navigate. He knew Phra Pricha, who had gone to India as part of Chulalongkorn's entourage and was a member, along with his father and uncle, of the faction who most strongly endorsed the king over the regent and other noble families.

18. As reported in the *London Gazette*, July 13, 1880, Prisdang was appointed "Second Secretary and Interpreter to the Special Embassy of His Majesty the King of Siam," along with Phya Ratna Kosa, the first secretary, and Jao Phraya Phanuwong, the ambassador. See also Prisdang, *Prawat yo*, 50.

19. Kullada, *Rise and Decline*, 95.

20. It is possible that Prisdang had encountered all these men before. According to Sumet Jumsai, he was associated with the publication in the 1870s of two newspapers affiliated with Young Siam: *Darunowat* and *Khot Khaorachakan*. Prisdang, Prince Devawongse, Prince Phanurangsi Sawangwong, and others are linked to the papers. Sumet Jumsai na Ayutthaya et al., *Phra ong jao prisdang lae khosanoe kieokap ratthathamanun chabap raek ph.s. 2427* [Prince Prisdang and the Proposal for the First Constitution in B.E. 2427/1885] (Bangkok: King Prajadhipok Institute, 2007), 52.

21. There is confusion over how many initial members existed: four, seven, eight, or nine, depending on one's source. See Kullada, *Rise and Decline*, 201n6; Prisdang, *Prawat yo*, 53. Wimonphan Pitathawatchai, *Somdet phrajao bormommawongthoe krom phraya Devawongsewaropakan* [Prince Devawongse], vol. 1 (Bangkok, 2004), 103.

22. Prisdang, *Prawat yo*, 52.

23. Nai phan-ek phiset.

24. Prisdang, *Prawat yo*, 52–53.

25. Manich, *Prince Prisdang's Files*, 7–8.

26. Manich Jumsai, comp., *Pramuan jotmai khong phra worawongthoe phra-ong jao Prisdang rachathut khon raek khong thai prajam thawip yurop* [Collected Letters of Prince Prisdang, First Thai Ambassador to Europe] (Bangkok, 1991), 7.

27. Prisdang, *Prawat yo*, 54.

28. Wichitwong, *Rachathut*, 132.

29. Manich, *Prince Prisdang's Files*, 30. Mason in effect operated as a bank through which money could be transferred to pay consular salaries to Siamese government officials in Europe because he had a business in Bangkok that facilitated the transfer of payment. Ibid., 146.

30. Ibid., 137.

31. Prisdang, *Prawat yo*, 55.

32. Manich, *Prince Prisdang's Files*, 18–19.

33. See ibid., 144.

34. Sumet, Postscript to Manich, *Prince Prisdang's Files*, 263.

35. Prisdang, *Prawat yo*, 54.

36. Ellis noted that Prisdang was "a highly intelligent gentlemen, speaking English remarkably well, and was very obliging to us; and without his assistance, for which we are much indebted, we should have had great difficulty in divining the theoretical scale." Alexander J. Ellis, "Appendix to Mr. Alexander J. Ellis's paper on 'The Musical Scales of Various Nations,' Read 25th March 1885," *Journal of the Society of Arts*, October 30, 1885, 1105.

37. Scattered letters now available for sale on the Internet prove this. In one letter dated 18 October 1881 by C. S. Aubrey Abbott to a Mr. Scoones, Prisdang is mentioned as searching for a tutor for King Chulalongkorn's brother, "who wishes to be prepared for entering a military college." http://www.historicalautographs.co.uk/catalogue.asp?content=British%20History%201800–1950.

38. NA KT 6.26/2, unsigned letter from Siamese official (likely Devawongse) to Prisdang, 9 October 1885.

39. NA KT 6.26/2, Prisdang to King Chulalongkorn, date illeg.

40. Manich, *Prince Prisdang's Files*, 3.

41. "Prince Prisdang, Death of a Siamese Diplomat," *Singapore Free Press and Mercantile Advertiser*, March 20, 1935, 6. These awards are included in the appendix to his autobiography along with certificates of Siamese honors and insignia.

42. Prisdang, *Prawat yo*, 38.

43. He was allowed to meet with the pope privately only. See A. Candilio and L. Bressan, "Sultan Abu Bakar of Johore's Visit to the Italian King and the Pope in 1885," *Journal of the Malaysian Branch of the Royal Asiatic Society* 73, no. 1 (2000): 48.

44. Prisdang, *Prawat yo*, 55, 62.

45. Isabel Hull used this felicitous turn of phrase about the language of ritual. Personal communication, 20 June 2104. See also Isabel V. Hull, "Prussian Dynastic Ritual and the End of the Monarchy," in *German Nationalism and the European Response, 1890–1945*, ed. Carole Fink, Isabel Hull, and MacGregor Knox (Norman: University of Oklahoma Press, 1985), 13–41.

46. The condescending piece can be found in the article "Stage Affairs in Paris," *New York Times*, September 25, 2.

47. Palgrave to H. A. W. Hervey, 24 September 1881, TNA: PRO, FO 69/78, cited in Brailey, *Two Views of Siam*, 16–17, 117.

48. NA R5 B 3/1, Prisdang to King Chulalongkorn. There is no pagination, and the specific dates are often, as in this letter, illegible.

49. Ibid.

50. Manich recounts this on the basis of Prisdang's files that were preserved at the Thai embassy in London. See Manich, *Prince Prisdang's Files*, 34–39.

51. Reginald S. le May, Walter Williamson, and E. Wyon Smith, *Descriptive Catalogue of the Postage Stamps and Post- and Letter-Cards of Siam* (Bangkok, 1920), 9; see also Manich, *Prince Prisdang's Files*, 175. For details about the treaty revisions on alcohol, see Phojai Thomya, "Botbat khong phra ong jao prisdang: suksa koranikanjeraja toklong nai nangsu sanya kiaokap sura kap nanaprathet" [The Role of Prince Prisdang: A Study of the Agreement in the Treaties Related to Alcohol with Foreign Countries, 1881–1886] (master's thesis, Chulalongkorn University, 2529/1986). See also various letters in file, NA KT 6.26/2, which includes advice to Prisdang regarding the specific problems that had arisen because of the illegal importation of spirits. Manich explains the tricky means by which the French obtained a quid pro quo regarding the hiring of French workers on the telegraph line in his *Prince Prisdang's Files*, 60, 216.

52. Manich, *Prince Prisdang's Files*, 147.

53. Manich quotes pages of Prisdang's notes from his passive-aggressive interview in December 1883 with the French minister of foreign affairs, Monsieur Clavéry, regarding the ratification of the spirits convention that Prisdang had worked on for over a year. Ibid., 201–17.

54. Some of the Frenchmen employed by Siam were notoriously ill behaved, abused Siamese subjects, drank to excess, were disorderly, and sometimes simply refused to work but still collected their paychecks, all because extraterritoriality privileges protected them from Siamese police and courts. The French had hired Monsieur Pavie, whom Prisdang later encountered in exile, to establish the telegraphic line between Bangkok and the disputed area of Battambang. Ibid., 60.

55. Prisdang, *Prawat yo*, 55, 58.

56. The Pali Text Society published a list of its subscribers and donors from 1882 to 1889, during which period Prisdang is listed as a subscriber throughout. See www.palitext. com/JPTS_PDF.htm. According to the society's administrator, Karen Wendland, Prisdang was a regular donor (typically ten pounds per year). Personal correspondence, 16 June 2014. King Chulalongkorn was a major donor as well and is listed as providing two hundred pounds the first year, which no doubt helped its founder launch the journal. Patrick Jory argues that the Siamese elite offered substantial financial assistance to keep the Pali Text Society afloat in the 1880s. Jory, "Thai and Western Buddhist Scholarship," 906.

57. Prisdang, *Prawat yo*, 62.

58. Ibid., 57.

59. Ibid., 58.

60. "Our London Letter," *Straits Times*, January 12, 1884. The letter, written by "our special Correspondent," was dated 30 November 1883.

61. Cetewayo refers to Cetshwaya kaMpande, the king of the Zulu kingdom who led the battle against the British in 1879.

62. "Pris-Dang It All!," *Moonshine*, December 15, 1883, 291.

63. "And they all began to make Excuse," *Moonshine*, December 6, 1883, 273. A special thanks to reference librarian Camille Andrews for tracking down copies of *Moonshine*.

64. This was confirmed in the *London Gazette*, December 14, 1883, 6439, which noted that on 12 December, "His Highness" Prince Prisdang had an audience with Queen Victoria at Windsor Castle in which he delivered his letter of recall, and "His Royal Highness" Prince Naret Worarit presented his credentials.

65. Newman to the Earl of Granville, 8 August 1883, TNA: PRO, FO 69/86.

66. Only one scholar has interpreted the move as a demotion. Udom, "Jaochai," 452–53.

67. Wichitwong refers to her as Mom Talap, a consort given to Prisdang by King Chulalongkorn in 1871. She traveled also with the wives of Prince Sonabanthit and Naret. See Wichitwong, *Rachathut*, 142. Mom Sadap, as Manich refers to her, arrived with her sister, Mae Tim, Prince Naret, and three of Naret's sons on the steamship *Sindh*. They arrived in Marseilles on 19 September. 1883. Manich, *Prince Prisdang's Files*, 124–25.

68. Manich, *Prince Prisdang's Files*, 101.

69. The original document is partially illegible, but Ida Aroonwong posits that the illegible name of the recipient is "Nong than khun phra nai wai." Phra nai is another way to refer to Jamuen, which makes the recipient's title Jamuen Wai. Surasak was given this title in 1878, so he would still have been so titled in 1882.

70. Nai krom refers to a prince who heads a government ministry or department, not to a nonroyal head of ministry.

71. NA KT 6.26/2, Prisdang to nong than, 3 November 1882. The author is grateful to Apikanya McCarty, Ida Aroonwong, and Pramin Kreuthong for painstakingly helping with the translation of this subtle, revealing letter.

72. Wyatt, "Family Politics," 117–19.

73. Letter from Newman, British acting consul general in Bangkok, to the Earl of Granville, British secretary of foreign affairs, 8 August 1883, TNA: PRO, FO 69/85, pp. 5–6.

74. He was born in 1830 and died in 1913. Upon his retirement in 1885, the Phra Khlang was formally divided into two ministries: the Treasury and the Ministry of Foreign Affairs, the latter headed by Prince Devawongse from 1885 until he passed away in 1923. See Wyatt, *Thailand*, 182–83.

75. NA KT 6.26/2, Prisdang to nong than, 3 November 1882. The letter has been dated with the help of Chairat Pholmuk and Pramin Kreuthong.

76. Prisdang, *Prawat yo*, 63.

77. The full maxim is *nua mai dai kin nang mai dai rongnan kraduk khwaen kho*.

78. Prisdang, *Prawat yo*, 63. Interpreted with assistance of Ida Aroonwong, personal e-mail communication, 23 June 2014.

79. Memo by E. H. French, 1892, TNA: PRO, FO 628/15/209; Captain H. M. Jones to Lord Salisbury, 24 August 1892, 2–4, TNA: PRO, FO 69/146.

80. "Six Siamese Students Sent to This Country in Preference to Europe," *New York Times*, January 19, 1891.

81. Vajiranana [Wachirayan], *Autobiography*.

82. Manich, *Prince Prisdang's Files*, 150–51.

83. Henry Norman, "The Future of Siam," *Contemporary Review* 64 (July–December 1893): 6.

84. J. W. Benson, the owner, threatened to air the debt publicly if the Siamese government refused to pay. Instead, in 1891 King Chulalongkorn declared that Benson's comments were libelous, that the shop had profited greatly from Siam already, and that from that point on no Siamese would shop there. See entire file in NA R5 B 3/2. According to Prisdang, one pound equaled 15 baht, so his debt was 27,465 baht.

85. See, for example, http://www.vintage-watches-collection.com/watch/jw-benson/vintage-jw-benson-watches-for-sale/andhttp://www.cjbalm.com/watches/watch-benson-history.htm.

86. Ads can be found, for example, in the *Singapore Straits Times*, November 7, 1874, 4; in *Allen's Indian Mail and Register of Intelligence for British and Foreign India, China and all parts of the East*, March 3, 1857, 167; and in the *Perth Gazette and West Australian Times*, July 11, 1873, 1.

87. "News by the Mail," *Bruce Herald* (New Zealand), September 1 (1882), 5.

88. Prisdang, "Confidential," in Brailey, *Two Views of Siam*, 55.

89. NA KT 6.26/2, letter from Prisdang dated 5 November (no year but must be early to mid-1880s).

90. The estimate comes from Manich, *Prince Prisdang's Files*, 145.

91. "A Foreign Prince Expected: Visit of Prince Prisdang of Siam to the Country," *New York Times*, February 25, 1882, 8. The article incorrectly notes that Prisdang spoke French fluently; he did not. Nor did he ever make it to America.

92. "Manila News: Madrid, 2nd May," *Straits Times Weekly Issue*, July 12, 1883, 9.

93. Wichitwong, *Rachathut*, 146.

94. "The New Siamese Embassy," *Straits Times*, August 14, 1883, 2.

95. Prisdang, *Prawat yo*, 59.

96. Manich, *Prince Prisdang's Files*, 245–52; quote is from 249.

97. Prisdang, *Prawat yo*, 60.

98. Prince Prisdang, "Confidential," 70–71.

99. Sumet, "Proposal for the First Constitution in Siam, 1885," in Manich, *Prince Prisdang's Files*, 254.

100. "Jaonai lae kharachakan krapbangkhomthun khwam hen jatkanplianplaeng rachakanphaendin r.s. 103," [The Princes and Royal Officials Offer their Opinion on Reforming the Administration of the Kingdom, 1885], in *Ekasan kanmuang kanpokkhrong thai (ph.s. 2417–2477)*, comp. Chai-Anan Samutwanit and Khattiya Kanasut (Bangkok: Thai Studies Institute, 1989), 40–61.

101. The original petition is reprinted, along with the king's response, in Chai-Anan Samutwanit and Khattiya Kanasut, *Ekasan kanmuang kanpok-khrong thai*, 40–66.

102. "Jaonai lae kharachakan," in Chai-Anan Samutwanit and Khattiya Kanasut, *Ekasan kanmuang kanpok-khrong thai*, 46.

103. Ibid., 69.

104. Ibid., 50.

105. Ibid., 50–51.

106. Sumet, et al., *Phra ong jao prisdang*, 35–37; Kullada, *Rise and Decline*, 105–6.

107. The petition and the king's response, like Prisdang's autobiography, have an interesting history, which is addressed in the concluding chapter.

108. "King Chulalongkorn's Speech on the Reform of the Government," unpublished translation by Noel A. Battye, 1969, of the speech as published in *Phraratchadamrat nai phrabatsomdet phrachulachomklao chaoyuhua. Songthalaeng phraboromaratchathibai kaekhai kanpokkhrong phaendin* [Speech Explaining the Governmental Reforms] (Bangkok: Sophonphiphanthanakon, 1927).

109. Sumet et al., *Phra ong jao prisdang*, 41–42. The same excuses were offered by King Prajiadhipok in 1927 when he wrote the introduction to the reprint of King Chulalongkorn's

speech on governmental reform (1888): Siam is not ready for a constitutional monarchy. He was overthrown five years later.

110. Kullada argues that the petitioners desired to increase the decision-making power of leading officials but did not consider increasing popular participation in the government. In other words, all those who signed the petition stood to gain from its implementation. Kullada, *Rise and Decline*, 105.

111. Prisdang, *Prawat yo*, 60. This is the reason most frequently cited for Prisdang's exile in 1890—that he angered the king not only by suggesting a constitutional monarchy but also by disclosing their private correspondence and making it public. Sumet et al., *Phra ong jao prisdang*, 31. Sumet, Postscript, 258.

112. Sumet pinpoints his departure from Paris on 26 February 1886. Sumet, Postscript, 258–59. However, Prisdang states (incorrectly) in his autobiography that he left with Naret and Sawat in January 1886. See Prisdang, *Prawat yo*, 61.

113. From letters to Florence Nightingale, 7, 13, and 25 January 1886, in the Lexbourne Collection, cited in Brailey, *Two Views of Siam*, 118–19n36.

114. Prisdang, *Prawat yo*, 61.

115. Manich, *Prince Prisdang's Files*, 217, 221.

4. BANGKOK

1. Manich, *Prince Prisdang's Files*, notes that he departed on 28 February 1886 from Marseilles. The entourage resurfaces in the *Straits Times Weekly Issue*, April 10, 1886, 1, which notes that they arrived on 10 April in Singapore. It is unclear as of yet exactly which day they arrived in Bangkok, but likely it was just a few days after reaching Singapore.

2. Prisdang, *Prawat yo*, 62 (emphasis added).

3. Bunphisit Srihong provides a meticulous overview of the scholarship on Prisdang in "Samphanthaphap rawang phrabat somdet phra julajomklao jaoyuhua kap phra-ong jao prisdang jak lakthan chanton su khamtham to nakwichakan lae nak-khian prawatsat-rathasat" [The Relationship between King Chulalongkorn and Prince Prisdang: From Primary Evidence to Questions by Scholars and Writers of Political History], *Ratthasatsan* 32, no. 3 (2011): 1–81.

4. Prince Naret was born May 2398/1853. In addition to his brief spell as ambassador to England and the United States, he also served as minister of the capital and minister of public works, among other positions. He died on 10 August 2468/1925, at the age of seventy-one. His mother was Jaojom Manda Klin. *Rachasakunwong*, 48. Prince Sonabandit was born on 1 April 2406/1863. He was promoted to Prince Bidyalabh (Phithayalap Phritithada). He was Naret's adviser when he was ambassador to England and the United States. He also served as governor (khaluang yai) of Monthon Phayap and the minister of the palace, among other positions. He died on 28 October 2456/1913, at the age of fifty. His mother was Jaojom Manda Wat (aka Thao Worajan under Rama V). *Rachasakunwong*, 63. Prince Svasti Sobhon was born on 22 December 2408/1865; became the minister of justice, special ambassador to Europe, and chief justice of the supreme court (San-Dika) under Rama VI; and died 10 December 2478/1925 at the age of seventy. *Rachasakunwong*, 67–68. He also was Devawongse's full brother, born to a queen.

5. Wichitwong, *Rachathut*, 158.

6. Phirasri Phowathong, "'Ubatihet' khong Phraworawongthoe Phra-Ong Jao Prisdang," *Sinlapa Watanatham* 35, no. 8 (June 2014): 124.

7. Prisdang, "Confidential," in Brailey, *Two Views of Siam*, 72.

8. "The Prince-Priest," *Straits Times*, February 9, 1897, 3.

9. Prisdang, *Prawat yo*, 64. The identity of his royally given wife, Mom Talap or Mom Sadap, remains a mystery. We don't know anything about her background or even her real name. The few facts included have been gleaned from various documents.

10. She must have been living in a house provided by the king, which may have been her parents' former home. But by 1882, the house was in disrepair, and Prisdang could not protect her or take care of the home, so he was considering returning the house to the king. Strangely, he notes, "From what I heard recently, the house has almost fallen apart, with such intimidation [of his wife by others] that no one dares to say anything even if it happens right in the bedroom." It is unclear who was harassing his wife, but he asked Surasak to take her in and show "deep mercy towards the suffering creatures," by which he meant his wife. NA KT 6.26/2, Prisdang to nong than, 3 November 1882.

11. Prisdang, *Prawat yo*, 64. Jao Phraya Surasakmontri (Joem Saeng-Chuto) had an arranged marriage when he was seventeen to a woman named Khit, but they split after two years because of different temperaments. He married again around 1882 to a woman named Lai, who died sometime between 1886 and 1887. He married again in about 1887 to Lai's younger sister, Liam. Lai and Liam were both granddaughters of Si Suriyawong. His son, Jao Phraya Surawongwaiwat (Won Bunnag), had sixty-five children, Lai and Liam being two of them.

12. Prisdang, "Confidential," 62–63.

13. Built during the reign of Rama I, Wang Tha Phra was given to Rama II's son, Prince Jetsabodin, who became Rama III. The palace housed the works of the Department of Artisans (Chang Sip Mu), a proto-public works and fine arts department run by Rama III's sons. First Prince Lakkhananukhun (Prince Chumsai's half brother) lived in Wang Tha Phra. After he died, Prince Chumsai, Prisdang's father, lived there and managed the Department of Artisans. At some point after he died it went to another of Prisdang's uncles, Prince Urai (Adulyalaksanasombat). In 1883 King Chulalongkorn bestowed the compound upon his half brother, Prince Naris (Narisranuwattiwong). For a history of the palace, see Nilwan Nildum, "The Architectural Heritage Management for Wang Tha Phra and Wang Thanon Na Phra Lan: From the Palaces of Builders and Craftsmen to the Art and Cultural Centre" (master's thesis, Silpakorn University, Bangkok, 2003), 10–12. Prisdang's former teacher at the Raffles Institution, Sir Robert Laurie Morant, moved into a house on the Wang Tha Phra compound between 1890 and 1894 while he tutored the crown prince, until 1894. Then it reverted to Prince Naris and remained in his family's hands until it became part of the Fine Arts Department. See Brailey, *Two Views of Siam*, 25. His descendants sold it to the government, which turned the compound into part of Silpakorn University. See cremation volume for Mom Rachawong Ying Thawi Lapha Puranasukhon (Chumsai) (Bangkok, 2528/1985), 21.

14. Phraya Rachamontri (Phu).

15. He borrowed the boat from Nai Sanphet, whose name is listed in a long letter from Prisdang to Prince Phanurangsi between May and August 1890, just as he was deciding to flee into exile. NA KT 6.26/2.

16. Perhaps as the youngest child of eight, Prisdang received no share in the inheritance and had no family home in which to live. It is unclear whether Prince Naris bought it or whether King Chulalongkorn reclaimed it from the Chumsais and gave it to Prince Naris. See Sumet, *Wang tha phra*, 47. For the confiscation of homes by the king, see Prisdang, *Prawat yo*, 64. Regarding inheritance, see Sumet Jumsai's comments in Ploenpote Atthakor, "Prisdang's Constitutional Dream," *Bangkok Post*, December 9, 2010, Outlook section. Ban Tha Chang at some point was purchased by Prince Naris.

17. Prince Prisdang to the Reverend Subhuti, 6 March 1887, Sri Lankan National Archives (SLNA) 5/63/17/707.

18. Order of King Chulalongkorn, cited in Phirasri, "'Ubatihet,'" 125n16. Phirasri found two documents in the archives—the bequeathal of Phumnithet and the letter from Rama V regarding the Jao Pan incident. These offered important keys to unlock the mystery of why Prisdang left in 1890.

19. NA R5 B 3/3, Prisdang to king, Bangkok, Monday [26?] September 1887. There is a crucial page (25) missing, which makes it difficult to precisely pin down some meanings.

20. It had been built for Mom Rachawong Lek Siriwong na Krungthep at the old palace of Prince Prasoetsak, Prisdang's cousin. Prince Prasoetsak (Phra Praphanthuwong Phra Ong Jao Prasoetsak) was the youngest son of Prisdang's uncle, Prince Matayaphithak. Matayaphithak was Prisdang's deceased uncle (his father's older brother), who had been the first husband of Mom Noi, Prisdang's mother.

21. This houseboat must have been different from the "picnic boat." It was loaned to him by Prince Chakraphan, who eventually demanded it back. Prisdang, *Prawat yo*, 64.

22. Ibid., 65.

23. Ibid. His total annual salary, including bonus and royal pension, was 5,600 Baht. If Prisdang's calculation that 15 baht was the approximate equivalent of 1 British pound, then he made 373 pounds per year.

24. According to Sumet, Phanurangsi's patronage smoothed out Prisdang's career. They had worked together on obtaining Siam's membership in the international telegraph association and postal union. Together they established Siam's Post and Telegraph Department in the mid-1880s. They also worked together as diplomats in Europe. Prisdang purchased items for Phanurangsi while Prisdang was in Europe. Sumet et al., "Phra ong jao prisdang," 12–13. On the history of the postal service in Siam, see Bonnie Davis, *Royal Siamese Postal Service (The Early Years)* (Bangkok: Siam Stamp Trading Co., 1983), 9, 11, 16.

25. Prisdang, *Prawat yo*, 66.

26. Ibid., 66–67.

27. My emphasis. *Phi ying* can mean an older female but more commonly is understood as older sister, even if, as in this case, she is not a blood relative. Prisdang means to signify a platonic but intimate relationship with an older female. Ibid., 66.

28. Bunphisit, "Samphanthaphap," 21.

29. NA R5 B 3/3, Prisdang to king; NA KT 6.26/2, Prisdang to Phanurangsi, May–August 1890.

30. The petition might have caused some bumps in his relationship with the king, but ultimately Prisdang claims that writing it was not a mistake but proof of his loyalty. From his review of the sources, Bunphisit argues that the Jao Pan incident was secondary and the rumors about Phi Si were primary. Bunphisit, "Samphanthaphap," 23–24, 26.

31. NA KT 6.26/2, Prisdang to Prince Phanurangsi, May–August 1890.

32. For a fuller explanation of these relationships, refer to Phirasri, "'Ubatihet.'" Mom Jao Sai was the daughter of a royal consort (Jaojom Manda Jin), born in about 1863, which means she was a daughter of Rama IV and therefore a half sister of King Chulalongkorn. She was the consort of Mom Jao Pan's father but was not Mom Jao Pan's mother.

33. Smith, *Physician in the Court of Siam*, 128.

34. Letter cited in Phirasri, "'Ubatihet,'" 127.

35. Ibid., 126.

36. The monthly salary cut was likely the pension of five chang and annual bonus of fifteen chang, not his salary of fifty chang received as director general of the Post and Telegraph Department. Ibid., 128.

37. Prisdang, *Prawat yo*, 64–65.

38. NA R5 B 3/3, Prisdang to the king, written Monday, fourth day of waxing moon 1249/either September or December 1887.

39. Trying to discover information about Si has been an object lesson in the gendered nature of history and document collection. Even female members of Siam's most powerful and famous Bunnag family are relatively undocumented and difficult to trace.

40. Surasak, *Prawatikan*, vol. 1. According to Surasak's memoirs, his older brother was alive in about 2425/26 (circa 1883), when the king appointed his brother to govern Suphanburi province and sent Surasak there to quash bandits raiding the area. Ibid., 1:163.

41. Prisdang sometimes referred to her as "Mae Si" or Mother Si.

42. The other members of the Young Siam Society were Prince Devawongse (president), Prince Thawiwong Thawalyaphan (Krommun Phuthawetdamrongsak), Jamuen Waiworanat (Joem Saeng Chuto), Jamuen Sisorarak (Mom Rachawong Lek Siriwong), Prince Svasti, Prisdang, and Nai Sanae Humphrae (But Phoenkul). The significance of these two associations diminished after the regent died in 1883 and the king began to exercise greater power. See Sumet et al., "Phra ong jao prisdang," 5.

43. Surasak, known as Luang Salayuthwithikan in 1871 and then as Jamuen Saraphai by about 1872, went with the king to Java and Singapore as well as to India. See Prayun Phitsanakha, *50 Jao phraya haeng ratanakosin* (Bangkok: Khlang Withaya Publications, 1962), 213.

44. Sumet et al., "Phra ong jao prisdang," 4n10.

45. Noel Alfred Battye, "The Military, Government and Society in Siam, 1868–1910: Politics and Military Reform during the Reign of King Chulalongkorn," (PhD diss., Cornell University, 1974), 221. On his military career, see ibid., 217–21. Surasak's memoirs express his undying loyalty and debt of gratitude to King Chulalongkorn. Surasak, *Prawatikan*.

46. In 1882, Prisdang's wife stayed with Surasak's sister at Sa Prathum, a palace in Bangkok, where Princess Sirinthon, daughter of King Bhumibol Adulyadej, resided as of 2016.

47. Prisdang, "Confidential," 56.

48. Battye, "Military, Government and Society," 223.

49. NA KT 6.26.2, Prisdang to Phanurangsi, May–August 1890.

50. Ibid.

51. Battye, "Military, Government and Society," 283–85.

52. NA KR 5 B 3.3, Prisdang to the king, written Monday, fourth day of waxing moon 1249/either September or December 1887, 6.

53. Ibid., 8.

54. Ibid., 9.

55. Ibid., 13. This is likely a reference to the king's inner circle of reform-minded supporters, many of whom were part of Young Siam and swore the oath of loyalty and brotherhood in 1881.

56. Ibid., 29.

57. Ibid., 35.

58. He uses the English term *rights*: "pen jao pen nai mi rai[t] yangdai." Ibid., 22–24.

59. NA KT 6.26.2, Prisdang to Phanurangsi, May–August, 1890. The letter noted that she should return to "serve the government," suggesting she had done so previously ("klap pai rap rachakan tamkhoei").

60. Ibid.

61. Ibid.

62. Ibid.

63. Ibid. Thanks to Ida Aroonwong and Chusak Pattarakulvanit for clarifying whose letters were exposed to the king.

64. Prisdang wrote, "The evil habits and customs of Siam and specially of the Court were discussed hotly in London when they [Princes Prisdang, Svasti, Naret, and Sonabandit] were together. . . . [But] Prince Sunabandit [*sic*] turned a spy and reported privately all conversations to the King." See Prisdang, "Confidential," 71–72.

65. NA KT 6.26.2, Prisdang to Phanurangsi, May–August, 1890.

66. The cause of her indebtedness is confusing. In the 1890 letter, Prisdang says that Si owed money to Phraya Suphan. Si asked the king for money to pay off this debt, and the king ordered Jao Phraya Rattanabodin to stop the debt collector. Devawongse sent a letter to Phi Si to inform her of this, but Surasak took the letter and the order from her. For more on Rattanabodin, see Nathawut Suthisongkram, *29 Jao phraya* (Bangkok, 2509/1966), 226–345.

67. NA KT 6.26.2, Prisdang to Phanurangsi, May–August, 1890.

68. Ibid.

69. See Wyatt, *The Politics of Reform*, 92–93nn14, 16.

70. Maryvelma O'Neil, *Bangkok: A Cultural History* (New York: Oxford University Press, 2008), 179–80.

71. His surveying work would serve him well in this position, but it is unclear who ended up serving as director. "Proposed Railway in Siam," *Straits Times Weekly Issue*, September 30, 1889, 10.

72. NA KT 6.26.2, Prisdang to Phanurangsi, May–August 1890.

73. Ibid.

74. This is a reference to the front palace king who attempted to overthrow King Chulalongkorn in 1874 and failing that, sought refuge in the British consulate.

75. NA KT 6.26.2, Prisdang to Phanurangsi, May–August 1890.

76. Ibid.

77. Ibid.

78. Prisdang, "Confidential," 69.

79. NA KT 6.26.2, Prisdang to Phanurangsi, May–August 1890.

80. NA R5 B 3/6, Phra Phitsanuthep to Phraya Maha Ammattayathibadi, 16 December R.S. 109 [1890].

81. *Koen kwa het.*

82. NA KT 6.26.2, Prisdang to Phanurangsi, May–August 1890.

83. Ibid.

84. NA KT 6.26/2, Prisdang to Phra Satja, 13 December 1890.

85. Bunphisit, "Samphanthaphap," 22.

86. NA KT 6.26.2, Prisdang to Phanurangsi, May–August 1890.

87. NA R5 B 3/4, Prisdang to Phanurangsi, 3 September 109/1890.

88. Battye, "Military, Government and Society," 223.

89. NA KR5 B 3/4, Prisdang to Phanurangsi, 3 September 109/1890.

90. NA KT 6.26.2, Prisdang to Phanurangsi, May–August 1890.

91. "Passengers: Arrived," *Hong Kong Daily Press*, September 10, 1890.

92. NA KR5 B 3/4, Prisdang to Phanurangsi, 3 September 109/1890.

93. NA KT 6.26.2, Prisdang to Phanurangsi, May–August 1890.

94. "Hongkong Hotel," *Hong Kong Daily Press*, September 25, 1890; "Passengers Departed," *Hong Kong Daily Press*, September 26, 1890.

95. Bunphisit, "Samphanthaphap," 24. A handwritten scribble on the back of the letters' envelope notes that they were handed to Phanurangsi the night before the ship left Hong Kong.

96. NA R5 B 3/5, Prisdang to Phanurangsi, 25 September 1890.

97. This is the Thai rather than the English portion of the telegram, which makes clearer sense. NA R5 B 3/6, telegram from Prisdang to Devawongse, 28 September 1890.

98. NA R5 B 3/6, telegram from Prince Prisdang to Devawongse, 10 October 1890.

99. Prisdang, "Confidential," 59.

100. This phrase, "thi non khong khao ronluekoen," comes from NA KT 6.26/2. Draft response by Prince Devawongse to A. D. Neubronner, Siam's consul in Penang, 11 August

1896. For a review of all the authors who have weighed in on the reasons for Prisdang's exile, see Bunphisit, "Samphanthaphap," and Phirasri, "'Ubatihet.'"

101. Prisdang, *Prawat yo*, 69–70.

5. COLONIAL SOUTHEAST ASIA

1. Prisdang, *Prawat yo*, 142.

2. Ibid., 82.

3. According to foreign observers at the time, this amounted to two thousand pounds, which was approximately Prisdang's annual salary when he worked in London as minister plenipotentiary.

4. "Envoy" is a closer translation, but this seems to refer to a number of people rather than a single individual.

5. NA R5 B 3/6, letter number 48, "Bok thi muang champasak" (dictated at Champasak), 16 December 109 [1890].

6. The letter upon which this one was based was a bit more specific. It claimed that Prisdang was obsessed with a specific actress named Copsey; see NA KT 6.26/2, letter from Phraya Sisinghathep, the minister of the interior, to the governor of Champasak. There is little evidence other than this about Prisdang's involvement with foreign women. He mentions an accusation of this sort in one sentence of his long 1890 letter to Phanurangsi explaining his resignation. "It's like the case of this 'farang' woman. I understood that what I did was good, appropriate, and honorable, but they had turned it into something devious that brought shame to me. Consequently, I was no longer trusted to be a royal ambassador. But when I learned about the conduct of the commissioner or the ambassador who replaced me, I stop grieving because I then realized that it's just the *karma* of mine and has nothing to do with my conduct." NA R5 B 3/4. An otherwise unrelated document in the British Public Records Office mentions a male valet named Copsey who worked for Prisdang in Paris who "had a sister, Emily, more beauteous than virtuous." In 1894, she had been spotted by the British with a M. Mass, "a French resident of sorts" in Cochin China. Copsey was suspected of having changed his name to Stivens, "a Cockney for Chiengmai, representing Leon Owens corsucation." The British memo warned, "The whole show is not only rotten but I believe it to be even criminally and dangerously so.... An ex-valet whose sister is *fille entretenue* [kept woman] of a French political officer in Cochin China seems to my mind rather out of place in Chiengmai." J. H. Merrifield to Col. H. R. Spearman, 19 October 1894, TNA: PRO, FO 628/16/224.

7. NA KT 6.26/2, Prisdang to Phra Satja, 13 December 1890.

8. NA KT 6.26/2, Prisdang (in English) to Your Royal Highness [Prince Phanurangsi?], 23 October 1890. The letter may, alternatively, been to Prince Devawongse.

9. NA KT 6.26/2, Prisdang to Phra Satja, 13 December 1890. This may have been a room rented from a Madame Alhi.

10. Ibid.

11. Thongchai Winichakul, *Siam Mapped: A History of the Geo-Body of a Nation* (Honolulu: University of Hawai'i Press, 1994); Auguste Pavie, *Pavie Mission Indochina Papers, 1879–1895,* trans. Walter E. J. Tips, vol. 1 (Bangkok: White Lotus Press, 1999).

12. Pavie, *Pavie Mission,* 1:436.

13. NA R5 B 3/6, Phraya Singhathep to Prince Sommut Amonphan and related enclosures, 24 December 109 [1890].

14. Penny Edwards, "Watching the Detectives: The Elusive Exile of Prince Myingoon of Burma," in *Exile in Colonial Asia: Kings, Convicts, Commemoration,* ed. Ronit Ricci (Honolulu: University of Hawai'i Press, 2016), 248–78.

15. NA R5 B 3/6, Phraya Singhathep to Prince Sommut Amonphan, 24 December 109 [1890].

16. Pavie, *Pavie Mission*, 1:441. Pavie reports that he left Saigon for Bangkok by steamer on 24 October and he left Saigon for Tonkin on November 22, which roughly corresponds to the dates given in the Siamese documents.

17. France required Siam to hire Frenchmen to work on the telegraphic line before it would sign conventions regarding spirits. Manich, *Prince Prisdang Files*, 62.

18. André Masson, Preface to Pavie, *Pavie Mission*, 1:9–10.

19. Handwritten on envelope by an unknown author in NA R5 B 3/6, Phraya Singhathep to Prince Sommut Amonphan, 24 December 109 [1890].

20. NA KT 6.26/2, Prisdang to Phra Satja, 13 December 1890.

21. Prisdang to Subhuti, 4 December 1890, SLNA 5/63/17/708. See also Ananda W.P. Gurugé, *From the Living Fountains of Buddhism* (Colombo, Sri Lanka: Government Printing Office, 1984).

22. Prisdang to Subhuti, 7 December 1890, SLNA 5/63/17/709.

23. NA KT 6.26/2, Prisdang to Phra Satja, 13 December 1890. I have not figured out who Phra Satja was or the precise nature of act he committed that made him decide to live in exile. Neubronner, the consul for Siam in Penang, refers to him as Lek Suriwongse, which might have been an incorrect reference to Mom Rachawong Lek Siriwong na Krungthep, who was a step-nephew of Prisdang. Born Mom Rachawong Lek Siriwong na Krungthep in about 1855, he lived a long life, not passing away until 1922. He was the grandson of Mom Noi, Prisdang's mother. Mom Noi originally was married to Prince Siriwong Kromamuen Matayaphithak. One of their sons was Phra Ong Jao Prasoetsak, who in turn was the father of Mom Rachawong Lek Siriwong. He rose in the military ranks to become Jamuen Sisorarak and became Surasak's (then known as Jamuen Waiworanat) assistant in the king's First Foot Guard. Jamuen Sisorarak (Lek Siriwong) was on duty when a madman fired shots into the camp, and he was blamed for carelessness on duty. For this, the king had him imprisoned in 1884. See Kullada, *Rise and Decline*, 99–100; and *Banyat chadok prachumnithan nai prathet ni tae boran 50 ruang phak thi 1* [Jataka Wisdom: Ancient Collected Tales from this Country], cremation volume for Mom Rachawong Lek Siriwong na Krungthep (Bangkok, 2467/ [1924?]), 6–10.

24. Prisdang, "Confidential," in Brailey, *Two Views of Siam*, 59.

25. Handwritten on envelope by an unknown author in NA R5 B 3/6, Phraya Singhathep to Prince Sommut Amonphan, 24 December 109 [1890].

26. The letters can be found in NA KT 6.26/2 and NA R5 3/6, which contain many of the same documents. NA R5 B 3/6, Phraya Singhathep to Prince Sommut Amonphan, 24 December 109 [1890]. For the rumor about Si sleeping with her husband's corpse, see NA KT 6/26/2, Phraya Sisinghathep, 3 November 1890.

27. NA R5 B 3/6, Phra Phitsanuthep to Phraya Maha Ammattahayathibodi, dictated 16 December 1890.

28. There is no signature for this handwritten note, but it is in NA R5 B 3/6, Phraya Sisinghathep to Prince Sommut Amonphan 24 December 109 [1890].

29. NA KT 6.26/2, Prisdang to Phra Satja, 13 December 1890.

30. NA R5 B 3/6, Neubronner to Prince Devawongse, 11 June 1891.

31. Brailey notes that "Phra Satcha [*sic*]" was a senior official in the Post and Telegraph Department up to 1890 who had worked in Peninsular Siam. Brailey, *Two Views of Siam*, 132–33n37. He no doubt extrapolated this from the Siamese documents about Phra Satja that exist in the archives. NA KT 6.26/2, Prisdang to Phra Satja, 13 December 1890. Confidential letters between Neubronner and Devawongse written in June 1891 mention Phra Satja but do not explain the reasons for his initial fall from grace. NA R5 B 3/6.

32. NA KT 6.26/2, Si to Phra Satja, 12 December 1890.

33. He said he had received three letters from Prisdang and one from Si. NA KT 6.26/2, Phra Satja Phirom to Prince Devawongse, 18 November 109 [1890].

34. Written in English.

35. This is likely a reference to Prince Bidyalabh (Sonabandit), who Prisdang claims acted as the king's spy in London and secretly reported the content of their conversations to the king. Prisdang, "Confidential," 71–72.

36. The English term was transliterated into Thai.

37. This is presumably a reference to the incident regarding Prisdang's attempt to hire Mom Jao Pan out from under Prince Svasti.

38. Here Prisdang claims that the king stopped paying his entire salary, but in chapter 3, the translation suggests it was only a portion of his salary—that given by the king to his royal kin.

39. NA KT 6.26/2, Prisdang to Phra Satja, 13 December 1890.

40. Ibid.

41. Ibid.

42. Ibid.

43. NA R5 B 3/6, Phraya Ammat from [illegible, name cut off], 31 May 1891.

44. NA R5 B 3/6, King Chulalongkorn to Phraya Maha Amat, 2 June 110 [1891].

45. Prisdang to Subhuti, 23 February 1891, SLNA 5/63/17/713.

46. Prisdang to Subhuti, 25 May 1891, SLNA 5/63/17/714.

47. NA KT 6.26/2, Frankfurter to Prince Devawongse, 4 August 1891. "Ruen is perhaps the younger royal sister."

48. Phraya Phuket came from a long line of Phuket governors who originally came from Madras, India, before trading in Siam and intermarrying with local women.

49. NA KT 6.26/2, A. D. Neubronner to Prince Devawongse, 1 August 1891.

50. "Siam News" [from the *Bangkok Times*, quoted in] *Singapore Free Press and Mercantile Advertiser*, 7 September 1891, 3.

51. NA R5 B 3/6, confidential letter from A.D. Neubronner [who used his Siamese title, Luang Thawip Siamkit] to Prince Devawongse, 11 June 1891.

52. NA R5 B 3/6, Sayamint (King Chulalongkorn) to Phraya Naithora (illegible), 25 June 110 [1891]. The king thought the governor of Trang was likely trustworthy, but because of Trang's relationship to Phuket, he didn't think it wise to send an order to Trang. The king worried that sending the order about having passports even to Songkhla and Saiburi might alert Prisdang and Satja that the Siamese government was aware of what they were doing.

53. NA R5 B 3/6, R. L. Morant to Prince Devawongse, 27 July 1891(emphasis in original).

54. NA R5 B 3/6, draft to consul in Penang from Prince Devawongse, 10 August 1891.

55. Prisdang, *Prawat yo*, 83.

56. Likely a reference to subjects, or the people.

57. Frank Swettenham to Sir Philip, "Private," 29 July 1891, *Selections of Papers Reflecting the Affairs of Siam, Part I, 1887–1892, Confidential* (London: August 1893), no. 33, pp. 30–31, cited in Brailey, *Two Views of Siam*, 81–82.

58. Brailey, *Two Views of Siam*, 26. It is unclear what was done with the memo after it was sent from Perak in July 1891 and personally delivered in 1892, but it appears to have made the rounds only after July 1892, when it provoked a vigorous response by British officials in Bangkok who discredited Prisdang and anything he might have to say about Siam. One would assume they were fed information about Prisdang from the minister of foreign affairs, Prince Devawongse, but this cannot be confirmed.

59. Sir Frank Swettenham, *Footprints in Malaya* (London: Hutchinson & Co., 1942), 100.

60. The king asked Prince Devawongse if Siam could protest against this by appealing to the importance of maintaining friendly relations. NA KT 6.26/2, Sayamint (King Chulalongkorn) to Prince Devawongse, 12 August 110 [1891].

61. They are both cited in an article about the transference of the territories to British Malaya in "New Territories," *Straits Times* (Singpaore), January 3, 1914, 10.

62. NA KT 6.26/2, Devawongse to King Chulalongkorn, 16 August 110 [1891].

63. NA KT 6.26/2, Phraya Akkharasena to the governor of Songkhla, August 110 [1891].

64. This series of letters dates from 24 February 110 [1891] to June 1892 and can be found in NA R5 B 3/6.

65. NA R5 B 3/6, handwritten note from King Chulalongkorn on the letter from Phraya Montri Suriyawongse to Prince Somom Amonphan (the king's secretary), 28 April 111 [1892]. It refers to Phra Worawongthoe.

66. Prisdang, "Confidential," 64–65.

67. Ibid., 71.

68. The letters, if they still exist, have not been made public.

69. Prisdang, "Confidential," 53.

70. Ibid., 75.

71. Ibid., 76–77.

72. Ibid., 50.

73. Smith, *Physician in the Court of Siam*, 99 (emphasis added).

74. Prisdang, "Confidential," 54–55.

75. This is according to Smith, *Physician in the Court of Siam*, 86. Under Chulalongkorn, Siam's revenue increased from 8,000,000 ticals in 1868 to 63,000,000 in 1910 (about 12,000,000 pounds). The Bunnag, for example, lost control of the Kalahom in 1886 after heading that lucrative ministry for over one hundred years, and they lost control of the Phrakhlang in 1885, after having run it more or less from 1822 to 1885. These were two of the three most powerful ministries that controlled the administration of the southern and western provinces, foreign trade and foreign affairs, and the gulf provinces. See Wyatt, "Family Politics," 119.

76. Brailey, *Two Views of Siam*, ix and 17.

77. Prisdang, "Confidential," 53.

78. Ibid., 49–50.

79. Ibid., 73.

80. Ibid., 53.

81. Ibid., 70.

82. Ibid.

83. Ibid., 58.

84. Ibid., 59.

85. Smith, *Physician in the Court of Siam*, 33. He was referring to the role of rank under Rama IV, but it continued to apply in King Chulalongkorn's reign.

86. Kullada argues that the king did not want to outright repress a prince for fear other elites might organize opposition, so instead he singled out key critics. He persecuted commoners like Thianwan, who was imprisoned for seventeen years. Kullada, *Rise and Decline*, 110.

87. Prisdang to Subhuti, 7 September 1891, SLNA 5/63/17/715.

88. "Diaries of Anagarika Dharmapala," entry for 5 November 1897, SLNA, microfilm 1944.

89. Memo by E. H. French, 1892, TNA: PRO, FO 628/15/209; and Captain H. M. Jones to Lord Salisbury, 24 August 1892, 1–10, TNA: PRO, FO 69/146.

90. E. H. French memo, 1892, TNA: PRO, FO 628/15/209.

91. Captain H. M. Jones to Lord Salisbury, 24 August 1892, TNA: PRO, FO 69/146. Jones had been appointed as Great Britain's minister resident and consul general to Siam in December 1888.

92. This is the Latin (and Italian) masculine term for Asian, but in this context may derogatorily refer to a stereotype of the corrupt Oriental.

93. Memo from Frank Swettenham to Sir Thomas Sanderson, 17 April 1893, TNA: PRO, FO 628/15/215, cited in Brailey, *Two Views of Siam*, 83–84.

94. Ibid., 84.

95. Brailey, *Two Views of Siam*, 21.

96. E. H. French memo, 1892, TNA: PRO, FO 628/15/209; Captain H. M. Jones to Lord Salisbury, 24 August 1892, TNA: PRO, FO 69/146.

97. For an eyewitness account, see H. Warrington Smyth, *Five Years in Siam, From 1891–1896* (1898; repr., Bangkok: White Lotus, 1994), 1:255–76. For a critical history of the Paknam incident and its import to Siam, see Thongchai, *Siam Mapped*, 141–63.

98. Brailey, *Two Views of Siam*, 21–22; 120n45. Archibald Philip Primrose, or Lord Rosebery, was the fifth Earl of Rosebery.

99. Scott dispatch to Rosebery, 28 November 1893, TNA: PRO, FO 17/1187, cited in Brailey, *Two Views of Siam*, 125n88.

100. Brailey, *Two Views of Siam*, 37.

101. NA R5 B 3/6, Prisdang to Jaokhun Thiphakosa, 20 June 1894.

102. NA R5 B 3/6, telegram from Phya Thipkosa in Penang to Prince Bidyalaph, Bangkok, 1 July 1894.

103. NA R5 B 3/6, Devawongse to Phraya Thipkosa, 2 July 113 [1894].

104. NA R5 B 3/6, Prince Devawongse to Prince Sommot Omphan, 2 July 113 [1894].

105. NA R5 B 3/6, King to Prince Sommot Amphan, no date.

106. Prisdang to Subhuti, 7 September 1891, SLNA 5/63/17/715.

107. NA R5 B 3/7, Devawongse to Neubronner, November 1896 (day unspecified).

108. "Notes from London," *Western Argus*, January 21, 1897, 5.

109. NA R5 3/7, Sommot (king's secretary) to Devawongse, 13/15 December 1896.

110. NA KT 6.26/2, Prisdang to King Chulalongkorn, 19 October 1896.

111. NA R5 B 3/7, Prisdang to King Chulalongkorn, 17 October 1896.

112. NA R5 B 3/7, Prince Devawongse to King Chulalongkorn, 5 November 1896.

113. Prisdang, *Prawat yo*, 82.

6. BRITISH CEYLON AND INDIA

1. NA R5 B 3/7, Devawongse to King Chulalongkorn, 5 November 1896.

2. O. M. Obesekera reported that Prisdang obtained an eight-month leave to be ordained, and that after eight months he would apply for an extension. NA R5 B 3/8, Obeyesekera to Prince Devawongse, 26 November 1896.

3. Subhuti had been in communication with King Chulalongkorn, through his various ministers, since at least 1877. Phya Phipat Kosa, undersecretary for foreign affairs, to W. [V.] Subhuti, 9 October 1877, SLNA 5/63/171 [final accession number not clear]. There are multiple letters between Prince Phanurangsi and V. Subhuti in the SLNA files 5/63/17. For example, Subhuti to Bhanurangsi [Phanurangsi], 23 November 1885, SLNA 5/63/17/5.

4. Anne Blackburn, *Locations of Buddhism: Colonialism and Modernity in Sri Lanka* (Chicago: University of Chicago Press, 2010), 171n42.

5. Prince Phanurangsi to V. Subhuti, 9 July 1886, SLNA 5/63/175/704. They were denied because of the "inability to procure the proper authority from the [British

colonial] Govnt to show the Relic." This must have caused some distress in the relations between Subhuti and the princes because Phanurangsi's letter assures Subhuti that he had shown the priest's letter to the princes and "they join in exonerating you from all blame."

6. The largest sect, in terms of the number of monks, was not the Amarapura but the Siyam Nikaya, according to Arnold Wright, *Twentieth Century Impressions of British Ceylon* (London: Lloyd's Greater Britain Publishing Co., 1907), 292.

7. NA R5 B 3/7, Prince Devawongse to King Chulalongkorn, 5 November 1896. The letter includes the article. It was published in the *Bangkok Times*, which received the story from the *Pinang Gazette*. No date given, but he says it was printed "today," which was 5 November 1896.

8. NA R5 B 3/8, Obeyesekera to Prince Devawongse, 26 November 1896.

9. Ibid. (including copies of newspaper articles). Obeyesekera wrote as a way to apologize for unwittingly welcoming Prisdang, whose poor relationship with the king was unknown to him. The incident demonstrated, in Obeyesekera's mind, the dire need for a Siamese consul in Lanka, a position that he humbly offered to fill.

10. "A Siamese Prince to Become a Buddhist Monk," *Overland Ceylon Observer*, October 29, 1896, 1210.

11. This temple was later renamed the Sri Subhuti Viharaya Temple.

12. NA R5 B 3/8, Obeyesekera to Prince Devawongse, 26 November 1896. On his desire to keep the ceremony quiet, see also "A Siamese Prince to Become a Buddhist Monk," 1210.

13. J. E. R. P., "Once a Prince, Now a Priest," *Ceylon Independent*, November 11, 1896. A handwritten copy of the article was included in NA R5 B 3/8, Obeyesekera to Prince Devawongse, 26 November 1896.

14. Ibid.

15. "The Ordination of a Siamese Prince as a Buddhist Priest," newspaper not cited, transcribed and enclosed in NA R5 B 3/8, Obeyesekera to Prince Devawongse, 26 November 1896.

16. NA R5 B 3/8, Obeyesekera to Prince Devawongse, 26 November 1896.

17. J. E. R. P., "Once a Prince, Now a Priest."

18. "The Ordination of a Siamese Prince as a Buddhist Priest."

19. Prisdang's hair is located in a gilded box behind a glass case in a small museum dedicated to the Venerable Subhuti and Jinawarawansa at the Waskaduwa temple outside Colombo.

20. J. E. R. P., "Once a Prince, Now a Priest."

21. Jinawon is Sanskrit for the Buddha. In English documentation, his priest name is rendered Jinavaransa, Jinawarawansa, Jinavaravangsa, Jinawarawamsa, and Chinaworawansa. The Thai is transliterated as Chinaworawong. Except when citing Thai sources, I use Prisdang's spelling, which he used to sign (in Roman script) his letters: Jinawarawansa.

22. NA R5 B 3/8, Chinaworawong [Prisdang] to King Chulalongkorn, 25 November 115 [1896.

23. NA R5 B 3/8, Obeyesekera to Prince Devawongse, 26 November 1896.

24. NA R5 B 3/7, H. S. Perera to the private secretary of the King of Siam, 7 November 1896. H. S. Perera may well have been related to Edward Perera, the man that some of the highest-ranking priests of the Siyam Nikaya, the sect most closely affiliated with Siamese royalty, wanted to have appointed as consul.

25. Ibid.

26. Blackburn, *Locations of Buddhism*, 162n27. His law firm was called Clark, Young and Company. Wright, *Twentieth Century Impressions*, 138.

27. NA R5 B 3/8, High Priest Subhuti to king of Siam, 8 December 1896.

28. Ibid.

29. Subhuti refers to Prisdang's ordination and sends pictures of Prisdang, a copy of a speech by Prisdang, and a biography of him to Henry Clarke Warren, a reclusive Sanskritist living in Boston. See letters from Subhuti to H. C. Warren, 14 January 1897 and 18 March 1897, SLNA 5/63/17/281.

30. In addition, the British government gave control over large amounts of monastic lands to the incumbents of temples, leading to the control of wealth by some monks who no longer obeyed a single monastic authority. Steven Kemper, *Rescued from the Nation: Anagarika Dharmapala and the Buddhist World* (Chicago: University of Chicago Press, 2015), 97. My summary of this moment in the history of Sri Lankan Buddhism is based on two excellent sources: Kitsiri Malalgoda's thorough and clarifying *Buddhism in Sinhalese Society, 1750–1900: A Study of Religious Revival and Change* (Berkeley: University of California Press, 1976), and Blackburn, *Locations of Buddhism*.

31. K. D. Paranavitana, "Scholar Monks of the Nineteenth Century and the Tragic Transformation of the High Priest Ven. Kapugama Dhammakkhanda Thero," *Journal of the Royal Asiatic Society* (Sri Lanka), n.s., 28 (1983–84): 134.

32. Malalgoda, *Buddhism in Sinhalese Society*, 92–98.

33. Ibid., 98.

34. Interview with Venerable Waskaduwe Mahindawansa Maha Nayaka Thero, 4 June 2015, at Dipaduttamarama Temple, Kotahena, Colombo. Krishantha Fedricks translated.

35. "Buddhism in Ceylon: The 'Princely Monk' Explains the Protection Desired from the King of Siam: The Prince-Monk Opposed, like Buddha, to All Caste," *Overland Ceylon Observer*, April 7 1897, 424.

36. Blackburn, *Locations of Buddhism*, 125.

37. Ibid., 168.

38. Ibid., 141. Sumangala was considered by the British to be the spokesperson for Buddhists in Lanka. Ibid., xi.

39. NA R5 B 3/9, Lankan priests to King Chulalongkorn, 16 March 1897.

40. Nine of the fourteen Lankan monks were the chief priests W. Sumangala, Wilikanda Kosdoga; Buddharakkita, Kelaniya Temple; H. Sumangala, Maligakanda, Colombo; Sri Sumangala, Panadura; W. Subhuti, Waskaduwa, Kalutara; Silakkandabhidhana, Ramanna Nikaya, Malwatte, Galle; Sumanathissa, Kalutara; Dhammarama, Kelaniya; and U.A. Nanatilaka, Walitara "for the united sects and strangers." See also Blackburn, *Locations of Buddhism*, 169n35, who adds Tibbatuvave and Kapiliade of Kandy.

41. NA R5 B 3/9, unsigned letter (last page missing) to Sumangala, 16 March 1897. There were several "Sumangalas," but only Hikkaduve was head of the Siamese Nikaya. In addition, the biographer of Hikkaduve, Anne Blackburn, concurs that the signature of the letter is that of H. Sumangala. Personal e-mail correspondence, 5 September 2014.

42. The Venerable Mahindawansa frequently used the Sinhalese term *tada*, or "hard," to refer to Jinawarawansa. "Law and order were important to him. He was strict about how money was spent. If, for example, ten Lankan rupees were donated for the construction of a temple, the funds could only be used for its construction." In other words, Jinawarawansa was known for his uncompromising character and incorruptibility. Interview with Mahindawansa. Thanks also to Professor Anne Blackburn for explaining the full range of meanings associated with tada—from hard, obdurate, and resolute to excessive, vehement, severe, harsh, and even strong or great. Personal communication, e-mail 24 June 2015.

43. Henry Steel Olcott, *Old Diary Leaves: The Only Authentic History of the Theosophical Society*, 6th ser. (1896–98; repr., Adyar, India: Theosophical Publishing House, 1935), 155–56.

44. Ibid., 156.

45. Diaries of Anagarika Dharmapala, entries for 28 October 1897, 29 October 1897, and 1 November 1897, respectively, SLNA microfilm 1944.

46. This can also be found in NA KT 6.26/2, Prince Prisdang, "Religious Manifesto," 25 March 1897 (not paginated). This version has nineteen points plus a "scheme."

47. NA R5 B 3/9, Jinawarawansa et al. to King Culalankarana [Chulalongkorn], 16 March 1897. Also printed in the *Ceylon Observer*, March 24, 1897, cited in full in Blackburn, *Locations of Buddhism*, 169.

48. Jinawarawansa, "A Religious Manifesto by the Buddhist Prince Priest," *Ceylon Observer*, April 3, 1897); NA KT 6.26/2, "Religious Unity of Ceylon with Siam," nos. 7, 8, 9, 13.

49. Jinawarawansa, "A Religious Manifesto" (emphasis in original). This is also cited in Blackburn, *Locations of Buddhism*, 173–74.

50. NA KT 6.26/2, "Private: Circular" by P. C. Jinavaravanse [*sic*], dated 23 March 1897 and stamped by the Ministry of Foreign Affairs, 11 April 116 [1897].

51. Ibid.

52. "Current Topics," *Overland Ceylon Observer*, April 29, 1897, 523.

53. "Buddhists and Roman Catholics," *Overland Ceylon Observer*, April 3, 1897, 410.

54. "Buddhism in Ceylon," 424.

55. Unless otherwise noted, the description of the king's arrival comes from "Arrival of the King of Siam at Colombo," *Ceylon Observer*, April 21, 1897. Anne Blackburn graciously shared copies of the articles from the *Ceylon Observer*.

56. "Paras from Our Contemporaries," *Overland Ceylon Observer*, December 30, 1897.

57. Olcott takes credit for drafting the letter to the king, which he did in consultation with Jinawarawansa and two Siamese sent in advance of the royal entourage to arrange the details of the royal visit. For a full account of the letter presented to the king, see Olcott, *Old Diary Leaves*, 158–62.

58. "Address of the Buddhist Priests to the King of Siam," *Overland Ceylon Observer*, April 19, 1897, 481–82.

59. Blackburn, *Locations of Buddhism*, 175.

60. "Arrival of the King of Siam at Colombo."

61. Blackburn, *Locations of Buddhism*, 187.

62. "King of Siam's Visit to Kandy," *Overland Ceylon Observer*, April 21, 1897, 482.

63. Maurizio Peleggi, *Lords of Things: The Fashioning of the Siamese Monarchy's Modern Image* (Honolulu: University of Hawai'i Press, 2002), 38.

64. "The King of Siam at Kandy," *Overland Ceylon Observer*, April 22, 1897, 496.

65. "Meeting of the Buddhists," *Overland Ceylon Observer*, May 3, 1897, 537 (emphasis in original).

66. "King of Siam and the Temple Authorities at Kandy," *Overland Ceylon Observer*, April 23, 1897, 499.

67. Olcott, *Old Diary Leaves*, 166–67.

68. "The King of Siam at Kandy," 496.

69. Ibid.

70. "The Arrival of the King of Siam," *Overland Ceylon Observer*, November 29, 1897, 1497.

71. "Current Topics," 523.

72. "The King of Siam and the Buddhist Authorities in Kandy," *Overland Ceylon Observer*, April 26, 1897, 506.

73. Olcott, *Old Diary Leaves*, 164–66. Emile Jottrand wrote in his diary that Rolin-Jaequemyns, Siam's chief legal adviser to the king, heard from the king that he had feigned devotion to the relic in order to get close enough to it to denounce it as a fake and to expose the Lankan priests as impostors. Mr. and Mrs. Emile Jottrand, *In Siam*, trans. Walter E. J. Tips (Bangkok: White Lotus, 1996), 364, cited in Peleggi, *Lords of Things*, 38–39.

74. Aleister Crowley, *The Confessions of Aleister Crowley: An Autohagiography* (New York: Hill and Wang, 1969), 250. Crowley thought the tooth to be that of a dog or crocodile but not that of a human.

75. "Meeting of the Buddhists," 537.

76. Blackburn, *Locations of Buddhism*, 183.

77. Olcott, *Old Diary Leaves*, 169–70.

78. Blackburn, *Locations of Buddhism*, 183–184.

79. Diaries of Anagarika Dharmapala, entry for 5 November 1897, SLNA microfilm 1944.

80. Olcott, *Old Diary Leaves*, 171.

81. Ibid., 314–15.

82. Prisdang, *Prawat yo*, 70.

83. Several letters in the Bangkok archives confirm that it was understood by Siamese authorities that the king had agreed to allow Jinawarawansa, who is sometimes referred to as Prisdang in the Thai documents, in his status as a monk to return to Siam. See for example, NA R5 3/8, Prisdang to Prince Sommot Amonphan, 14 December 1897; and NA R5 3/8, Prince Sommot Amonphan to Prisdang, 10 January 116 [1898].

84. Letter from Jinawarawansa to W.C. Peppé, 9 April 1898, courtesy of Chris Peppé.

85. NA R5 3/8, Prisdang to Prince Sommot Amonphan, 14 December 1897.

86. NA R5 3/8, Prisdang to Prince Sommot Amonphan, 18 December 1897.

87. NA R5 3/8, Sommot Amonphan to Prisdang, 10 January 116 [1898].

88. NA R5 3/8, Prisdang to Prince Sommot Amonphan, 25 February 1898.

89. Blackburn's description of Anagarika Dharmapala, born Don David Hevavitarna, applies equally well to Jinawarawansa. Blackburn, *Locations of Buddhism*, 104.

90. Diaries of Anagarika Dharmapala, entries for 14, 17, and 18 December 1897, SLNA microfilm 1944.

91. Ibid., entry for 1 February, 1898.

92. See Kemper, *Rescued from the Nation*, 98.

93. Jinawarawansa, "An Open Letter," 28 December 1897, *The Theosophist* 19, no. 5 (February 1898): 292.

94. Lumbini has been declared a UNESCO World Heritage Site, but one scholar continues to contest it as fraudulent. See "Lumbini on Trial: The Untold Story," http://www.lumkap.org.uk/Lumbini%20On%20Trial.htm. See also "World Heritage Site: Lumbini," http://www.worldheritagesite.org/sites/lumbini.html.

95. Charles Allen has reconstructed a precise timeline of the disinterring of the relics to prove that there was no way that they were faked by Dr. Führer. See Charles Allen, "What Happened at Piprahwa: A Chronology of Events Related to the Excavation in January 1898 of the Piprahwa Stupa in Basti District, North-Western Provinces and Oude (Uttar Pradesh), India, and the Associated 'Piprahwa Inscritpion,' Based on Newly Available Correspondence," *Zeitschrift für Indologie und Südasienstudien* 29 (2012): 1–19. See also the website created by Peppé's descendants: www.piprahwa.com.

96. Copies of several of these photos of poor quality exist in Bangkok's National Archives as well, replete with Sinhalese titles explaining who Prisdang was.

97. Charles Allen, *The Buddha and Dr. Führer: An Archaeological Scandal* (London: Haus Publishing, 2008), 203.

98. Peppé to Subhuti, 14 May 1898, SLNA 5/63/17/57; 16 September 1898, SLNA 5/63/17/59; Vincent Smith to Subhuti, 17 April 1898, SLNA 5/63/17/137.

99. Peppé to Subhuti, 14 May 1898, SLNA 5/63/17/57.

100. Jinawarawansa's letter to Vincent Smith explains that he copied the inscription from the vase found at Piprahwa and sent it to Subhuti along with the transliteration and translation of the inscription that the British had. Subhuti would compare the two. Letter from Jinawaransa to V.A. Smith, 9 April 1898, courtesy of Chris Peppé.

101. Letter from Jinawarawansa to Peppé, 9 April 1898, courtesy of Chris Peppé.

102. Ibid.

103. My summary of Prisdang's activities in India on behalf of the relics comes from Allen, "The Prince-Priest: Gorakhpur Division, 1898," in *The Buddha and Dr. Führer*, 201–34.

104. See Blackburn, *Locations of Buddhism*, for a discussion of his role in Sinhalese and regional Buddhist politics, and for his changing relationship with Olcott and the Theosophical Society, esp. chapter 4.

105. Andrew Huxley, "Mr. Houghton and Dr. Führer: A Scholarly Vendetta and Its Consequences," *South East Asia Research* 19, no. 1 (March 2011): 59–82.

106. For a full discussion of the history of this scandal, see Allen, *The Buddha and Dr. Führer*, and the PBS special narrated by Allen, "The Bones of the Buddha," July 13, 2013, http://www.pbs.org/wnet/secrets/bones-of-the-buddha-watch-the-full-episode/1073/.

107. Allen, *The Buddha and Dr. Führer*, 176, 178. In lieu of being fired, Dr. Führer resigned. He became a monk in Burma in 1903, after which he allegedly went to Siam. See http://dhammalokaproject.wordpress.com/early-western-buddhists/the-first-western-buddhist-monks.

108. The article is cited by Andrew Huxley in a 2013 lecture, but I have not located the original yet. It was likely published in the *Straits Times* (Singapore). Andrew Huxley, "T.W. Rhys Davids and the Forged Relics of the Buddha" (lecture, School of Oriental and African Studies, University of London, February 27, 2013), https://www.youtube.com/watch?v=6RAY97DFu3c.

109. Allen, "What Happened at Piprahwa" and *The Buddha and Dr. Führer*, 235–70. Andrew Huxley lists other scholars who argue the relics were fake in his "Dr. Führer's Wanderjahre: The Early Career of a Victorian Archaeologist," *Journal of the Royal Asiatic Society*, 3rd ser., 20, no. 4 (2010): 489. See also Huxley, "T. W. Rhys Davids."

110. Letter from Dr. W. Hoey, commissioner, Gorakhphur Division, to the chief secretary to the government, N.-W. Provinces and Oudh, 13 April 1898, courtesy of Chris Peppé.

111. *1899 Foreign Department, External A Pros. April 1899, nos. 92–11*, quoted in Allen, *The Buddha and Dr. Führer*, 206. Allen quotes from British documents in the National Archives of India but does not cite each quote specifically.

112. Allen, *The Buddha and Dr. Führer*, 208. Subhuti also wrote to Siamese authorities, requesting a portion of the relics. See letters from Prince Sommot, King Chulalongkorn's secretary, to Subhuti, 28 February 1899, SLNA 5/63/17/683, and 8 November 1899, SLNA 5/63/17/689 and 5/63/17/731.

113. NA R5 3/7, Prisdang to King Chulalongkorn, 28 July 1898. Prisdang typically called his country Muang Thai, not Siam. But for the sake of consistency in English, I have rendered it Siam.

114. Ibid.

115. NA R5 B 3/7, Draft of the letter of instruction by King Chulalongkorn. See also Prisdang, *Prawat yo*, 71.

116. Devawongse to George Greville, 21 November 1898. The letter is in the private collection of Sumet Jumsai.

117. Quoted in Allen, *The Buddha and Dr. Führer*, 209.

118. Letter from Jinawarawansa to W. C. Peppé, 6 August 1898, listed in Charles Allen, "Preliminary Handlist of Transcripts of the William Claxton Peppé Correspondence from the Papers of Neil Peppé, Esq." Copy provided to author by Chris Peppé.

119. Wichitwong, *Rachathut*, 145. In 1885, Pan Sukhum was known as Khun Wijitworasan, and Prince Ratburi was called Prince Rabi.

120. By the time Phya Sukhum went to India in February 1899, he was superintendent commissioner of monthon Nahkhon Sri Thammarat (1895–1905), administered from Songkhla. He was in charge of modernizing the provincial administration of the southern provinces bordering British Malaya. Pan Sukhum was later promoted to Jao Phraya Yomarat, and was the minister of the capital. From that post he allegedly threatened to arrest Prisdang when he returned to Siam in 1911 to attend the monarch's cremation ceremony.

121. "Presentation at Gorakhpur," *Amrita Bazar Patrika*, February 28, 1899, 6.

122. Sommot to Subhuti, 28 February 1899, SLNA 5/63/683.

123. NA R5 B 3/7, Young cites the original in a response to Devawongse, 4 March 1899 (in English).

124. NA R5 B 3/7, Prisdang to Devawongse, 2 March 1899 (in English).

125. NA R5 B 3/7, draft letter from Devawongse to Young, March 1899. The king approved the draft, 16 March 1899. In a bizarre coincidence, Devawongse cites the first and standard Pali dictionary, compiled by Robert Childers with the assistance of Jina-warawawansa's preceptor, Subhuti.

126. NA R5 B 3/7, royal secretary to Prince Devawongse, 16 March 1899.

127. NA R5 B 3/7, Jinawarawansa to King Chulalongkorn, 18 May 1899.

128. Prisdang, *Prawat yo*, 71.

129. Allen, *The Buddha and Dr. Führer*, 212–13. Prisdang enshrined his portion in the Ratna Chetiya at Dipaduttamarama, which he had begun building in 1908. Allen, *The Buddha and Dr. Führer*, 213.

130. "Where the Buddha Rests," *Nation* (Bangkok), May 30, 2011, http://www.nation multimedia.com/2011/05/30/life/Where-the-Buddha-rests-30156444.html.

131. An undated document in the Sri Lankan National Archives entitled "The Sacred Relics of Lord Buddha to Be Received from Siam" notes that the portions were divided among Lankan sects. See SLNA 5/63/17/731. The *Ceylon Observer* reports on the confusion among the low-country Lankan Buddhists who apparently could not decide on whom to send to Bangkok. The king gave a portion to Mandalay, one to Rangoon, one to Anuradhapura, one to Kandy, and one to Colombo, but the deputations sent by Ceylon "representing various communities far more exceed the three portions which His Majesty has assigned to the Island, viz., the Anuradhapura sent one, Kandy sent two, and Colombo sent three." Presumably exasperated, the king of Siam gave them each one portion and said they had to mutually agree on the place of deposit and if they could not agree, then the portion would go to the Siamese sect in Colombo. See "Buddhist Relics," *Ceylon Observer*, March 15, 1900, weekly edition, 365. In 2015, the Venerable Mahindawansa reported that no one has heard of those relics since they were distributed and no one knows where they are. He claims that only his temples in Waskaduwa and Dipaduttamarama have portions of the Kapilavastu relics. Interview with Mahindawansa.

132. Diaries of Anagarika Dharmapala, entry for 28 November 1899, SLNA microfilm 1944.

133. "Local News," *Ceylon Observer*, November 21, 1900, weekly edition, 1546.

134. Prisdang, *Prawat yo*, 72.

135. Ibid., (mis)numbered appendix 38, 147.

136. NA KT 6.26/2, acting consul for Siam J. S. Clark to Phya Phibat Kosa (Phraya Phiphatkosa), 26 December 1900, and 4 January 1901, 130–32.

137. Prisdang, *Prawat yo*, 72–73.

138. "Local News," *Overland Ceylon Observer*, November 4, 1901, 1544.

139. Aleister Crowley, *Why Jesus Wept* (Paris: privately printed, 1904), http://www. 100thmonkeypress.com/biblio/acrowley/books/why_jesus_wept1_1904/jesus_wept_1st_text.pdf. Crowley dedicated it to several others as well. A hard copy of the play can be

found in Aleister Crowley and I. B., *The Works of Aleister Crowley* (Fowers, Scot.: Society for the Propagation of Religious Truth, 1905).

140. Crowley, *Confessions*, 385.

141. Sumet Jumsai, "Notes on The Ven. P.C. Jinavaravansa," foreword to P. C. Jinavaravansa, "The Ratna Chetiya Dipaduttamarama, Colombo," *Journal of the Royal Asiatic Society of Sri Lanka* (*RASSL*) 48 (2003): 214. The little island is known today as Galgodiyana, a small island south of Matara.

142. Prisdang, *Prawat yo*, 73.

143. Ibid.

144. I am grateful to an anonymous reader for pointing out the oddity of the Prince Priest's type of skeleton meditation.

145. F. F. Martinus, *A Guide to Buddhist Temples* (1907; repr., New Delhi: Asian Educational Services, 1999), 12.

146. "The Governor at Matara," *Overland Ceylon Observer*, March 1, 1897, 365.

147. *The Life of Nyanatiloka Thera: The Biography of a Western Buddhist Pioneer*, comp. and ed. Helmuth Hecker and Bhikku Nanatusita (Kandy, Sri Lanka: Buddhist Publication Society, 2008), i. Anton Gueth, ordained as Nanatiloka in Burma in 1904, was born in Wiesbaden, Germany, in 1878 and died in 1957 in Colombo, Ceylon. He was the second European to be ordained as a Buddhist monk. He met Prisdang in 1905 on the island, where they lived in small huts made of coconut leaves (37). Nyanatiloka mentions that a twenty-year old Dutchman, the son of a rich businessman in Amsterdam named Bergendahl, came. In addition, a German man named Stange came with a man he identified as Polish, born in Prussia, and named Dr. Sobczak. Only Bergandahl and Stange became novices (28). The young Dutchman had a "pathological mental condition" (28).

148. Venerable Mahindawansa explained that Jinawarawansa became the abbot because Subhuti sent him there. Interview with Mahindawansa.

149. Robert Aldrich, *Cultural Encounters and Homoeroticism in Sri Lanka: Sex and Serendipity* (London: Routledge, 2015), 41–42. I am grateful to the art historians Janice Leoshka and Michael Charlesworth for bring Farrer and his wonderful writing to my attention.

150. Reginald Farrer, *In Old Ceylon* (London: Arnold, 1908), 34.

151. Ibid., 1–2.

152. Ibid., 40.

153. Martinus, *Guide to Buddhist Temples*, 6.

154. Interview with Mahindawansa.

155. For example, a chief justice in Matara and Mudaliyar Naganather, head shroff of the National Bank in Nuwara Eliya, visited him in 1905. See "The Siamese Prince Priest at Nuwara Eliya," *Ceylon Observer*, May 12, 1905, weekly edition, 689; and "Here and There," *Ceylon Observer*, November 21, 1905, weekly edition, 1693. In 1908 Miss F. D. Petit, sister of Sir Dinshaw Manickjee Petit, Baronet (and philanthropist and wealthy mill owner, in India), her secretary, her cousin, and others visited. See "The Parsee Lady Millionaire," *Ceylon Observer*, October 3, 1908, weekly edition, 1648.

156. This is noted in Guruge's published copies of Subhuti's correspondence. Jinawarawansa to Subhuti, 17 June 1904, in Ananda W. P. Gurugé, *From the Living Fountains of Buddhism* (Colombo, Sri Lanka: Government Printing Office, 1984), 200n2.

157. The quote comes from Farrer, *In Old Ceylon*, 34. On Jinawarawansa's personal contributions to the museum-library, see Prisdang, *Prawat yo*, 74. Regarding donations, see "Address by the Prince Priest," *Independent*, March 22, 1905, included in Prisdang, *Prawat yo*, app. 15, 116.

158. Both speeches are reproduced as appendixes 15 and 16 in Prisdang, *Prawat yo*, 114–18, and 119–27. They were originally published in the *Independent* (Ceylon), on 22 March 1905 and in the *Morning Times* (Ceylon), 17 August 1906.

159. "Address by the Prince Priest," in Prisdang, *Prawat yo*, app. 15, 114–18; "The Secret of Ceylon's Future Welfare," *Morning Times*, August 17, 1906, in Prisdang, *Prawat yo*, app. 16, 119–27.

160. Address by the Prince Priest," in Prisdang, *Prawat yo*, app. 15, 117.

161. Prisdang, *Prawat yo*, 120 (emphasis in original).

162. Ibid., 121.

163. Ibid., 122–23 (emphasis in original). His views differ little from those of many turn-of-the-century reformers of women and women's education. Their prescriptions presumed all women would become mothers who would remain in the home educating their children.

164. "Secret of Ceylon's Future Welfare," in Prisdang, *Prawat yo*, app. 16, 125 (emphasis in original).

165. "The Kotahena Girls' Free School," *Ceylon Observer*, August 17, 1906, weekly edition, 1245.

166. "H.I.H. Prince Arisugawa in Colombo," *Overland Ceylon Observer*, April 25, 1905, 596; "Outstation News: Kurunegala," *Ceylon Observer*, May 25, 1905, weekly edition, 752; Local News," *Ceylon Observer*, July 26, 1905, weekly edition, 1062; "The Approaching Visit of the Japanese Prince and Princess," *Ceylon Observer*, July 31, 1905, weekly edition, 1093; "The King of Cambodia in Colombo, *Ceylon Observer*, August 10, 1906, weekly edition, 1207; and "The Visit of the German Crown Prince," *Ceylon Observer*, December 12, 1910, weekly edition, 1933.

167. See, for example, "Departure of T. E. Sir Henry and Lady Blake," Supplement to the *Ceylon Observer*, July 10, 1907); "The Late Hon. Mr. Herbert Wace," *Ceylon Observer*, May 30, 1906, weekly edition, 827; and "The Late Sir Alexander Ashmore, K.C.MC.," *Ceylon Observer*, December 8, 1906, weekly edition, 1391 [or 1891, number illegible].

168. "Visitors at Kotahena Temple," *Ceylon Observer*, October 14, 1908, weekly edition, 1528; "Here and There," *Ceylon Observer*, January 20, 1911, weekly edition, 85.

169. "Mr. Keir Hardie in Colombo," *Ceylon Observer*, November 14, 1907, weekly edition, 1810.

170. Dr. Ananda Coomaraswamy, "Notes on Indian Dramatic Technique," *The Mask: A Quarterly Journal of the Art of the Theatre* 6, no. 2 (October 1913): 113. Bhikku P.C. Jinavaravamsa, "On Craftsmen in Siam," in *The Indian Craftsman*, ed. Ananda K. Coomaraswamy (London: Probsthain and Co., 1909), 119–27.

171. It cost $25.20 and was purchased in the early 1900s. Personal correspondence with Laura Weinstein, the Ananda Coomaraswamy Curator of South Asian and Islamic Art, Museum of Fine Arts, Boston, 10 December 2014.

172. *Buddhism: An Illustrated Review*, vol. 1, no. 4 (November 1904): 661–62.

173. Blackburn, *Locations of Buddhism*, 131. *Annual Colonial Report: No. 396 Ceylon for 1902* (Presented to Parliament, London, 1903), 70.

174. "Outstation News: Anuradhapura," *Ceylon Observer*, June 7, 1905, weekly edition, 812.

175. "Correspondence: Excise Commission Report, Feb. 7, 1911," *Ceylon Observer*, February 10, 1911, weekly edition, 120; and "The New Excise Proposals," *Ceylon Observer*, March 6, 1911, weekly edition, 371.

176. P. C. Jinawarawansa, "The Ratna Chetiya of Dipaduttamarama, Colombo," republished with an introduction by Sumet Jumsai, *Journal of the Royal Asiatic Society of Sri Lanka* 48 (2003): 217.

177. Prisdang, *Prawat yo*, 76.

178. NA R6 B 1/15, P. C. Jinawarawansa to Paramindra Mahavajiravudh [King Vajiravudh], 8 November 1910.

179. Ibid.

180. "Criminal Trespass at the Kotahena Temple," *Ceylon Observer,* February 3, 1911, weekly edition, 178.

7. BANGKOK

1. Malcolm Smith, *Physician in the Court of Siam*, 93–94, explains that the king had also suffered from diabetes for years. Given his popularity and how well recorded King Chulalongkorn's life was, there are remarkably few descriptions of his final days or of the symptoms that led to his death.

2. Smith, *Physician in the Court of Siam*, 93.

3. William F. Strobridge, "Mrs. Hamilton King's Bangkok Diary, 1911," *Journal of the Siam Society* 63, pt. 1 (1975): 90.

4. K. Van Dort, "A Royal Cremation," *Century Magazine*, September 1911, 751–55. Much of my description comes from Van Dort and Mrs. Hamilton King, two of the thousands who witnessed the procession.

5. Strobridge, "Mrs. Hamilton King's Bangkok Diary," 92.

6. Van Dort, "A Royal Cremation," 754–55.

7. The wreath and candles are mentioned in "A King's Funeral Pyre," *The Press* (New Zealand), April 26, 1911, 9, http://paperspast.natlib.govt.nz/cgi-bin/paperspast?a=d&d=CHP19110426.2.40.

8. Strobridge, "Mrs. Hamilton King's Bangkok Diary," 91.

9. *Siam Directory 1910* (Bangkok: Siam Observer Office, 1910), 51, 55, 56, 62, 72, 77.

10. He left Lanka in February 1911 but did not specify the date. He went first to Penang, then Singapore, where he boarded a different ship that then sailed to Bangkok. The ship out of Lanka was full of people heading to Japan to see the crown prince of Germany. Some Siamese were on board, escorting the "king's son" (unspecified) back for the funeral. See Prisdang, *Prawat yo*, 77–78.

11. This was Mom Rachawong Suwaphan Sanitwong, who was likely related through Prisdang's brother Prawit, whose son had married into the Sanitwong family. The first person Prisdang had an audience with when he returned in early March was Prince Sai Sanitwong. Wichitwong, *Rachathut*, 170.

12. Prisdang, *Prawat yo*, 79.

13. Ibid., 78.

14. Ibid., 79.

15. Ibid.

16. Upon disembarking in Bangkok, the first place he visited was "the house in Bangrak," where Mom Rachawong That Chumsai na Krungthep took him. He was visited by Jao Phraya Surasak, Mom Rachawong Lek Siriwong na Krungthep [Phra Satja?], and Mom Jao Phoem. He went to visit Phra Ong Jao Sai first and then Prince Devawongse. Ibid., 78.

17. Sumet et al., *Phra ong jao prisdang*, 20.

18. This is the Thai transliteration of the Pali term for *anagarika*, literally "homeless one," but meaning a person who gives up all possessions, including his home, to commit fully to Buddhist practice. While he was in Lanka, Prisdang questioned Anagarika Dharmapala for adopting this title.

19. Prisdang, *Prawat yo*, 83–84.

20. Wichitwong, *Rachathut*, 171.

21. NA KT 6.26/5, letter number 69/882 from the Ministry of the Palace (Jao Phraya Mahithon) to Prince Traidos Prabandh, minister of foreign affairs, 2 July 1924.

22. Mom Jao Ying Prapha was dead by the time it was decided and may even have passed away before he initiated the lawsuit. She was to be the subject of one of his chapters of the unwritten future autobiographical volumes.

23. NA R6 B 1/15, Prisdang to King Vajiravudh, 18 May 1915.

24. Prisdang, *Prawat yo*, 80.

25. Ibid.

26. Ibid., image 32, no page.

27. Prince Yugala Dighambara, also known as the Prince of Lopburi, lived from 1882 to 1932. http://en.wikipedia.org/wiki/Yugala_Dighambara.

28. NA R6 B/15, letter number 67/1678 from Jao Phraya Thammathikoranathibodi (minister of the palace) to King Vajiravudh, 27 December 1918. The correspondence reveals the king's and official's distrust of Prisdang.

29. Prisdang, *Prawat yo*, 79.

30. Sumet says King Vajiravudh closed down the *Siam Observer*, but the king published several arresting articles such as "Jews of the East" with the paper as late as 1914, suggesting that he had shut down a different newspaper. Sumet, *Wang tha phra*, 24.

31. Damrong wrote later that Prisdang had a dubious past. *Rawaengphit* means suspicious, distrustful, or dubious. Letter from Prince Damrong to Prince Narit, 4 March 1937, in Naritsaranuwattiwong, Damrong Rajaubhap, and Sirindhorn, *San somdet* (Bangkok: Munnithi Somdet Jaofa Krom Phraya Naritsaranuwattiwong, 1991), 289.

32. Sathian Koset [Anuman Rachathon], *Fuenkhwamlang* [Recollections of the Past], vol. 2 (Bangkok, 1968), 61; Wichtwong, *Rachathut*, 97–99.

33. NA R6 B 1/15, Prisdang to King Vajiravudh, 25 July 1912.

34. NA R6 B 1/15, letter number 17/2459 from the king's royal secretary to Prisdang. Prisdang claimed he received the salary for his role in investigating the case of "Kho Nanthawisan," which is a reference to a Buddhist parable. Prisdang, *Prawat yo*, 80.

35. James Ingram lists exchange rates, baht to British pound, in his *Economic Change in Thailand since 1850* (Stanford: Stanford University Press, 1955), 336, 154. The baht was fixed at thirteen baht per pound until 1919. The US inflation guide provides calculations for equivalent amounts in the 2000s. http://www.dollartimes.com/inflation/inflation.php?amount=1&year=1918.

36. NA R6 B 1/15, Prisdang to King Vajiravudh, 6 April 2459/1916.

37. NA R6 B 1/15, Prisdang to King Vajiravudh, 23 July 2460/1917.

38. Brendan Whyte and Suthida Whyte, "The Inscriptions on the First World War Volunteers Memorial, Bangkok," *Journal of the Siam Society* 96 (2008): 176.

39. NA R6 B 1/15, Prisdang to King Vajiravudh, 27 December 2460/1917.

40. NA R6 B 1/15, Prisdang to King Vajiravudh, 17 December 1918.

41. Ibid.

42. NA R6 B 1/15, Jao Phraya Thammathikoranathibodi to King Vajiravudh, 27 December 1918.

43. NA R6 B 1/15, letter number 123/1375 from royal secretary to Jao Phraya Thammathikoranathibodi, 31 December 2461/1918.

44. NA KT 6.26/7, correspondence between Prince Devawongse and Jao Phraya Mahithon, royal secretary, 4–5 June 1923.

45. NA R6 B 1/15, Prisdang to the secretary of the Palace Ministry, 6 July 1925. See also Wichitwong, *Rachathut*, 172.

46. Prisdang, *Prawat yo*, 81.

47. NA R6 B 1/15, letter number 263/23365 from Traidos to King Vajiravudh, 25 March 1925.

48. NA KR 6 B 1/15, Prisdang to the secretary of the Palace Ministry, 6 July 1925.

49. There was additional spirited correspondence about Prisdang's being presumptuous and bending the truth about filling a position in the Ministry of the Palace, but the ministry did not want to hire him, and it also refused to "bother" the king with the issue. NA R6 B 1/15, letter number 40/1228 from Jao Phraya Thammathikoranathibodi to Jao Phraya Mahithon, 19 October 2468/1925.

50. Wichitwong, *Rachathut*, 172.

51. Mani Siriworasan, *Chiwit muan fan* (Life Is a Dream), vol. 1 (Bangkok: Chuanphim, 2533/1990), 26–28.

52. Phraya Rachanuphan (Pia Bunnag) was the son of Jao Phraya Phanuwong Maha-kosathipbodi (Thuam Bunnag), who in turn was the Siamese ambassador to England in 1879 for whom Prisdang served as an interpreter.

53. Badman's and B. Grimm & Company are among the stores listed in his account of personal debts handed over to the king in 1918. The ad for Harry Badman and Company comes from the 1912 *Siam Directory*.

54. For his debt to B. Grimm & Company, see NA R6 B 1/15, Prisdang to His Majesty King Vajiravudh, 17 December 2460/1919. He was an "ordinary member" of the Siam Society in at least 1926 and 1928 but likely much longer. See *Journal of the Siam Society* 20, pt. 1 (1926): 272.

55. Mani, *Chiwit muan fan*, 28.

56. Hecker and Nanatusita, *The Life of Nyanatiloka Thera*, 88.

57. Ibid., 89–90.

58. Aree Chaisatien interviewed Sumet Chumsai for his article "Secrets of Solid Rela-tions with Japan Revealed," *Nation* (Bangkok), May 7, 2007. See also Sumet, *Wang tha phra*, 24.

59. Jinanan is referred to as "Chinnanan" in the Siamese correspondence.

60. I quoted the English translation of the original French letter sent to Phanuvong because the Thai version is one of Prisdang's earlier drafts. He claimed he could not find the original. NA KT 6.26/3, Prisdang to Phanuvong, 11 January 1922.

61. Ibid.

62. NA KT 6.26/3, Fernand Pila to Prince Devawongse, 22 March 1922.

63. NA KT 6.26/7, letter number 22030 from Prisdang to Traidos, 25 March 2464/1922.

64. NA KT 6.26/7, letter number 77/22147 from Devawongse to Monsieur Fernand Pila, Envoy Extraordinary and Minister Plenipotentiary of the French Republic, Bangkok, 27 March 1922.

65. NA R6 B/15, members of the Southern Buddhist Association (Galle), Ceylon, to the King of Siam, 23 September 1925.

66. NA R6 B/15, letter number 6/13899 from minister of foreign affairs, Traidos, to the Galle Buddhist Association, 22 October 1925.

67. Prisdang, *Prawat yo*, 84.

68. Ibid., 38.

69. Ibid., 39.

70. Ibid., 142–45.

71. See, for example, "Prince Prisdang Dies at 83," *New York Times*, March 18, 1935, 21. See also *Bangkok Times*, March 18 and 19, 1935; and *Sinhala Bauddhaya* [Sinhala Bud-dhist], March 30, 1935, 1.

72. Sumet et al., *Phra ong jao prisdang*, 23–24.

73. Letter from Prince Damrong to Prince Narisaranuwattiwong, 4 March 1937, in Naritsaranuwattiwong, Damrong Rajanubhap, and Sirindhorn, *San somdet*, 289.

8. AFTERLIFE

1. Papers of Reginald Farrer, Royal Botanic Garden, Edinburgh, 235 GB RJF 2/1/2, 5 February 1908. I am grateful to Michael Charlesworth for bringing Farrer's letter to my attention.

2. William Reddy develops the notion of "emotional refuge" in his *The Navigation of Feeling: A Framework for the History of Emotions* (Cambridge: Cambridge University Press, 2001), 49.

3. Prisdang, *Prawat yo*, 63.

4. The image is housed in the museum at Waskaduwa Temple outside Colombo.

5. "Prince Prem Purachatra at Ceylonese Buddhist Ceremony," *Singapore Free Press and Mercantile Advertiser*, August 25, 1937, 6.

6. Prince College website, Colombo, Sri Lanka, http://princecollege.wix.com/01#! about.

7. Prawat yo phraworawongthe phra-ong jao prisdang ru phrachinaworawong haeng sri langka [A Biographical Note on His Highness Prince Prisdang or Reverend Jinavaravansa ("The Prince Priest")] (Bangkok: Chaloemnit and Didi Books, 1993).

8. Duvindi Illankoon and Saveen Jeewandara, "Little Known Thai Temple with a Long History," *Sunday Times* (Colombo), June 23, 2013, online edition, http://www.sunday times.lk/130623/plus/little-known-thai-temple-with-a-long-history-49651.

9. See, for example, General Shantha Kottegoda, a former commander in the Sri Lankan Army who fought in the Sri Lankan civil war against the "terrorists" (Tamil nationalists/separatists) and was appointed ambassador to Thailand sometime after 2011. "From Top Military Commander to a Life of Diplomacy," http://www.slembbkk.com/ srilankanews/121313.pdf. Ethnic Malay Muslims in Thailand's southern provinces are also unequally incorporated into the majority Buddhist Thai nation.

10. Sumet Jumsai, "Notes on the Ven. P.C. Jinavaravansa," foreword to P. C. Jinavaravansa, "The Ratna Chetiya Dipaduttamarama, Colombo," *Journal of the Royal Asiatic Society of Sri Lanka* (RASSL) 48 (2003): 215.

11. Illankoon and Jeewandara, "Little Known Thai Temple"; Ven. Waskaduwe Mahindawansa Nayaka Thera, "Thai Prime Minister's Visit to Sri Lanka—Its Religious Significance," *Daily News* (Sri Lanka), August 14, 2003, http://archives.dailynews.lk/2003/ 08/14/fea03.html.

12. Benjamin Batson, ed., *Siam's Political Future: Documents from the End of the Absolute Monarchy* (Ithaca: SEAP Publications, 1974), 7–8.

13. *Jaonai lae kharachakan krap bangkhom thus khwamhen chatkan plianplaeng rachakan phaendin ro. So. 103 lae phrarachadamat*, cremation volume for Mom Sanit Kritsadakon (Bangkok: Krom Sinlapakon 2510/1967). Cited in Sumet et al., *Phra ong jao prisdang*, 71, 64.

14. For this critique of Chai-anan, see Sumet et al., *Phra ong jao prisdang*, 73.

15. Chai-anan Samudavanija [Samutwanit], *Plaen phattana kanmuang chabap raek khong thai* [The First Thai Political Development Plan] (Bangkok, 1970); see especially 105–7.

16. David Streckfuss, "Kings in the Age of Nations: The Paradox of *Lèse-Majesté* as Political Crime in Thailand," *Comparative Studies in Society and History* 37, no. 3 (July 1995): 445–75; and David Streckfuss, *Truth on Trial* (London: Routledge, 2011).

17. Bunphisit in particular carefully appraises the secondary scholarship by Chai-Anan Samutwanit, Mom Luang Manich Jumsai, Mom Luang Tui Jumsai, Sumet Jumsai, Suphot Jaengrew, Wichitwong na Pomphet, Thanet Aphonsuwan, Suthachai Yimpraset, Wimon-phan Pitthawatchai, Komphon Jampaphan, and Nigel Brailey—nearly all of whom have informed this narrative of Prisdang as well. Bunphisit, "Samphanthaphap," l, 3–18. To this illustrious list, I would add Sulak Siwalak, "Siamese Society from the Perspective of its Tenth Intellectual," *International Network of Engaged Buddhists* (2014): 1, http://www. inebnetwork.org/news-and-media/6-articles/490-siamese-society-from-the-perspective-of-its-tenth-intellectual.

18. Brailey, *Two Views of Siam*, is most frequently cited as the source of this rationale.

19. Prisdang, "Confidential," in Brailey, *Two Views of Siam*, 55.

20. Bunphisit, "Samphanthaphap," 26.

21. This is also noted by Bunphisit, ibid., 27.

22. Ploenpote, "Prince Prisdang's Constitutional Dream," *Bangkok Post*, December 9, 2010.

23. Professor Sumet Jumsai and his wife, Suthini, arranged for this postage stamp to be issued. Personal communication, 12 October 2015. They generously supplied me with a sheet of these stamps.

24. David Streckfuss, *Truth on Trial in Thailand: Defamation, Treason and Lèse-Majesté* (London: Routledge, 2011).

25. This exile community encompasses the political spectrum: from royalists such as Prisdang (1890), Prince Damrong Rajanubhap (1933), and King Prajadhipok (1935) to suspected communists such as Pridi Phanomyong (1949) and Kulap Saipradit (1958); student activists in the 1970s; and Buddhist social critics such as Sulak Sivaraka (Sulak Siwarak) (1976, 1991). In the 2000s, the neoliberal populist Thaksin Shinawatra (2006) and public intellectual Giles Ungpakorn (2009), both accused of lèse majesté, similarly moved into exile for fear of political persecution, but they too remain closely connected to Thailand's embittered political divide. Many more fled in 2014 after yet another military coup that initially called itself, without irony, the "Council for Reforming the Democratic Regime of Government with the King as Head of State."

26. An important exception is Aum Neko, a transgender political activist who lives in exile in France. http://prachatai.org/english/node/5082. I am grateful to Chris Baker for bringing Aum Neko to my attention.

27. His experience is instructive for what it reveals about the selective (not arbitrary) reification of social discrimination in law, arrest warrants, and other institutional forms by which the state implements power. Social politics, rumor, and other noninstitutionalized forms of power are momentarily reified to target a specific individual. Laws and policing are not equally applied but are deployed selectively.

28. Duncan McCargo, "Network Monarchy and Legitimacy Crisis in Thailand," *Pacific Review* 18, no. 4 (December 2005): 499–519.

Bibliography

Archival Materials: Thailand

Thailand's National Archive sources are cited as "NA," followed by the reign number, the ministry or department from which the source comes, and numbers that refer to a division and subdivision in the ministry or department. For example, NA R5 R B 3/4 refers to the National Archives, reign of Rama V, and the Department of the Royal Secretariat (Rachalekhanukan). The B refers to Bettalet, the section of collected documents called "miscellaneous." The number 3 refers to the collection of files about Prisdang within "Miscellaneous," and the number 4 refers to the fourth set of files in the Prisdang collection. An English translation follows the Thai transliteration below.

Fifth Reign (R5) Documents

B Bettalet (Miscellaneous), Series 3 Phra ong jao prisdang (Prince Prisdang)

3/1 Rai-gnan phra ong jao prisdang khran ok pai pen rachathut wiset (R.S. 100–103). (Prisdang's Reports Issued When He Was Special Envoy, 1881–1884.)

3/2 Ruang phra ong jao prisdang pen ni hang bensan London (16 ph.y. 104–9 m.k. 110). (Prince Prisdang's Debts to the Benson Store, London, 16 November 1884–9 January 1892.)

3/3 Phra ong jao prisdang krapthun chijaeng hetkantangtang thi koetkhun nai suanpra ong (R.S. 106). (Prince Prisdang Informs the King of Various Incidents That Personally Happened to Him, circa 1887.)

3/4 Priwet ruang phra ong jao prisdang kho bangkhom la pai yu muang chianghaikon (3 ph.kh.–24 k.y. 109). (Private Matter of Prisdang Who Asks to Resign and Live Briefly in Shanghai, 3 May–24 September 1890.)

3/5 Khwamkhatkhong nai suan phra ong jao jao prisdang (27 k.y. 109). (Personal Objections of Prince Prisdang, 27 September 1890.)

3/6 Phra ong jao prisdang (28 k.y. 109–2 k.kh. 113). (Prince Prisdang, 28 September 1890–2 July 1894.)

3/7 Phra ong jao prisdang lae ruang phra rachathan gnoen pai kuakun kankep khongboran prathet india (19 October 11–17 May 118). (Prince Prisdang and the Issue of Royal Funds to Support the Collection of Indian Antiquities, 19 October 1896 to 17 May 1899.)

3/8 Phra ong jao prisdang upasombot (25 ph.y. 115–10 m.kh. 116). (Prince Prisdang Is Ordained, 25 November 1896–10 January 1898.)

3/9 Phra ong jao prisdang ruang muang langka (16 mi.kh. 116). (Prince Prisdang in Lanka, 16 March 1898.)

Sixth Reign (R6) Documents

B Bettalet (Miscellaneous) Series 1/15 Phra Chinaworawong (Phra ong jao prisdang) 20 ph.y. 2453–26 ph.y. 2468. (Monk Chinaworawong [Prince Prisdang], 20 November 1910/11–26 November 1925.)

Fifth and Sixth Reigns

KT   Krasuang Tangprathet (Ministry of Foreign Affairs)
     Series 6.26/2-7 Phra worawongthoe phra ong jao prisdang (Prince Prisdang).

Archival Materials: Great Britain

The National Archives (TNA), Public Records Office (PRO), Kew, Foreign Office (FO),
     series 69 Siam; 628 Siam Confidential Print.
Papers of Reginald Farrer, Royal Botanic Garden, Edinburgh, GB 235 RJF 2/1/2, 5
     February 1908.

Archival Materials: Sri Lanka

Diaries of Anagarika Dharmapala. Sri Lankan National Archives (SLNA), microfilm
     1944.
Sri Lankan National Archives (SLNA), 5/63/17 series.

Newspapers

Amrita Bazar Patrika
Bangkok Post
Bruce Herald (New Zealand)
Ceylon Independent
Ceylon Observer
Ceylon Observer (Weekly Edition)
Daily News (Sri Lanka)
Hong Kong Daily Press
Independent (Ceylon)
London Gazette
Moonshine (London)
Morning Times (Ceylon)
Nation (Bangkok)
New York Times
Overland Ceylon Observer
Press (New Zealand)
Singapore Free Press and Mercantile Advertiser
Sinhala Bauddhaya (Ceylon)
Straits Times
Straits Times Weekly Issue
Western Argus (Australia)

BLOGS

Dhammaloka Project. "The First Western Buddhist Monks." http://dhammaloka
     project.wordpress.com/early-western-buddhists/the-first-western-buddhist-
     monks.

"Lumbini on Trial: The Untold Story" (blog). http://www.lumkap.org.uk/Lumbini%20 On%20Trial.htm.

WEBSITES

Blavatsky Study Center, HPB Photo Gallery. "Theosophical Society, Adyar, Madras, India, 1890." http://www.blavatskyarchives.com/hpbphotos28.htm.
Bloy, Marjorie. "A Web of English History." http://www.historyhome.co.uk/peel/ p-health/pubheal.htm.
Government of Thailand. "King Mongkut Memorial Park of Science and Technology." http://www.waghor.go.th.
Piprahwa project. www.piprahwa.com.
World Heritage Site: Lumbini. http://www.worldheritagesite.org/sites/lumbini.html.

PRIMARY AND SECONDARY SOURCES

Aldrich, Robert. *Cultural Encounters and Homoeroticism in Sri Lanka: Sex and Serendipity*. London: Routledge, 2015.
Allen, Charles. "The Bones of the Buddha." PBS, July 13, 2013. http://www.pbs.org/ wnet/secrets/bones-of-the-buddha-watch-the-full-episode/1073.
——. *The Buddha and Dr. Führer: An Archaeological Scandal*. London: Haus Publishing, 2008.
——. "What Happened at Piprahwa: A Chronology of Events Related to the Excavation in January 1898 of the Piprahwa Stupa in Basti District, North-Western Provinces and Oude (Uttar Pradesh), India, and the Associated 'Piprahwa Inscription,' Based on Newly Available Correspondence." *Zeitschrift für Indologie und Südasienstudien* 29 (2012): 1–19.
Aree Chaisatien. "Secrets of Solid Relations with Japan Revealed." *The Nation* (Bangkok), May 7, 2007.
Aubin, David. "Eclipse Politics in France and Thailand, 1868." In *The Heavens on Earth: Observatories in Nineteenth-Century Science and Culture*, edited by David Aubin, Charlotte Bigg, and H. Otto Sibum, 86–117. Durham, NC: Duke University Press, 2010.
Baker, Chris, and Pasuk Phongpaichit. *The Palace Law of Ayutthaya and the Thammasat: Translation and Commentary*. Ithaca: SEAP Publications, forthcoming.
Barmé, Scot. *Woman, Man, Bangkok*. Lanham, MD: Rowman & Littlefield, 2002.
Batson, Benjamin A. *The End of the Absolute Monarchy in Siam*. Singapore: Oxford University Press, 1984.
Battye, Noel Alfred. "The Military, Government and Society in Siam, 1868–1910: Politics and Military Reform during the Reign of King Chulalongkorn." PhD diss., Cornell University, 1974.
Blackburn, Anne. *Locations of Buddhism: Colonialism and Modernity in Sri Lanka*. Chicago: University of Chicago Press, 2010.
Bradley, Dan Beach. *Dictionary of the Siamese Language*. Bangkok, 1874.
Brailey, Nigel. *Two Views of Siam on the Eve of the Chakri Reformation: Comments by Robert Laurie Morant and Prince Pritsdang*. Whiting Bay, Scot.: Kiscadale Publications, 1989.
Buddhism: An Illustrated Review 1, no. 4 (November): 661–62.
Bunphisit Srihong. "Samphanthaphap rawang phrabat somdet phra julajomklao jaoyuhua kap phra-ong jao prisdang jak lakthan chanton su khamtham to nakwichakan lae nak-khian prawatsat-rathasat" [The Relationship between King Chulalongkorn and Prince Prisdang: From Primary Evidence to Questions for Scholars and Writers of Political History], *Ratthasatsan* 32, no. 3 (2011): 1–81.

Candilio, A., and L. Bressan. "Sultan Abu Bakar of Johore's Visit to the Italian King and the Pope in 1885." *Journal of the Malaysian Branch of the Royal Asiatic Society* 73, no. 1 (2000): 43–53.

Chaen Patchusanon. "Suriyupparakha temkhrat ph.s. 2411" [The Full Solar Eclipse of 1868], *Nawikkasat* 62, no. 11 (November 1979): 124–41.

Chai-anan Samudavanija [Samutwanit]. *Plaen phattana kanmuang chabap raek khong thai* [The First Thai Political Development Plan]. Bangkok, 1970.

Chai-anan Samudavanija [Samutwanit], and Khattiya Kannasut, comps. *Ekasan kanmuang kanpok-khrong thai (ph.s. 2417–2477)* [Documents about Thai Politics and Administration]. Bangkok: Thai Studies Institute, 1989.

Chula Chakrabongse, Prince. *Lords of Life: A History of the Kings of Thailand.* 1960. Reprint, London: Alvin Redman, 1967.

Chulalongkorn, King. "Phraboromarachowat nai rachakan thi 5 chapab thi 2." In *Ekkasan kan muang kanpokkhrong thai* [Documents on Thai Politics and Administration], edited by Chai-anan Samudavanija and Khattiya Kannasut, 103–7. Bangkok: The Social Association of Thailand, 1975.

Cook, Nerida. "Tale of Two City Pillars: Mongkut and Thai Astrology on the Eve of Modernization." In *Patterns and Illusions: Thai History and Thought*, edited by Gehan Wijeyewardene and E. C. Chapman, 279–312. Singapore: ISEAS, 1992.

Coomaraswamy, Ananda. *Mediaeval Sinhalese Art.* Broad Campden, UK: Essex House Press, 1908.

——. "Notes on Indian Dramatic Technique." *The Mask: A Quarterly Journal of the Art of the Theatre* 6, no. 2 (October 1913): 109–28.

Crowley, Aleister. *The Confessions of Aleister Crowley: An Autohagiography.* New York: Hill and Wang, 1969.

——. "Why Jesus Wept." Paris. Privately printed, 1905.

Damrong Rajanubhap [Rachanuphap], Prince. *Khwamsongjam* [Memoirs]. Bangkok: Khlang Withaya Publications, 1951.

Davis, Bonnie. *Royal Siamese Postal Service (The Early Years).* Bangkok: Siam Stamp Trading Co., 1983.

Department of Fine Arts. *Jaonai lae kharachakan krapbangkhomthun khwam hen jatkanplianplaeng rachakanphaendin r.s. 103 lae phra rachadamrat nai phrabatsomdet phrajulajomklaojaoyuhua son thalaeng phraboromarachathibai kaekhai kanpokhrong phaendin* [The Princes and Royal Officials Offer Their Opinion on Reforming the Administration of the Kingdom, 1885, and King Chulalongkorn's Speech Announcing the Correction of the Government of the Kingdom]. Bangkok: Department of Fine Arts, 1983.

Edwards, Penny. "Watching the Detectives: The Elusive Exile of Prince Myingoon of Burma." In *Exile in Colonial Asia: Kings, Convicts, Commemoration*, edited by Ronit Ricci, 248–78. Honolulu: University of Hawai'i Press, 2016.

Ellis, Alexander J. "Appendix to Mr. Alexander J. Ellis's Paper on 'The Musical Scales of Various Nations,' Read 25th March 1885." *Journal of the Society of Arts*, October 30, 1885, 1102–7.

Farrer, Reginald. *In Old Ceylon.* London: Arnold, 1908.

Gurugé, Ananda W. P. *From the Living Fountains of Buddhism.* Colombo: Government Printing Office, 1984.

Harris, Townsend. *The Complete Journal of Townsend Harris.* Rev. ed. with introduction by Mario Emilio Cosenza and preface by Douglas MacArthur II. Rutland, VT: Charles E. Tuttle, 1959.

Hecker, Helmuth, and Bhikku Nanatusita, comps. and eds. *The Life of Nyanatiloka Thera: The Biography of a Western Buddhist Pioneer.* Kandy, Sri Lanka: Buddhist Publication Society, 2008.

Hull, Isabel V. "Prussian Dynastic Ritual and the End of the Monarchy." In *German Nationalism and the Euorpean Response, 1890–1945*, edited by Carole Fink, Isabel Hull, and MacGregor Knox, 13–41. Norman: University of Oklahoma Press, 1985.

Huxley, Andrew. "Dr. Führer's Wanderjahre: The Early Career of a Victorian Archaeologist." *Journal of the Royal Asiatic Society*, 3rd ser., 20, no. 4 (2010): 489–502.

——. "Mr. Houghton and Dr. Führer: A Scholarly Vendetta and Its Consequences," *South East Asia Research* 19, no. 1 (March 2011): 59–82.

——. "T. W. Rhys Davids and the Forged Relics of the Buddha." Inaugural lecture for the School of Oriental and African Studies, University of London, 27 February 2013. https://www.youtube.com/watch?v=6RAY97DFu3c.

Illankoon, Duvindi, and Saveen Jeewandara. "Little Known Thai Temple with a Long History." *Sunday Times* (Colombo), June 23, 2013, online edition. http://www.sundaytimes.lk/130623/plus/little-known-thai-temple-with-a-long-history-49651.html.

Ingram, James. *Economic Change in Thailand since 1850*. Stanford: Stanford University Press, 1955.

"Jaonai lae kharachakan krapbangkhomthun khwam hen jatkanplianplaeng rachakanphaendin r.s. 103" [The Princes and Royal Officials Offer Their Opinion on Reforming the Administration of the Kingdom, 1885]. In *Ekasan kanmuang kanpok-khrong thai (ph.s. 2417–2477)*, compiled by Chai-Anan Samudavanija and Khattiya Kannasut, 40–61. 1885. Reprint, Bangkok: Thai Studies Institute, 1989.

Jinawarawansa [Prince Prisdang Chumsai]. "On Craftsmen in Siam." In *The Indian Craftsman*, edited by Ananda K. Coomaraswamy, 119–27. London: Probsthain and Co., 1909.

——. "An Open Letter," dated 28 December 1897. *The Theosophist* 19, no. 5 (February 1898): 291–94.

——. "The Ratna Chetiya of Dipaduttamarama, Colombo." Republished with an introduction by Sumet Jumsai in *Journal of the Royal Asiatic Society of Sri Lanka* 48 (2003): 213–36.

Jones, Robert B. *Thai Titles and Ranks: Including a Translation of Traditions of Royal Lineage in Siam by King Chulalongkorn*. Ithaca: Cornell Southeast Asia Program Data Paper 81, 1971.

Jory, Patrick. "Republicanism in Thai History." In *Clio in a Phanung: Ten Essays on the Cultural and Intellectual History of Thailand*, edited by Maurizio Peleggi, 97–117. Ithaca: SEAP Publications, 2015.

——. "Thai and Western Buddhist Scholarship in the Age of Colonialism: King Chulalongkorn Redefines the Jatakas." *Journal of Asian Studies* 61, no. 3 (August 2002): 891–918.

Joti Kalyanamitra. *Phon ngan 6 sattawat khong chang thai* [Six Hundred Years of Work by Thai Artists and Architects]. Bangkok: Fine Arts Commission, 1977. In Thai and English.

Jotmaihaet sadet phraphat tang prathet nai rachakan thi 5 sadet muang singapo lae muang batawia khrang raek lae sadet praphat india [Records of Rama V's Travel Abroad for the First Time to Singapore, Batavia, and India]. 2nd ed. Cremation volume for Phra Jao Boromawongthoe Kromaluang Adison Udomdet. Bangkok, 1925.

Kemper, Steven. *Rescued from the Nation: Anagarika Dharmapala and the Buddhist World*. Chicago: University of Chicago Press, 2015.

Kulap, K. S. R. "Prawat Phraya Rachamontri (Phu)" [The History of *Phraya* Rachamontri (Phu)]. *Sayam Praphet* 4, no. 16 (March 27, 1901): 545–55.

Kullada Kesboonchoo Mead. *The Rise and Decline of Thai Absolutism*. London: RoutledgeCurzon, 2004.

Laut, Ernest. "La Mort de Chulalongkorn, Roi de Siam." *Le Petit Journal*, November 6, 1910. Illustrated supplement.

Lek Siriwong na Krungthep, Mom Rachawong. *Banyat chadok prachumnithan nai prathet ni tae boran 50 ruang phak thi 1* [Jataka Wisdom: Ancient Collected Tales from this Country]. Cremation volume. Bangkok, 1924.

le May, Reginald S., Walter Williamson, and E. Wyon Smith, 1920. *Descriptive Catalogue of the Postage Stamps and Post- and Letter-Cards of Siam*. Bangkok, 1920.

Loos, Tamara. "Besmirched with Blood: An Emotional History of Transnational Romance in Colonial Singapore." *Rethinking History* 16, no. 2 (June 2012): 199–220.

———. "Renegade Royalist: Autobiography and Siam's Disavowed Prince Prisdang." In *Clio in a Phanung: Ten Essays on the Cultural and Intellectual History of Thailand*, edited by Maurizio Peleggi, 63–77. Ithaca: SEAP Publications, 2015.

———. *Subject Siam: Family, Law, and Colonial Modernity in Thailand*. Ithaca: Cornell University Press, 2006.

Malalgoda, Kitsiri. *Buddhism in Sinhalese Society, 1750–1900: A Study of Religious Revival and Change*. Berkeley: University of California Press, 1976.

Manich Jumsai, comp. *Pramuan jotmai khong phra worawongthoe phra-ong jao prisdang rachathut khon raek khong thai prajam thawip yurop* [Collected Letters of Prince Prisdang, First Thai Ambassador to Europe]. Bangkok, 1991.

———. *Prince Prisdang's Files on His Diplomatic Activities in Europe, 1880–1886*. Bangkok: Chaloemnit, 1977.

Mani Siriworasan. *Chiwit muan fae* [Life Is a Dream]. Vol. 1. Bangkok: Chuanphim, 1990.

Martinus, F. F. *A Guide to Buddhist Temples*. 1907. Reprint, New Delhi: Asian Educational Services, 1999.

McCargo, Duncan. "Network Monarchy and Legitimacy Crisis in Thailand." *Pacific Review* 18, no. 4 (December, 2005): 499–519.

McFarland, George B., ed. *Thai-English Dictionary*. Stanford: Stanford University Press, 1941.

Merry, Sally Engle. "Rethinking Gossip and Scandal." In *Toward a General Theory of Social Control*. Vol. 1, *Fundamentals*, edited by Donald Black, 271–302. Orlando: Academic Press, 1984.

Moffat, Abbot Low. *Mongkut the King of Siam*. Ithaca: Cornell University Press, 1961.

Mongkut, King. Letter (in English) to Sir Henry Ord, 8 July 1868. http://www.siamese-heritage.org/jsspdf/1921/JSS_022_1b_EnglishCorrespondenceOfKingMongkut Continued.pdf.

Morris, Rosalind. "Three Sexes and Four Sexualities: Redressing the Discourses on Gender and Sexuality in Contemporary Thailand. *Positions* 2, no. 1 (1994): 15–43.

Murashima, Eiji. "The Origins of Modern Official State Ideology in Thailand." *Journal of Southeast Asian Studies* 19, no. 1 (1988): 80–96.

Narisaranuwattiwong, Prince, and Damrong Rajanubhab, Prince. *Prawat sawek-ek mom jao prawit* [History of Court Official Mom Jao Prawit]. Bangkok, 1926.

Naritsaranuwattiwong, Damrong Rajanubhap, and Sirindhorn, Princes. *San somdet* [Royal Correspondence]. Bangkok: Munnithi Somdet Chaofa Krom Phraya Naritsaranuwattiwong, 1991.

Nathawut Suthisongkram. *29 jao phraya* [29 Jao Phraya] Bangkok, 1966.

Nilwan Nildum. "The Architectural Heritage Management for Wang Tha Phra and Wang Thanon na Phra Lan: From the Palaces of Builders and Craftsmen to the Art and Cultural Centre." Master's thesis, Silpakorn University, Bangkok, 2003.

Norman, Henry. "The Future of Siam." *Contemporary Review* 64 (July–December 1893): 1–13.

Olcott, Henry Steel. *Old Diary Leaves: The Only Authentic History of the Theosophical Society.* 6th ser. (1896–98). Adyar: Theosophical Publishing House, 1935.

O'Neil, Maryvelma. *Bangkok: A Cultural History.* New York: Oxford University Press, 2008.

Pallegoix, D. J. B. *Sapha, Phacana, Phasa Thai: Dictionarium Linguae Thai.* 1854. Reprint, Paris: Gregg International, 1972.

Paranavitana, K. D. "Scholar Monks of the Nineteenth Century and the Tragic Transformation of the High Priest Ven. Kapugama Dhammakkhanda Thero." *Journal of the Royal Asiatic Society* (Sri Lanka), n.s., 28 (1983–84): 123–64.

Pasuk Phongphaichit, and Chris Baker. *Thailand: Economy and Politics.* Oxford: Oxford University Press, 1997.

———. *Thailand: Economy and Politics.* 2nd ed. Oxford: Oxford University Press, 2002.

Pavie, Auguste. *Pavie Mission Indochina Papers, 1879–1895.* Vol. 1. Translated by Walter E. J. Tips. Bangkok: White Lotus Press, 1999.

Peleggi, Maurizio. *Lords of Things: The Fashioning of the Siamese Monarchy's Modern Image.* Honolulu: University of Hawai'i Press, 2002.

The Penal Code for the Kingdom of Siam (Draft Version). Bangkok: A. P. Mission Press, 1908.

Phirasri Phowathong. "'Ubatihet' khong phraworawongthoe phra-ong jao prisdang" [The "Incident" of Prince Prisdang]. *Sinlapa Watanatham* 35, no. 8 (June 2014): 116–31.

Phlai-noi. *Jao tang chat nai prawatisat thai* [Foreigners in Thai History]. Bangkok: Ruamsan Co., 1995.

Phojai Thomya. "Botbat khong phra ong jao prisdang: Suksa koranikanjeraja toklong nai nangsu sanya kiaokap sura kap nanaprathet" [The Role of Prince Prisdang: A Study of the Agreement in the Treaties Related to Alcohol with Foreign Countries, 1881–1886]. Master's thesis, Chulalongkorn University, 1986.

Phrarachadamrat nai phrabatsomdet phrajulajomklao jaoyuhua (King Chulalongkorn). *Songthalaeng phraboromarachathibai kaekhai kanpokkhrong phaendin* [Royal Speech Explaining the Governmental Reforms]. Bangkok: Sophonphiphanthanakon, 1927.

Ploenpote Atthakor. "Prisdang's Constitutional Dream." *Bangkok Post*, Outlook section, December 9, 2010.

Prasong Sukhum. *Jak yomarat thung sukhumwit* [From Yomarat to Sukhumwit]. Bangkok: Chulalongkorn University Publications, 2000.

Prawat yo phraworawongthe phra-ong jao prisdang ru phrachinaworawong haeng sri lanka [A Biographical Note on His Highness Prince Prisdang or Reverend Jinawarawansa, "The Prince Priest"]. Bangkok: Chaloemnit and Didi Books, 1993.

Prayun Phitsanakha. *50 Jao phraya haeng ratanakosin* [50 Chakri Era Jao Phraya]. Bangkok: Khlang Withaya, 1962.

Prisdang, Prince. "Confidential. Notes on Siamese Administration, Relations with Foreign Powers and Life in the King's Palace at Bangkok, Written for me/ Mr. Swettenham (British Resident in Perak) in October 1891 by a Siamese Gentleman of Rank—Now in Disgrace" (1891). In *Two Views of Siam on the Eve of the Chakri Reformation: Comments by Robert Laurie Morant and Prince*

Pritsdang, introduced and edited by Nigel Brailey, 49–79. Whiting Bay, Scot.: Kiscadale Publications, 1989.

———. *Prawat yo naiphan ek phiset phra worawongthoe phra ong jao pritsdang tae prasut pho. so. 2392 thung 2472* (Bangkok 2472/1930) [Abbreviated History of Special Colonel Prince Prisdang, from 1850–1930]. 1930. Reprinted in the cremation volume for Luang Aneknaiwathi (M. R. W. Narot Chumsai). Bangkok, 1970.

Rachasakunwong (Royal Genealogy). 7th rev. ed. Bangkok, 1969.

Reddy, William M. *The Navigation of Feeling: A Framework for the History of Emotions.* Cambridge: Cambridge University Press, 2001.

Royal Institute. *Romanization Guide for the Thai Script.* 1968. Reprint, Bangkok: Royal Institute, 1982.

Sathian Koset [Anuman Rachathon]. *Fuenkhwamlang* [Recollections of the Past]. Vol. 2. Bangkok: Suksit Siam, 1968.

Schaffer, Simon, Lissa Roberts, Kapil Raj, and James Delbourgo. *The Brokered World: Go-Betweens and Global Intelligence, 1770–1820.* Sagamore Beach, MA: Science History Publications, 2009.

Siam Directory. Bangkok: Siam Observer Office, Bangkok, 1910.

Skinner, G. William. *Chinese Society in Thailand.* Ithaca: Cornell University Press, 1957.

Smith, Malcolm. *A Physician at the Court of Siam.* 1947. Reprint, Kuala Lumpur: Oxford University Press, 1982.

Smith, Samuel J. "Events in Siam Connected with the Eclipse of 1868." *Siam Repository* 1 (January 1869): 2–3.

Smyth, H. Warrington. *Five Years in Siam, From 1891–1896.* Vol. 1. 1898. Reprint, Bangkok: White Lotus, 1994.

So Sethaputra, *New Model Thai-English Dictionary.* Bangkok: Thai Watana Phanit, 1991.

———. *New Model Thai-English Dictionary.* Vols. 1, 2. Bangkok: Thai Watana Phanich, 1965.

Stoler, Ann. "Matters of Intimacy as Matters of State: A Response." *Journal of American History* 88, no. 3 (December 2001): 893–97.

Streckfuss, David. "Kings in the Age of Nations: The Paradox of *Lèse-Majesté* as Political Crime in Thailand." *Comparative Studies in Society and History* 37, no. 3 (July 1995): 445–75.

———. *Truth on Trial in Thailand: Defamation, Treason and Lèse-Majesté.* London: Routledge, 2011.

Strobridge, William F. "Mrs. Hamilton King's Bangkok Diary, 1911." *Journal of the Siam Society* 63, pt. 1 (1975): 86–104.

Sulak Sivaraksa. "Siamese Society from the Perspective of Its Tenth Intellectual." International Network of Engaged Buddhists. http://www.inebnetwork.org/news-and-media/6-articles/490-siamese-society-from-the-perspective-of-its-tenth-intellectual.

Sumet Jumsai. "Notes on The Ven. P.C. Jinavaravansa." Foreword to P. C. Jinavaravansa, "The Ratna Chetiya Dipaduttamarama, Colombo." *Journal of the Royal Asiatic Society of Sri Lanka* (RASSL) 48 (2003): 213–36.

———. "A Postscript." In *Prince Prisdang's Files on His Diplomatic Activities in Europe, 1880–1886,* by Manich Jumsai, 262–67. Bangkok: Chaloemnit, 1977.

———. "Prince Prisdang and the Proposal for the First Siamese Constitution, 1885." *Journal of the Siam Society* 92 (2004): 105–16.

———. *Wang tha phra* [Tha Phra Palace]. Bangkok: Krung Siam, 1971.

Sumet Jumsai et al. *Phra ong jao prisdang lae khosanoe kieokap ratthathamanun chabap raek ph.s. 2427* [Prince Prisdang and the Proposal for the First Constitution in B.E. 2427/1885]. Bangkok: King Prajadhipok Institute, 2007.

Supot Jaengrew. "Phra ong jao prisdang 'kraduk sanlang' khong ong somdet phrapiyamaharat." *Sinlapa Watanatham* 14, no. 12 (October 1993): 155–59.

Surasakmontri, Jao Phraya. *Prawatikan khong jomphon jaophraya surasakmontri* [The History of Army Field Marshal Jao Phraya Surasak Montri]. Vols. 1–4. Bangkok: Khuru Sapha, 1961.

Terwiel, B. J. *Thailand's Political History: From the Fall of Ayutthaya in 1767 to Recent Times.* Bangkok: River Books, 2005.

Thanet Aphonsuvan. "'Rasadon rakchat': Warasutthai khong khwamkhit kanmuang sayam phra ong jao prisdang lae khosanoe kiaokap ratathamanun chabap raek ph.s. 2427" ["Popular Patriotism": Doomed Siamese Political Thought of Prince Prisdang and the Proposal for the First Constitution, 1885.] *Sinlapa Watanatham* 29, no. 11 (September 2008): 112–19.

——. "Riakrong rattathamanun khrang raek samai rachakan thi 5" [The First Call for a Constitution during the Reign of Rama 5]. *Sinlapa Watanatham* 24, no. 12 (October 2003): 73–83.

Thawi Lapha Puranasukhon (Chumsai), Mom Rachawong Ying. Cremation volume. Bangkok, 1985.

Thongchai Winichakul. *Siam Mapped: A History of the Geo-Body of a Nation.* Honolulu: University of Hawai'i Press, 1994.

Udom Pramuanwithaya. "Jaonai nakkanthut khon raek khong sayam thung 13 prathet" [The First Siamese Prince Diplomat to 13 Countries]. In *Nung roi jaofa lae senabodi* [100 Jaofa Princes and Ministers], 446–55. Bangkok: Khlang Withaya, 1962.

Vajiranana [Wachirayan Warorot], Prince-Patriarch. *Autobiography: The Life of Prince Patriarch Vajiranana.* Edited and translated by Craig J. Reynolds. Athens: Ohio University Press, 1979.

Vajiravudh, King [Asvahabu]. *Jews of the Orient.* Bangkok: Siam Observer Press, n.d. Originally serialized in the *Siam Observer* in July 1914.

Van Dort, K. "A Royal Cremation." *Century Magazine*, September 1911, 751–55.

Van Esterik, Penny. *Materializing Thailand.* New York: Berg, 2000.

Vella, Walter. *Chaiyo! King Vajiravudh and the Development of Thai Nationalism.* Honolulu: University of Hawai'i Press, 1978.

Wechsler, Maxillian. "From Top Military Commander to a Life of Diplomacy." *The BigChilli*, 20 February 2013. http://www.thebigchilli.com/features/category/diplomats/2.

White, Luis. *Speaking with Vampires: Rumor and History in Colonial Africa.* Berkeley: University of California Press, 2000.

Whyte, Brendan, and Suthida Whyte. "The Inscriptions on the First World War Volunteers Memorial, Bangkok." *Journal of the Siam Society* 96 (2008): 175–92.

Wichitwong na Pomphet. *Rachathut haeng krung sayam* [Siam's Diplomatic Envoys]. Bangkok: Saengdao, 2004.

Wilson, Constance. "State and Society in the Reign of Mongkut, 1851–1868: Thailand on the Eve of Modernization." PhD diss., Cornell University, 1970.

Wimonphan Pitathawatchai. 2004. *Somdet phrajao bormommawongthoe krom phraya thewawongwaropakan* [Prince Thewawong]. 2 vols. Bangkok: DMG, 2004.

Wright, Arnold, ed. *Twentieth Century Impressions of Ceylon: Its History, People, Commerce, Industries, and Resources.* London: Lloyd's Greater Britain Publishing Co., 1907.

———. *Twentieth Century Impressions of Siam*. London: Lloyd's Greater Britain
    Publishing Co., 1908.
Wyatt, David. "Family Politics in Seventeenth and Eighteenth Century Siam." In
    Studies in Thai History, 107–30. Chiang Mai: Silkworm Books, 1994.
———."King Chulalongkorn the Great." In *Studies in Thai History*, 276–88.
———. *The Politics of Reform in Thailand: Education in the Reign of King Chulalongkorn*.
    New Haven: Yale University Press, 1969.
———. *Thailand: A Short History*. 2nd ed. New Haven: Yale University Press, 2003.

Index

Page numbers in italics refer to figures.

1885 reform proposal, 45–49, 58, 61, 141; as reason for Prisdang's exile, 50, 72, 81, 87, 160–162; scholarship on, 159–162
1891 confidential memo, 44, 46, 74, 86–95, 161, 176n34

Abeyesekera, G. M., 131–132
Abhidhamma Wheel of Life, 153, *154*
absolute monarchy, 68, 87–89, 159, 162–166; establishment of, 5, 25, 135; overthrow of, 3, 150, 156; reform proposal, 47–48 (*see also* 1885 reform proposal)
Allen, Charles, 197n95
Amarapura Nikaya sect, 99, 104, 106
anagarika, 202n18
Ananda, King (Rama VIII), 158
Anuman Rachathon, Phraya, 140
Anuradhapura riot, 128
applied engineering. *See* engineering
architecture, 19, 21, 31
aristocrats, nonroyal, 5, 31, 40, 58, 111, 140. *See also* elite society; nobles
Arisugawa, Prince, 127
Aroonwong, Ida, 172, 182n69
Article 112, Criminal Code, 165. *See also* lèse majesté
astrologists, Siamese, 10–14
Aubin, David, 176n21
Aum Neko, 206n26
autobiography, Prince Prisdang Chumsai, 1–3, 8, 155; publication of, 149–150, 174n7; scholarship on, 160; second and third proposed volumes, 2, 3, 73, 150, 176n5, 202n22; self-censorship in, xii, 3, 9, 72, 73, 164, 165
Ayutthaya, 106

Baker, Chris, 176n37
Bangkok Times, 99
Ban Tha Chang (property), 17, 19, 52–53, 57, 178n53, 185n16
Battambang, 78, 79
behavioral and speech norms, 6–9, 162–166

belonging, 7, 36, 141, 162–163
Benson, J. W., 44–45
Besant, Annie, 114
Bhumibol Adulyadet, King (Rama IX), 158, 160
Bidyalabh, Prince (Phitthayalap), 94, 191n35. *See also* Sonabandit, Prince
Birdpore estate, 114
Blackburn, Anne, 110, 195nn41–42, 197n89
blacklisting, 89, 154, 165. *See also* rumors and gossip
Blake, Henry and Lady, 124, 126, 127
Bodh Gaya, 114, 118, 119, 155
Bond Street, 44
"bones hanging around his neck," ix, xii, 43–44. *See also* scapegoating
Borapah (Borapha) Railway Company, 65
border areas, 4, 45, 47, 60, 76–77, 85–87, 92–93, 153
Boston Museum of Fine Art, 127
Bowonniwet Temple, 156
Bradley, Dan Beach, 13
Brailey, Nigel, 88, 190n31
British Burma, 4, 13, 25, 45, 77
British Ceylon. *See* Lanka
British colonial officials, 33–34, 42–43; and Buddhist relics and sites, 111, 118, 128, 155; discrediting Prisdang, 90–91, 191n58; and monastic lands, 195n30; reception of Chulalongkorn, 109
British India: Buddhist relics, 113–123, 153–155; Chulalongkorn's travels in, 20
British Malaya, 13, 82–86, 153
British Singapore, 11, 15, 20–21, 27, 50, 58, 84, 118, 119
Buddhism, Theravada: fraternities, 104–106; monastic lands, 195n30; unification efforts, xi, 4–5, 96, 103–113, 153, 155
Buddhist era (P.S.) dates, 172
Buddhist life-story (Jataka), 1–2
Buddhist monks: Europeans ordained as, 145, 200n147; Lankan, 195n40. *See also* Jinawarawansa (Prisdang Chumsai); Subhuti

217

Printed in the USA
CPSIA information can be obtained
at www.ICGtesting.com
LVHW092137191023
761571LV00015BA/335/J